PAUL BURGESS

A Mishmash
OF LIFE

THE ROYAL NAVY YEARS

PAUL BURGESS

A Mishmash OF LIFE

THE ROYAL NAVY YEARS

MEMOIRS
Cirencester

Published by Memoirs

MEMOIRS
PUBLISHING

25 Market Place, Cirencester, Gloucestershire, GL7 2NX
info@memoirsbooks.co.uk www.memoirspublishing.com

A MISHMASH OF LIFE: The Royal Navy Years
All Rights Reserved. Copyright © 2013 Paul Burgess

No part of this book may be reproduced or transmitted in any form or
by any means, graphic, electronic, or mechanical, including
photocopying, recording, taping or by any information storage or
retrieval system, without the permission in writing from the copyright
holder. The right of Paul Burgess to be identified as the editor/author
of this work has been asserted in accordance with the Copyright,
Designs and Patents Act 1988 sections 77 and 78.

The views expressed in this work are solely those of the author and do
not necessarily reflect the views of the publisher, and the publisher
hereby disclaims any responsibility for them.

ISBN: 978-1-909544-64-2

CHAPTER ONE

WALKING AWAY from home left me with mixed emotions. I was leaving behind a family that I loved, and a home that I cherished.

Christmases, birthdays, holidays, happy times, sad times, all mixed together in the mishmash of my life.

Getting off the bus at Oxford railway station, I made my way onto the platform, showing my navy travel warrant to the ticket collector. My orders were to get from Oxford to Paddington station in London, then to proceed to Waterloo Station and report to the Royal Navy Regulating Office. I found the regulating office and was met by a regulating petty officer. There were a number of new recruits already assembled, some of whom I knew, these being some of the lads I had previously met at the Reading recruiting office and at the Navy medical examination building in Southampton.

We were gathered together and escorted to the platform from which the train to Maidstone was due to leave. There were about eight of us. We got aboard the train and as it gently pulled away from the station we were all wondering what lay ahead of us.

CHAPTER ONE

On arrival at Maidstone station we were greeted by a G.I. petty officer and a Women's Royal Navy driver. Our transport was a Bedford truck painted, of course, in Navy Blue with the big white letters R N written on the side. It had a canvas cover stretched over a metal frame. The Petty Officer yelled out his order to throw our suitcases into the back of the truck and then to follow them. We did this without hesitation, for the heavens opened and the freezing rain came down in a deluge.

Our destination was *H.M.S. Pembroke*, in Chatham. As the truck made its way down Dock Road towards the Barracks Gates I remembered that on the 4th of December 1951 a squad of cadets had been ploughed into by a double decker bus killing twenty three of them. As I remember, it was a very foggy night and visibility was down to nil.

I wondered what my fellow recruits and I would be facing in the coming weeks.

Arriving at the guard house, we disembarked from the truck and were signed in; we were then marched by our petty officer G.I. to a barrack block called Grenville, and this would be our mess deck for the duration of our stay at *H.M.S. Pembroke*. Grenville block was some three stories high and we were to be accommodated on the 2nd floor; the other accommodation block was Anson block, identical to Grenville in layout, joined together by a building that contained the main galley and dining room.

CHAPTER ONE

A courtyard also separated the two accommodation blocks. This was where a set of davits had been installed and a ship's whaler was slung. I found this amusing, thinking that *H.M.S. Pembroke* was a land-based establishment and would be imposable to flounder and sink. Anyway, these were my first observations.

Back in our mess we were allocated a locker and a bunk which was two tiered. I was allocated a top bunk that would prove to be interesting when trying to get in or out of it!

After stowing our clothing into the allocated lockers and being issued with a key, we were marched off to collect our bedding; this consisted of two sheets, two pillowcases, one pillow, two blankets, and one counterpane.

The counterpane was central to how your bunk was made. It was made of a heavy woven material with a blue and white fleck with an anchor embroidered into the centre. When the bunk bedding was made up an inspection would be carried out; if the anchor was not perfectly positioned in the centre of the bedding, it would be stripped off by the inspecting officer and the bunk would have to be remade.

All this would be revealed in time. As for now, time was getting on and we new recruits were getting very hungry. It was now late afternoon and darkness was creeping up on us. Our petty officer, we were informed, would be our instructor along with a chief petty officer; these two men would become our mentors, and would replace our previous mentors, our parents or guardians, which meant being tied to mother's apron strings was of now a thing of the past!

After having a meal we returned to our mess. We had experienced a very long day. There were fifteen of us, brought together from all parts of the United Kingdom—Jocks, Geordies, Scousers, Yorkies, Janners, Brummies, Taffys and Cockneys; we were like a soup mix of many ingredients that our new-found instructors and mentors would blend together.

Being very tired and unfamiliar with our new surroundings we decided to turn in for the night.

Getting into a bunk with someone already asleep in the lower one could be difficult for the novice. Out pipes and out lights orders had already been given over the tannoy system, the system adopted by the navy to relay orders to all parts of a ship or establishment; these loudspeakers were everywhere so that no order or instruction could be missed.

Some of these orders were followed up by a visit from the Officer of the watch or a duty Chief Petty Officer; any infringement could result in a harsh punishment.

Out pipes and out lights had been ordered, and the mess lights were automatically extinguished, leaving what we found out to be police lights, which were like little blue lamps that illuminated the exits and stairways from the mess deck.

I had been to the toilet before returning to my allotted bunk, and in the darkness I fumbled trying to get a foothold on the bottom bunk to propel myself into

CHAPTER ONE

the top bunk. Unfortunately my foot found its way into the groin and testicles of my new-found bunk mate, who let out a yell enough to awake the dead! My other mess mates weren't dead but some had gone into a deep slumber, and the painful yell had awakened the whole mess. "What the f**k's going on!" one voice shouted, and my compatriot replied, "This stupid Oxford bastard trod on me balls!" By this time I had got into my bunk and had slithered under the covers. Before dozing off into a furtive sleep, I was aware of a few sobs and sniffles from some of the occupants of the bunks around me. Some of these lads were still attached to their mothers' apron strings.

Dawn was breaking and the tannoy came alive with a bugle call, this being what we would recognize as reveille. The bugle call on this occasion was accompanied by two instructors with clubs bashing on the metal lockers shouting at us: "Wakey, wakey, rise and shine, the sun's burning your eyes out, hands off your cocks and into your socks!" Without hesitation we were out of our bunks.

Standing at some assemblage to attention, we were ordered to get washed and dressed, then go to the dining room for breakfast, after which we were to return to our mess.

Returning to the mess we were confronted and addressed by our petty officer and chief petty officer, who were G I's, the abbreviation for Gunnery Instructors. We were informed that we were going to the

CHAPTER ONE

slops. "Where the hell is that?" some of the lads blurted out. The reply from our instructors informed us that it was the clothing stores. The Navy had a language of its own—in time we would be indoctrinated into it.

At the slops we were issued our uniforms and every bit of kit we required for our respective trades. We were measured for our No.1 suits that would be made to measure by a Naval tailor; Bernard's was the Navy contractor that would provide the uniform. Navy dress code was governed by numbers: No.1 was going ashore rig, No.2 was the same as No.1 without a lanyard, No.3 was the everyday uniform. No.1 and two uniforms had gold badges, No.3 uniforms had red badges; other working rigs were conducive to whatever trade you were employed in: No.8'ts were the normal daytime rig of the day for duties that included sweeping, cleaning, painting and any other work that was required to keep the ship or establishment in pristine condition.

Badges for this clothing were made of a cotton fabric with the branch insignia embossed in blue.

All of this would be revealed as our day progressed. Some of us recruits were to become cooks; others would be officers' stewards, stores ratings, writers, all put under the heading of the S & S division, short for Supply and Secretariat.

After the kit issue we reassembled in the mess, which was our new home,

For the next four weeks, we were informed, we would be transferred to *H.M.S. Ceres* that was

CHAPTER ONE

established near Wetherby in Yorkshire. I was in wonderment why a Navy establishment would be installed so far from the sea.

Our instructors were now faced with a bunch of recruits who had no idea of how to dress, except for a couple of lads that had been sea cadets, who knew how the navy uniform would be worn.

Our instructors, with the assistance from the sea cadet recruits, eventually got us into our new garb, from underwear up; our uniforms were called a square rig, dating back to the days of sail.

Because it was winter, sea jerseys were worn under the tunic. The blue collar that was tied down around the middle of your anatomy was very uncomfortable but after a while you could get used to it. Bell bottom trousers were a major part of the uniform. The main difference from other service uniforms was that the creases had to be horizontal as opposed to vertical; five or seven creases were acceptable, seven creases representing the seven seas and if preferred the five creases representing the five oceans.

After struggling to get into our uniforms we were ordered to stand to attention by our bunks. Our Chief and Petty Officer instructors carried out their inspection, commenting in no uncertain terms what they thought of the individual they were inspecting! When my turn came, the petty officer yelled out: "Burgess, you look like a scran bag!" I asked, "What's that, sir?" and he yelled at me again, saying, "You don't

CHAPTER ONE

speak unless you're asked to!" I kept my mouth shut after that.

Uniforms were issued, dress of the day was put on, and we were marched off with studded boots, kit bags slung over our shoulders filled with all items of clothing, everything from underwear, socks, white fronts, tee shirts, and in my case, all the other items issued to cook recruits; with our chef's whites, we had probably twice the amount of kit than any other branch.

We had four pairs each of tee-shirts, chef, white trousers, cooks' caps, aprons, and galley boots.

Galley boots were of a special design with buckle fasteners and rubber rings built into the boot, to give a grip on the galley deck when a ship was being tossed around in unfriendly seas.

A ship's galley can be a very dangerous place during the stormy weather that I would come to experience.

However, we were destined to be marched to the wash house or what was known to the initiated as the dohbey room, where large galvanized tubs were in abundance, along with wash boards, mangles like Mum used to have; and neatly piled up was what we would learn was one pound blocks of pussers soap.

We were not given the luxury of Persil, Tide, Lux or any other washing powder; in our case it was down to the nitty-gritty of Nelson's time!

We were ordered to tip out our kit onto the wash room deck and fill our tubs with hot water that was in plentiful supply.

CHAPTER ONE

This was demoralizing! Our kit was brand new and spotless, albeit with our names having been stamped on every bit of it; even our boots had our names imprinted under the arch of the boot. There was no excuse for not knowing what belonged to you!

Hot water cascaded into the tubs. No soap suds were in sight. With the plugs in place over the drain holes the tubs were filling fast; when full the water was turned off, and we were instructed to put the wash boards into the tubs, followed by our kit; taking a bar of soap we started to get some froth going, and washing and scrubbing with scrubbing brushes provided we got into the art of dohbeying.

After washing our kit we hung it up to dry in a drying room. We were then marched back to our mess. Another part of our kit that had been supplied was a housewife. (Not the female kind, although we could have done with one!) This was a small blue canvas satchel that contained sewing needles of different sizes, black and white thread, darning wool, a thimble, and a pair of small scissors.

As stated, our kit had been marked with each individual's name, except for our sea jerseys: this we had to do ourselves.

Out came the housewife, and under the watchful eye of our instructors we threaded our needles with white thread. When this was done we were given instructions on how to make a chain stitch. We had to embroider our surname into the tail of our sea jerseys. This was not the only sewing we had to do; all of our branch insignia badges had to be sewn onto our uniforms and any other clothing where it was required.

When our kit had dried we collected it and back in the mess we had to iron it. Ironing boards and irons were provided, not enough for one each, so we had to learn how to share; this was all part of the Part One of recruit training; with a group of fifteen young lads being brought together there was bound to be some friction.

This would evolve in time, but as for now, the ironing of our dried kit was to be done in our own time.

During the morning and afternoon parts of the day we would be given a break period of fifteen minutes; these we would come to know as stand easy. In the morning we would get a cup of milk and a biscuit, a quick puff of a fag or a draw on a pipe if you smoked. The Navy with its many historical traditions could afford it. The senior service was to give each rating a tot of rum, which was issued at 11.50 a.m. each day. Another perk was that an issue of duty-free tobacco was allowed once a month on shore bases and home based ships; if a ship was on foreign service there was no restriction on the duty-free tobacco allocation.

"Tot time," as the rum issue was affectionately called, was piped throughout the ship or establishment as "up spirits"; in the navy each rating, which is what we had now become, was issued a station card, either port or starboard. This depicted your watch; port was red, starboard was green. The card also stated one of three conditions in respect of entitlement for rum issue;

CHAPTER ONE

these were G. T. or U.A. G meant you were allowed grog, the rum issue; T meant that you were temperance and refused to take the grog, and for this you would receive three pence a day in payment. U.A. stood for under age: you had to be eighteen years old before you could draw your tot.

Another booklet we were issued with was a pay book; this book, of a green colour, was made of parchment paper, and would be part of your navy life forever. As the name implies, a pay book was presented to the paymaster every two weeks on pay parade; it contained your photograph and official number. Every member of Her Majesty's Navy had an official number (mine was C/M 944560), which got ingrained in your mind and had to be repeated on many occasions throughout one's service.

Your pay book not only contained your photograph and official number; recorded in it was all the inoculations and immunizations that you had to suffer, everything from Yellow fever, Cholera, Typhoid fever and so on—all administered by the scratching of the skin or injected by hypodermic syringe, none of which was a pleasant experience.

A pay book also acted as a passport for entering or passing through other N.A.T.O. countries.

At the time foreign countries were far distant from our minds. We were still in the infancy of being new recruits, and going through the pangs of induction into Her Majesty's Navy.

After our kit issue and kit inspection, we were

CHAPTER ONE

marched off to the dentist; this was not a very good experience.

Assembled in a waiting room we sat in fear of what lay ahead of us. When my turn came I was escorted into the surgery by a W.R.N.S. dental assistant's nurse. I was directed to sit in the chair encompassed by all sorts of dental paraphernalia, not unlike what I had to endure at the school dentist some years previously, the only difference being that the drill mechanism had an electric motor instead of a foot treadle to make it whirr inside your mouth.

The dentist was a lieutenant. "Open up," he said. I obeyed and opened my mouth wide, and in went the mirror followed by the dreaded pick and scraper. After prodding and probing, he commented to the dental nurse that I needed a couple of small fillings. Owing to the fact that they were only small cavities, he said it was not required for me to have any cocaine. The drilling started, and so with mouth wide open the torture began, white knuckles gripping the arms of the dentist chair! The noise from the drill in my mouth and from the electric motor that was driving it, together with the smell from the drill bit boring into the enamel of my tooth, did not make this one of the best experiences of my life.

After the dentist came our encounter with the medical branch, or S.B.A.'s

These were the angels of mercy that would administer the injections and inoculations. S.B.A. was

CHAPTER ONE

an abbreviation for Sick Berth Attendant, and our first encounter was to get our T.A.B. injection. T.A.B. was an abbreviation for Typhoid Anti Bacteria. We gathered at the sick bay, rolled up our left sleeves to expose our upper arms, and a number of S.B.A.'s were at the ready with cotton wool soaked in ether in one hand and a hypodermic syringe in the other. Needles were injected into the arm, plungers were pushed, and the serum found its way into our bodies.

It was not long before the reaction to the injection set in. We were in the mess and our instructors were in the process of giving instructions as to the next stage of our training.

We looked a sorry sight! Left upper arms were swelling with big red blotches and were as painful as hell, noses started to run, eyes became bloodshot and watery, and then came the shakes and shivers! Our instructors in their wisdom ordered us to stay where we were and because of our deterioration took off to summon medical attention; they returned with a leading sick berth attendant who looked us over and, clearly not happy with our physical condition, he left to get the Medical Officer. After further checks on us it was decided that our mess would be quarantined and made into a temporary sick bay ward; a sick birth attendant would be in attendance at all times to monitor our conditions. The reason why our mess was turned into a ward was because there were not enough cots in the sick bay to accommodate us.

CHAPTER ONE

This was an interruption to our scheduled joining routine as our confinement to the mess lasted close to a week before we were fit enough to continue our training. Our confinement was thought to be caused by an out-of-date typhoid vaccine; of course, this would never be admitted but we nevertheless all made a full recovery and continued with our training.

·

CHAPTER TWO

WITH THE FIRST PART of our induction into the navy completed, we were ready to embark on the next phase. This included squad drill, marching and counter marching, with slow marching drilled into us by our instructors so that we all could and would respond in unison to a given order.

Learning to march is not that difficult unless one has two right arms and two left feet; unfortunately we had a couple of our squad that had both! Little Jock, as we called him, couldn't march for toffee; he was the worst and would drive our drill instructor into fits of rage that he meted out on all of us.

Our training was to be carried out and completed within a strict time frame, but we were already behind because of close to one week having been taken out of the training program caused by the bad vaccine that we had been injected with.

Other interruptions to the training program would take place, and I became one of them.

Every morning we would have to be on parade and fell in on the parade ground. I may say that the parade ground was a great expanse of gritted tarmac and concrete, and had been pounded on since Nelson's time. This time recruit Burgess was about to be a hiccup in the system.

We had fallen in on the parade ground for the daily inspection to check that we were dressed correctly, wearing our uniforms correctly. Because we were doing squad drill training, No.3s were our rig of the day with the addition of gaiters to hold the bottom of your bellbottoms in place. After the inspection and the usual deliberations from our drill instructor along the lines of what a shower of shit we were, he announced, as he did on a daily basis, that if anyone wanted to report sick, that person should forthwith step forward—and I did.

Being tall and not as bad as the others at marching and drill instruction, I was always positioned as the right-hand marker and the rest of the squad would fall in on me; being in this position the step and stride would fall on me in response to the given order from the instructor, whether it was quick march, slow march, or double march.

After stepping forward the instructor ordered me to report to the sick bay and to double march. The sick bay was established at the farthest end of the parade ground, probably two to three hundred yards away. I did as I was told until I thought I was out of his sight, then slowed to a limp. On entering the sick bay reception area I was confronted by a sick berth attendant. After his enquiry as to what my problem was, I showed him, taking off my gaiters, boots and socks,

CHAPTER TWO

the red swollen and bleeding welts above my ankles. He said, "I bet that's painful!" and I replied, "You can have them if you want."

It was agreed that the M.O. should take a look at my condition that had been caused by the top edge of my boots wearing away at my skin in the affected area.

I was ordered into the doctor's surgery. The S.B.A. had already informed him of my complaint, and I sat down on a chair as ordered. The doc checked out my condition, and after getting me to walk a few paces, observing me from a distance, he asked if I had any questions. I said, "Can I be excused boots?" The reply was short and sweet: "NO!" My prescription was a wad of cotton wool to be tucked into my boots around the affected places.

My drill instructor was pleased to see me back and welcomed me back into the fold.

Taking up my position of right-hand marker, the squad drill commenced. Gritting my teeth to help overcome the excruciating pain from my ankles, I was determined not to let my classmates down.

Orders were barked out at us and we did our best to comply. Mistakes were made and had to be corrected, and Little Jock was the main culprit—he couldn't march to save his life!

After hours from the daily training routine some of us got together to try and get him coordinated, to get his feet and arms to go in the right direction when marching; this was not only for his benefit but also for

CHAPTER TWO

the rest of us, as we were assessed as a group, not an individual—at least at this stage of our training, anyway.

When our instructors were satisfied that we were competent enough to march and respond to parade ground orders, our parade ground training was put up a notch.

Rifle drill would be the next stage of our parade ground training. We assembled at the armoury, a solid brick-built building with strong steel doors attached. We were each issued with an Enfield 3.0.3 rifle, and a webbing belt that had a scabbard attached containing what was known as a pig sticker bayonet, or if you were not careful, an eye sticker bayonet.

Our instructors thought that we were now competent enough to handle this new equipment, having learnt how to dress in the new khaki webbing with the attached scabbard and pig sticker bayonet. We reassembled on the parade ground and were put through the basic rudiments of rifle drill.

We were taught how to shoulder arms, ground arms, pick up arms, present arms, reverse arms, and to carry out the given orders yelled at us by our drill instructors, or parade commander.

After four weeks of intense training we were transferred to *H.M.S. Ceres* in Yorkshire.

We travelled as a group under the watchful eye of our instructors. On arrival we had to carry out a joining routine not unlike the one at *H.M.S. Pembroke*, the difference being that we had our kit with us, carried in

CHAPTER TWO

the kit bags that was standard issue to all navy ratings with each individual's name clearly stamped on the bottom of it; no matter where you went, if you were carrying your kit bag, everyone knew your name.

H.M.S. Ceres must have been the most landlocked establishment in the Royal Navy. It was still winter, with snow on the ground and a constant fog swirled around the establishment, so it was difficult to get our bearings.

Because of the weather our training continued in classrooms where basic seamanship was being taught—knots and lines, the various parts of a ship such as what was forward and what was aft, midships, the stern, and all the other parts of a ship that we would need to know.

After a few days the fog cleared and it was back to the parade ground for more square bashing and rifle drill.

We had a new chief instructor who was decent and fair to us. Unfortunately there was one instructor who was a pure bastard, who was short and stocky.

I had made friends with a Scots lad, Ronnie, who was about the same size and build as me; we were being marched from one instruction class to another by our class leader. Ronnie and I were having a quiet chat when a bellowing voice yelled out: "HALT THAT SQUAD!" The order was obeyed—we came to an immediate halt and stood to attention. The bullying chief G.I. came over to us and started berating us in language that I won't print. He was carrying a bunch of files under his arm, and in a rage he continued to ball us out, yelling at us that we don't speak when marching within the confines of the establishment. He then took the files from under his arm and started to beat Ronnie around the head with them, knocking his cap off into the slushy, partly melted snow.

After the Chief's tantrum we were released, after Ronnie retrieved his cap before he could be charged for being improperly dressed, and we were marched off to our next class.

Back in the mess I apologized to Ronnie for him getting belted. I should have received the same punishment—since I was the one talking to him at the time. Ron replied, "Not to worry," saying we were still mates.

H.M.S. Ceres was in the process of closing down or, in Navy terminology, decommissioning. The snow was gone along with the fog, and we discovered that we were only a couple of miles from Wetherby Race Course. This brightened the lives of some of the lads among us who, when given a Saturday off and a race meeting would take place, would descend upon the race track to try and enhance their pittance of Navy pay.

Not far from the base was the village hall which we renamed The Snake Pit. Dances were held on a Saturday night and, of course, all of us little randy buggers would be there trying to get off with the village maidens. We didn't get much time to get up to any hanky-panky as we had to be back on board by 22 hundred hours—navy time for 10 o'clock.

Because *H.M.S. Ceres* was being decommissioned, a

CHAPTER TWO

decommissioning ceremony and parade had to be carried out.

It fell to our class to be the final honour guard. We were dressed in our No.1 uniforms, this time with pure white gators, white webbing belts, our rifles with white shoulder straps; the bayonets on our rifles were the proper ones, not the pig sticker type.

We fell in and were inspected by our divisional officer: boots were polished, uniform creases were razor sharp, caps were worn correctly with chin straps down; after a few minor adjustments we were ready to carry out our duty as the last honour guard that *H.M.S. Ceres* would ever have.

All the ship's company divisions were in place, the Captain was on his dais, local people of distinction were in attendance, and the Captain took up the salute; being the right-hand marker, I would be the one to set the pace of the march past while our chief G.I. would be marching close by to keep a check on me.

With our divisional officer at the head of the honour guard the order was given, "By the left, quick march!" We stepped off in unison and marched along the parade ground towards the captain's dais; at a given time we were ordered, "Eyes right!" This is a salute to the Captain and the commission that he holds. After marching past the dais the "Eyes front!" order was given. Being the right-hand marker, I was not required to do the "Eyes right" salute as it was my job to maintain the step and direction of the squad.

CHAPTER TWO

After the decommissioning ceremony, our regular training schedule came to a halt and would continue when we returned to *H.M.S. Pembroke*. For the next two weeks we were employed on what was called work ship duties. I got lucky, for down the road from the main establishment was the W.R.N.S. camp called Moreland's. I was escorted there by the Buffer—this was the name given to the Chief or Petty officer responsible for a ship, or establishment's cleanliness and tidiness.

My job was to go around all of the buildings and collect the fire extinguishers, and take them to a designated storeroom. A red painted hose cart was provided for me to carry out my task. I might add that not all of the accommodation had been vacated as small contingents of W.R.N.S. were still in residence.

I found this out when entering one mess to collect the fire extinguishers. I was confronted by a half-dressed W.R.N. who was in the process of putting her stockings on. Seeing me, she let out a stream of expletives! I didn't hang around and scarpered back out the door from where I had entered. (On reflection I must say that God had been good to her in the ample proportions that he had provided her for a body!) Seeing that the establishment was still partly occupied I was very careful when I entered other buildings in my quest to retrieve the fire-fighting equipment.

One perk of the job was that the Moreland's galley was still operational and I could take a stand easy when

CHAPTER TWO

I wanted to. I had made friends with the galley staff, and even with the voluptuous W.R.N. that I had disturbed putting her stockings on who had forgiven me.

All good things come to an end and it was back to Chatham and *H.M.S. Pembroke* for us. I believe that when the Navy left *H.M.S. Ceres*, it became a civilian establishment, namely an open prison; all they had to do was put bars on the windows and lock the gates. Whether this was true I'm not sure but it sounded feasible.

On arrival back at *H.M.S. Pembroke* the final stages of our Part One training would continue. Although we had been the final honour guard at *H.M.S. Ceres*, we still had to do a passing out parade at Pembroke, for this was the one where we would be scrutinized by the watchful eye of the Lieutenant Gunnery instructor. We were provided with arm bands with a number on it—mine was 13. (I wondered if this was an omen!) After being put through our drill routines bellowed out by our drill instructor, we came to a halt, standing at attention with our rifles in the shoulder arms position, and awaited our fate.

The Lieutenant from his dais in his best parade ground voice started off in his deliberations as to what level of competence we had achieved.

He began, "With the exception of numbers thirteen, nine, seven, six, three, and two, all have failed!" I let out a sigh of relief; being the right-hand marker I could have been held responsible for the failures, but as I had passed the inspection I was off the hook, so to speak; all

CHAPTER TWO

those that had failed would go through more intensive parade ground training to bring them up to an acceptable standard.

During this part of our training we had to be interviewed by a P.S.O.—a Personal Selection Officer; she was a W.R.N. Lieutenant, and I might add that she was a very attractive lady, wearing full make up with golden blonde hair trying to hide under her officer's cap.

I was invited to take a seat in front of her desk. She then went on to ask some questions about my background and family life. I explained in the best way I could, saying, "When I was born I had a mum and a dad; they got divorced and mum remarried a man that had two daughters from his first marriage; they became my stepsisters; they later had a daughter between them, who became my half-sister; my dad remarried a women who had two sons from her previous marriage, so I inherited two step-brothers; so in all in all I had two stepsisters, two step-brothers and a half-sister." This, I explained, was the Mishmash of life that I had to contend with!

She responded with a smile, saying I was very mature for my age; my thoughts were, "If I could get you on a date you would find out just how mature I am!"

Other parts of our training included fire-fighting, which I enjoyed the most. Handling fire-fighting equipment, such as foam generators, water jets and spray, we dealt with fires from bilges to flight decks; a written test was part of the training, and for the first time in my life I achieved 100% and was congratulated by our instructors.

Another requirement was to pass the swimming test. Understandably, being in the Navy and not being able to swim could be an embarrassment.

H.M.S. Pembroke had an indoor swimming pool. We were ordered to assemble at the pool at a given time, and a P.T.I. was there to greet us. (P.T.I was an abbreviation for Physical Training Instructor.) Later on he would be known as 'clubs'—this was due to the badge worn on his tee-shirt, the insignia being crossed India clubs.

We were asked who could swim. Most of us could but a few of the lads stated they were non-swimmers. Those of us who were swimmers were ordered to strip off and put on a boiler suit; when this was done we had to dive into the water at the deep end, which was ten foot deep, and swim three lengths of the pool; the pool was twenty-five yards long, and some of the lads floundered because of the weight of water and drag on the boiler suits. I was fortunate—I passed this test without any problems.

The next test was to jump into the pool from a platform that was about ten feet high above the water at the deep end, still wearing the wet and soggy boiler suit. Those of us who had passed the first stage of the test assembled on the platform. The P.T.I. stood at the side of the pool with the non-swimmers who were holding a long pole; their job was to pull out anyone who got into difficulty; the procedure was that on the given order one at a time we would jump into the water; on surfacing we had to tread water and take off the boiler suit and hold it over our heads. If anyone got into difficulty the pole would be there to grab hold of so that you could be pulled to the side of the pool safely.

Those of us who passed the swimming test became safety swimmers; this meant that for the lads who were to be initiated into the ways of swimming we would be there to help them if they got into difficulty.

One of our classmates was petrified! He was on the platform at the deep end and was ordered to jump in. It was a very emotional experience to see someone in so much fear. The P.T.I. did his best to coax him to jump. We were all ready and willing to help him, some of the lads with the pole, myself and couple of us in the pool ready to help him when he hit the water; but it was to no avail—his fear of water got him his discharge: it was a sad experience to see one of our classmates leave.

I must admit that others that were unable to swim had a lot of guts to jump from a ten-foot platform into a pool of water with a P.T.I., a pole and a bunch of new recruits to save them if they got into difficulties.

Another stage of our training was to be put into the gas chamber. We were first given instructions as to how to wear a gas mask. This was a horrible looking contraption but, that said, it could save your life. It consisted of a rubber mask with two eye pieces, an exhaust valve to allow exhaled breath to escape, and a

CHAPTER TWO

flexible tube was attached to the mask, the other end being attached to a canister containing soda lime. The soda lime would filter out the gas and impurities in the atmosphere. The mask was held in place by webbing straps that could be adjusted to fit the individual.

All this equipment was held in place in a canvas webbing bag that was held in place by straps around the neck and body. After being instructed on the use of the gas mask and its benefits, we were marched to the gas chamber. My thoughts on hearing the words 'gas chamber' sent shivers down my spine! It evoked thoughts of Auschwitz, Buchenwald, and other Nazi internment camps where my dad had helped to liberate the longsuffering Jewish people.

Arriving at the gas chamber, we were confronted with a brick building not unlike the armoury; the door had a window in it, and in the centre of the building was a sturdy table. In the middle of the table was a hot plate. Our instructor gave the order for us to put on our gas masks, and we were then instructed to walk in line around the table; we were told that when we heard a rapid bang on the door we were to remove our gas masks; after these instructions the instructor disappeared out of the door and slammed it shut behind him.

A dim light was provided that illuminated the table and hot plate. We gingerly walked around the table and, looking towards the hot plate, we noticed that two capsules had been placed on it; these slowly melted and a vapour cloud engulfed the chamber. Walking around with our gas masks on, we were not affected. Then came the bash on the door, the signal to remove our face masks; most of us did but a couple of lads were hesitant, which prolonged our agony. Walking around the table with eyes streaming and throats choking, we were finally released from our hell.

The object of the exercise was to give us confidence in the equipment we were provided with. On this occasion the Navy proved its point. Other lectures were given in biological warfare where the gas mask could be a life saver. Nerve gas was a particular nasty substance; as its name suggests, the gas could attack the nervous system; the gas mask or respirator was effective in giving protection against this toxin; another antidote was a serum called atropine, which would be injected into the body by an injection automatically given by a clever device about the size of a matchbox. Three doses were supplied; any more than that and you could die of atropine poisoning.

The signs and symptoms were graphically given to us. One must understand that this was the beginning of the cold war and the world was still a very dangerous place. Russia was asserting itself under Stalin and, thank God, General Eisenhower was equal to him.

However, we new recruits had completed our Part One training and were about to start Part Two training; cooks would learn how to be cooks, stewards would learn how to be stewards, stores ratings would learn how to become stores ratings, and so on.

CHAPTER THREE

OUR PART TWO training was about to begin. We trainee cooks were introduced to the new instructor who would be our mentor for the next eight weeks.

Chief petty officer cook Amphil was a good instructor and gently eased us into the art of culinary expertise. This was considerably different from the square-bashing and bellowing of our G.I. instructors.

Although we still had to attend the Friday Divisions parade, and of course, Sunday church parade, *H.M.S. Pembroke* could accommodate those of the Church of England and Church of Scotland affiliates, where services would be held in the St George's Chapel close to the dockyard. Those of the Roman Catholic faith were also accommodated. Any other rating that had a faith outside of these regimes were given other duties around the establishment, mainly in Tin Pan Alley, the name given to the scullery where the dish washing took place; this was also where men under punishment would spend their time. I would find out what this entailed in due course.

After church parade we were let loose, unless the two participating padres decided to have a whaler race with Protestants against the Catholics.

CHAPTER THREE

Two whalers would be tied up to the jetty; whalers were a standard boat of the Navy, of the clinker-built construction painted, of course, in battleship grey.

Because I had some experience in rowing from my days on the river Thames I was nominated as stroke, which put me directly in front of the Padre who was the cox'n. The oars were like tree trunks and weighed a ton! We let slip, the padre standing at the stern with the tiller firmly in his hand giving the orders to pull; we responded, although most of the lads were novices, probably only having played with toy boats in a bath tub! We managed to get to a plausible start line, and our opponents were in no better shape.

Our course was to row downstream passing the destroyer *H.M.S. Defender* and the cruiser *H.M.S. Swiftsure* that was tied up alongside the jetty.

We were rowing on the River Medway that was tidal and part of the Thames estuary.

When both crews were in position, the order was given to start the race. We were off, the Padre yelling his lungs out using language that would never be heard from a pulpit! Our opposition team was getting the same treatment from their monsignor. Rowing downstream was not too difficult. The return part of the race would be entirely different. Rowing against the tide was a lot harder, oars catching waves and knocking some of the lads off their stroke. One of the lads nearly lost his oar, bringing forth a stream of expletives from the Padre as to the poor bugger's birthright and being stupid to say the least.

CHAPTER THREE

The race finished in a disputed draw. The last we saw of the Padre and the Monsignor were two men of the cloth walking away from the jetty remonstrating with each other with loud acoustics and much evidence of gesticulations of hands and arms.

As for us competitors, we retired to the mess to nurse our sore bums caused by the hard wooden seats of the whalers, and our aching muscles from pulling a ton of wood in the shape of a whaler across a stretch of unfriendly water.

We did get some time off to go ashore. One Saturday Ronnie and I decided to take a trip to Margate. We caught a train, meeting two girls on the way; they came from London, and were on their way to visit an aunt who lived in Margate. We got to know each other in a very intimate way, Ronnie and I in our best No.1 uniform and the girls in their Sunday best. Everything was going well until the train guard interrupted us and put paid to our amorous shenanigans.

On arrival at Margate we went our different ways, the girls going off to visit auntie, and Ronnie and I off to investigate the pleasures of Margate. I had been to Margate once before on a day trip organized by Mum and Ernie. I remembered Dreamland, the fairground and Pleasure Park.

We found Dreamland and wandered around looking at the various side shows and rides. We decided to take a ride on the dive bomber. We paid our fare to the ride operator who opened the door for us to get in. He took

CHAPTER THREE

a moment, looking inside the cockpit, then turned to us and said it looked like it had dried out. Ronnie and I looked at each other and wondered if there had been a shower of rain that had occurred before we arrived in Margate. We would soon find out! We got strapped in and the ride started. Going round in a vertical ark was fine, with centrifugal force holding us passengers in our seats and whatever was riding with us in place; then it was time for the real thrill bit of the ride—when the dive bomber would go upside down with just the leather seatbelts holding us in place. The problem was that the previous occupants of our seats had been sick and the contents of their stomachs were sloshing around within the cab—under our seats; the ride operator we later found out had thrown a bucket of water into it to flush it out, so a mixture of putrid vomit and stagnant water cascaded upon us! After getting off the ride and leaving the ride operator in doubt of his birthright, we left Dreamland which had become a nightmare, and headed to the nearest public washrooms and toilets to clean up as best we could.

We decided to leave Margate and return to the sanctuary of *H.M.S. Pembroke*. We were scrutinized by the quartermaster at the guardhouse when we reported to retrieve our station cards; we did our best to explain the unseemly condition we were in. He laughed at us and sent us on our way to get properly cleaned up.

Returning to the mess we were confronted with some of our mess mates, who informed us that an altercation

CHAPTER THREE

had taken place. We enquired what had happened and one of the lads explained that one of the Geordie lads had got into a punch-up with one of the Cockney boys. What it was about was unclear; as previously stated, regional honour was always in the forefront. Fortunately the two pugilists had settled their differences, the Cockney lad nursing a black eye and the Geordie lad nursing a fat lip. After the punch-up they became the best of mates.

Things settled down until most of us were getting short of kit. We would do our dohbeying and hang it out to dry in the drying room. Going to collect it so we could iron it, we found it was missing. It came to light that one of us was taking it, wearing it, then when it was dirty would stuff it into a spare locker!

A bunch of us set up a surveillance on the drying room under the supervision of the mess deck Killick, otherwise known as the leading hand of the mess.

Finally our observations paid off and the culprit was caught in the act! He was taking our freshly laundered clothing, and was putting it into his own locker; he was confronted by all of us, and had no option but to confess to his misconduct.

Punishment would be hard. The Royal Navy was run on trust of your officers and men, and this recruit had crossed the line in respect of honesty and trust. He was a mess mate who had crossed the line; our kit that was all soiled was retrieved from the spare locker where it had been hidden, and we were in debate as to what the punishment would be—all unofficial, of course, but this was the lower deck taking care of its own problem. We were interrupted in our deliberations by the entrance of the duty N.C.O. into the mess who enquired what was going on; this was a man of great stature, a Royal Marine Colour Sergeant who also had been awarded the M.B.E. The Killick of the mess conferred with him and explained the situation. The outcome was that we would be left alone to mete out the punishment and he would return within the hour to make sure that all was well within the mess.

A bathtub was prepared with rather hot water. Pussers hard soap was thrown in followed by the miscreant. A scrubbing brush appeared and he got scrubbed from head to foot. After cleaning him up we tossed all of our kit that he had soiled on top of him and made him wash it, dry it, and iron it and return it to each of us in a good condition.

We never had any more problems with missing kit.

Back to cookery school, we were taught the basics and were supplied with a cookery book called the *B. R. Five*, which was the Manual of Naval Cookery. It laid out the basics of various culinary dishes and what to watch out for in some ingredients that could be harmful. I remember being informed from our instructor that we should always be aware of weevils in flour, and flour that, when exposed to dampness when stored, could cause rope disease; this meant that if flour with rope disease was used in bread baking, the loaf would be sour and strands of it could be pulled out from the crust like a shank of rope—hence the name rope disease.

After eight weeks of instruction it came to the passing out exam, where our culinary skill would be put to the test; all of us were given a menu that instructed us to prepare and cook a meal for four people.

My menu instructed me to make a consommé soup, as a starter, followed by a braised beef steak with Duchess Potatoes and green beans; for sweet I was instructed to make four individual Bakewell tarts.

All was going well; the soup was good, the braised beef was passable although the cow it came from probably died of old age—however, this was the Navy so you had to deal with things as they came; the Duchess potatoes came out good along with the green beans; but the Bakewell tarts were a disaster—the basic short crust pastry was like a rock, the jam was hard and although the almond cake filling was passable, I think the flour that I had to use was old and probably contaminated with some of the things listed in the *B. R. Five*.

My instructor, seeing my predicament and frustration, came to my rescue. He took my disaster away and replaced it with another that was on the menu of another class that was still in training in the classroom next door. Unfortunately my benefactor had also made a mistake and had forgotten to put the jam into his Bakewell tarts!

Standing by my dishes ready for the tasting and comments from the inspecting officer, I stood in trepidation as to what the outcome would be.

Comments were made and notes were written

CHAPTER THREE

down. It would be a few days before the outcome would be known.

Instead of being allowed to stand around kicking our heels waiting for our results, we were put to work on the Buffer's party. We were mustered outside of Grenville block where the Buffer would allocate our cleaning duties; for some it was to sweep the roads; some would be employed in cleaning the numerous figureheads salvaged from ships gone by that were positioned in prominent places around the establishment.

My turn came, my name being called. I stood to attention. The Buffer then told me what my duty would be. I was escorted to a toilet block which, in Navy terms, was called the heads, and a bucket of baizal was issued. (Baizal was the Navy name given to a strong disinfectant containing caustic soda and other unpleasant substances.)

However, my job was to clean the urinal.

Looking at it with the black tarred splash back and what was supposed to be a white ceramic gulley that was designed to take the flow of pee into a drain, my thoughts flowed back to the Napoleonic wars, as Chatham was home to *H.M.S. Victory* where she had been built.

Looking at the encrusted lime scale that had formed over many years stuck to the tarred back splash and the supposed-to-be white china glazed gulley, I got to work with a scraper and, with lashings of my baizal disinfectant solution, I did the best I could with what I had—a scraper, chipping hammer, a bucket of baizal and a lot of elbow grease. I was very happy when the work day ended! The Buffer made an inspection and was satisfied with my endeavours, for I had removed some hundred and fifty years of encrusted pee put there by many hundreds of matelots relieving themselves after a good night on the town.

We got to do other things to occupy us: there was an Upper Yards-man program in place for lower deck ratings of exceptional ability to become officers.

One Sunday morning we were herded into the back of a lorry. Accompanied by a couple of Upper Yards-men, we were driven at about thirty miles an hour for one hour, when the lorry came to a halt and we were instructed to get out.

Not having a clue as to where we were, we looked at each other in a bemused way. Our Upper Yards-men informed us that we were on the Pilgrims Way and would walk back along the route as far as it would take us to Chatham. The Upper Yards-men had a map and compass and would guide us back to *H.M.S. Pembroke*.

During our trek we found a pub and got some refreshment. What we didn't know was that our chief G.I. was following us on his motorbike, hugging the country roads close to the Pilgrims Way.

We had lost little Jock since he was having a hard time keeping up with us, not only because he couldn't march but because walking or rambling was beyond his capabilities. We finally left the Pilgrims Way and found ourselves on the road into Chatham when a motorbike passed us. At this point we were footsore and weary, and imagine our surprise when we noticed that the motorbike (ridden of course by our G.I.) had a passenger on the pillion passenger seat, who we recognized: little Jock, wearing a big grin on his face and waving at us!

On another Sunday after church parade, a couple of the lads and I took a walk along the jetty to have a look at the ships tied up there. *The Defender* was still there with *Swiftsure* not far away. A submarine was also tied up there. This was something new and attracted our attention. Looking down at her, I noticed she looked small in comparison to the larger surface vessels. Someone appeared on the casing coming out of the forward hatch. It was the cox'n, who saw us and invited us onto the boat. We didn't hesitate and we were given a stem-to-stern tour of the boat! The cox'n said she was being recommissioned after undergoing an extensive refit in Chatham dockyard. *H.M. Submarine Tapir* and her crew were about to be put to the test by F.O.S.M., short for Flag Officer Submarines, before she would take up her duties in support of the Australian Navy.

Finely, our draft chits arrived; some lads were drafted to Scotland to ships and establishments like *H.M.S. Lochinvar* in the Forth Estuary and other places around the coast of Britain where the Royal Navy had a presence.

We still had a week or two before our drafts would be carried out.

CHAPTER THREE

In a letter from Mum I was informed that my cousin Mona was coming home for a holiday from America. Mona had married an American Airman and was living in New Jersey.

It brought back memories of Mona's wedding. Auntie Evelyn and Uncle Tom along with John and his buddies put on a fantastic ceremony. Mona and John were married in St Luke's church in Cowley, the same one where I had been an altar boy when at school. After the wedding ceremony we went to the old Cowley Community Centre that Aunt Evelyne had hired for the reception. I was about twelve at the time. Our American friends had access to many goodies that were in short supply to us and were very generous in providing cigarettes and alcoholic beverages to indulge in! The wedding cake took centre stage as they do, speeches were made and formalities were undertaken and all was well.

The time came for Mona and John to depart on their honeymoon, which was going to be in London. Aunt Tilley had come up from London to attend the wedding. Mona and John announced that they had to leave to catch the train, and Aunt Tilley, hearing this, asked Mona if she could travel back to London with them! Mona and John had no objection, so Aunt Tilley travelled with Mona and John on the journey to London.

John had booked a suite at the Cumberland Hotel. Unfortunately Aunt Tilley insisted in accompanying them! According to Mona they had a drink in the hotel lounge and after a very long day were very tired and

CHAPTER THREE

wanted to start their honeymoon. Aunt Tilley was being rather pushy and wanted to see the suite that John had booked. John was polite but firm, stating that Mona and he needed time to relax and that Aunt Tilley should go home, also to relax.

Back in Oxford, the reception and the frivolities were coming to an end. I had a pocketful of Chesterfield cigarettes that had been left standing in a glass Shippam's paste pot. Uncle Charlie, who had travelled up from Swindon, thought he was pouring a cup of tea from one of the old brown betty teapots! He had already had a skinful and was three sheets to the wind; unfortunately, what he was pouring into his cup was a brown coloured liquid that consisted of every dreg from every drink that had been left. Mum and Auntie Evelyne had started to clear away the tables and to start the washing up using the teapots to empty the leftover drinks into, and needless to say Uncle Charlie became six sheets to the wind and had to be carried out.

I put in a request form for a weekend leave and it was granted. I travelled to Oxford by train and met with the family. Mona was the reason for me being there and we had a very good reunion.

Traveling back to *H.M.S. Pembroke* on a Sunday was a bit problematic; train schedules ran on a Sunday service, and unfortunately for me I missed my connection at Waterloo. My leave expired at 22.00hrs and I arrived at 22.45hrs.

Arriving at the guard house, I reported to collect my

CHAPTER THREE

station card, which had been withdrawn. I was now in the rattle, another Navy term ('in the shit'!); I was cautioned and told to be ready for Commander's report the following morning.

There were a number of us miscreants at this parade, all of us having done something that we shouldn't have done! Our respective divisional officers were there to defend or prosecute us. As for me, it was the Master at Arms that prosecuted me—for the sin of being 45 minutes adrift (another navy term for being late). I was given 14 days No.9's. I need to explain that Navy punishment was meted out by numbers—I think No.1 was being hung from the yard arm.

My No.9 punishment involved 14 days loss of pay and left me with extra duties and having to respond to the pipe over the tannoy system; men under punishment were mustered so that we could be counted and be given our extra duties.

This would not be the only time that I would be a man under punishment!

CHAPTER FOUR

MY PUNISHMENT ended and my draft chit arrived. I was instructed to report to *H.M.S. Dryad*.

My mates also received their drafts. We all celebrated together with a lot of backslapping and shaking of hands! We had survived our training schedules and the soup mix that we were in some three months before had been blended into a fine bunch of young lads, ready to take up their duties in Her Majesty's Royal Navy.

* * *

H.M.S. Dryad was a shore Establishment not far from Portsmouth, snuggled in the confines of the village of Southwick just over Portsdown Hill.

Southwick House was the centre of the Establishment which came to fame during WWII where the D-Day landings were planned and executed. Field Marshall Montgomery had his command mobile caravan that he used during the great tank battle at El-Alamein parked on what was to be the parade ground. General Eisenhower also had taken up residence there. This was a time long before my arrival as a junior assistant cook.

CHAPTER FOUR

H.M.S. Dryad holds many fond memories. The Establishment was now the training school for radar and sonar operators, held together by officers and instructors and of course by us other ships' company members of the Supply & Secretariat Division. Our captain was John Fieldhouse who would become Lord Fieldhouse later in his career when he was one of the masterminds behind the success of the Falklands war in 1982.

I was introduced to Chief Cook Riddle who was a jovial chap, then to the rest of the Petty officers, leading hands and cooks. I would be under their charge and direction for my time serving at *H.M.S. Dryad*.

I completed my joining routine, being issued my bedding, and getting the stamp from each department that I had to report to, then returning it to the regulating office for scrutiny; this done, I went to my allocated mess.

These accommodation buildings were of a wartime construction, slabs of pre-formed concrete put together with a corrugated asbestos roof on top and a concrete floor with a skimming of some sort of composite black material that would shine when polished with Ronnuck floor polish and a lot of hard work with floor buffers and Dixon electric floor polishers.

I was allocated a bunk by the Killick of the mess. This was a lower bunk; the one above me had not yet become occupied. The mess accommodated cooks, stewards and stores ratings. As an aside, stores ratings in Navy language were known as Jack Dustys; cooks could be called Slushies, and Stewards, Po Jerkers; seamen were called Dabtoes; sick bay attendants were called a sick bay Tiffy—more of an endearment than a disparagement.

A number of civilians were employed in the establishment. Some worked in the main galley alongside of us, all being retired ex-Navy men—some having served during World War Two. *Dryad* was served by the main galley where I was employed and the wardroom galley that was established within the main building of Southwick House; the officers' cooks were accommodated in our mess.

H.M.S. Dryad, as previously stated, was different from many other establishments. It was positioned in the Hampshire countryside, within a vast estate. A pig farm was tended by Jim, a rating of the engine room branch; he was issued with an old Shire horse along with a cart and a shovel to take care of his duties. A vegetable patch was also tended by Jim. The produce found its way to the captain and wardroom's dinner table, well prepared and offered up by the Officers' cooks; two of them would become good mates of mine.

Being such a large estate, a game keeper was needed. This fell to another rating who was a leading Officer's cook. He was allowed to carry a double-barrelled shotgun when on game keeping duty around the woods and copses on the estate. Sometimes I would go with him and shoot the odd crow or other vermin that would threaten the pheasants or other game birds.

CHAPTER FOUR

The central appliance of any galley is the cooking range. *H.M.S. Dryad* was supplied with a monster; it was made of cast iron and had been converted from being a coal fired range to using fuel oil to heat it. Four ovens and numerous hot plates were positioned on the surface.

Other cooking vessels included a number of coppers heated by steam and boiling water. A steam hose was supplied; this was a clever device: a hose was attached to a steam pipe outlet on the end of which was a steel rod perforated with holes; it could be placed in any container to heat up or cook anything from soup to custard.

There were ladles as big as buckets, spoons as big as shovels and a large array of galley dishes made of aluminium that anything from rice pudding to roast potatoes could be cooked in. Five-gallon bowls were in abundance, (mainly used for soaking dried peas or beans) and for putting what we called strongers—a soft soap solution that we would use to scrub the galley deck that was made of red tiles and would be cleaned after every meal with mops, brooms, and squeegees. I will explain later regarding my problem in defining the difference between a five-gallon bowl containing dried peas and another one containing cold strongers that needed revitalizing to scrub out the galley.

I was gradually introduced to my duties. Some of the Petty Officers and leading hands were married and lived in the married quarters not far from the Establishment, so my only connection with them was when I was on duty.

For the rest of us, our home was the mess. We made

CHAPTER FOUR

it as comfortable as we could within Naval regulations that were permitted. The central part of the mess was the cast iron coke-burning stove that stood on a concrete plinth in the centre of the mess. We had a number of chairs that had arms attached, padded with some sort of stuffing and covered with a dark red imitation leather material.

In the dark winter months we would get close to the old stove to take in the heat that it provided, taking turns to replenish the coke and stoke it up with a long poker. On top of the stove was the maker's emblem cast into the metal; this was a tortoise with the words embossed on the outer edge SLOW BUT SURE. It did take time for it to heat up, but once going it provided a lot of warmth and comfort to us.

Reading books was a great pastime. One evening I was reading a novel and something struck me as funny. I read it out loud. One of my mates was also engrossed in his book and responded by reading out loud the sentence that he was reading. The connection was spontaneous: reading out loud, taking a sentence or a paragraph from two different people reading two different books was hilarious! It went something like this: reading from my book, 'She went into the room.' My mate reading from his book would take his turn, 'Now she's on the floor,' and so on.

Being cooks and having access to the galley, the duty cook would make a fanny of Kye and bring it up to the mess. Kye was the Navy term for cocoa, while a fanny was a small bucket with a pouring lip; however, on this particular night, Buck was the one that was doing the honours.

Buck had closed down the galley, turned off all the lights and was making his way to the mess. From what he later told us, he heard a rattling sound, looked around and saw that the galley lights were on. He was sure that he had turned off the lights before leaving and was certain that he had secured the galley for the night. Feeling in his pockets for the keys, he couldn't find them; he put the fanny of Kye down and, returning to the galley, he found the door was unlocked, and he went in. He found the keys on the edge of the range. Taking a quick look round, he turned off the lights, locked the galley doors and legged it back to the mess, picking up the fanny of Kye on the way. He was as white as a sheet!

One member of the mess had a smile on his face. He was a leading cook, not a bad chap. Ships' messes are very confined and nobody can keep secrets for long, and it was a known secret that this particular leading cook came from a family whose father was a man of the cloth. They had an altercation, from which the outcome was that the father was for the white arts but the son was for the black arts; in these confines we become part of each other—something that can make life very interesting.

A new messmate arrived and he was allocated the bunk above me. He was a Geordie lad, built like a brick shithouse. He was a Steward and had hands like hams and a nose that was flattened. When he got in his bunk

CHAPTER FOUR

my nose was about six inches from his bum, separated by his mattress.

He snored and kept the whole mess awake for the bigger part of the night. He had a gentle disposition although his size could be a bit disconcerting.

A week or two went by and most of the lads reported for duty with red eyes and yawning because of lack of sleep—all because of Geordie's snoring. Something had to be done.

We decided to have a run ashore, taking Geordie with us. Finding out that the Yorkshire Grey was his favourite pub in Portsmouth, we accommodated him, and after a few pints of his favourite ale, namely Newcastle Brown, the rest of us imbibing our own proffered beverage, it came to the matter in hand: me being in the bunk below him was nominated to address the situation.

In trepidation of what his response would be to the words that were about to be spoken from my mouth, I braced myself and came out with it: I said, "Geordie, me old mate, do you mind if I say something a bit personal?" He replied in his great Geordie accent, "Nay lad, gawe ahead." I said, "You don't half snore!" We were astounded by his response. We were expecting a punch-up, but he started to laugh, and apologized for keeping us awake at night.

He was aware that he did snore in a lot of decibels and had forgotten to warn us. Being the elected spokesman, so to speak, I asked him what could be done

CHAPTER FOUR

to resolve the problem, and he replied, "All you have to do is get your finger and thumb and squeeze my nose when the snoring starts."

Back at Dryad this action would be put to the test, me being nominated to do the nose tweaking since Geordie had been allocated the bunk above me.

Our run ashore was over. Back in the mess we turned in. Getting into our respective bunks, we waited for Geordie to start his nightly rendition of snoring. It didn't take long! Hushed whispers were coming at me from all directions to get up and tweak Geordie's nose. I quietly got out of my lower bunk and, keeping low, gingerly put my right hand in the direction of his face. Darkness has its problems: not being able to see Geordie's face, let alone his nose, I furtively let my hand find its way across his physiology, crawling like a spider. He didn't flinch since his Newcastle Brown ale had sent him into a deep slumber. Although his snoring was at a great crescendo, I found his nose and gave it a hard tweak. If I was going to have a fistful of those great hams of hands of his, I would make it worth my while.

My fears were relieved when there was no retaliation. I had survived and my messmates could sleep in peace. Needless to say that for the duration of my stay at *H.M.S. Dryad* my nightly duty was to squeeze Geordie's nose.

Another leading cook arrived. He was drafted from *H.M.S. Messina*, a Tank landing craft that had been used in the Christmas Islands for the duration of the British atomic bomb tests. He came from Manchester and was a flamboyant character. He needed to be, for he had been classified as P.7. R, a Navy term for unfit for sea duty.

Ted, as was his name, had what was diagnosed as coral poisoning. His face was pockmarked, and his back was covered in pimply yellow and red-headed pustular eruptions. His treatment was that he had to go into the shower with the water temperature as hot as he could bear it; he would run in, brace his back muscles, and this would pop the pustular eruptions and the water from the shower would wash away the infected puss that was under his skin.

A sick bay tiffy was always in attendance on Ted's daily shower routine, ready to get him dried off and to administer a powder that would disinfect and soothe his skin condition; one must not forget that the skin is the largest organ of the human body.

Although Ted's condition was diagnosed as coral poisoning, I had my own doubts; the fact that atomic bomb tests were taking place, and Ted among others had been swimming in the waters around Christmas Island, albeit that coral reefs were in abundance, the chances of radioactive water was not inconceivable and could have been contributory to his condition.

Back in the galley I had to deal with one of my own mess ups. Tot time was over and the dinner time service was over. Jan, the leading cook of the watch, instructed me to get the bowl of strongers ready for scrubbing the galley floor. Unfortunately a five-gallon bowl was in position under the tap of one of the coppers containing

CHAPTER FOUR

boiling water. I thought the brackish water in the bowl was strongers that needed a bit of livening up, so I got a handful of soft soap and dropped it into the bowl, adding in a dash of boiling water from the copper and started to agitate it with a scrubbing broom. To my horror dried peas started to rise to the surface. Oh shit! I was going to be in deep and murky trouble! I was about to scrub the galley floor with tonight's mushy peas!

Fortunately no one was in sight. I found a large sieve, placed it in a sink and poured the contents of the bowl into it; it saved the peas but strands of soft soap were in evidence. I turned on the tap and washed and washed those damned peas until all traces of soap were gone, returning them to the bowl and filling it with fresh water. Nobody was any the wiser, and they were the cleanest peas that the Navy had ever had.

Lieutenant Erwin was my Divisional Officer. He was a man of compassion and very protective and proud of the men in his division.

One morning during one of his unannounced inspections, he stopped to have a chat. He said, "Burgess, you're quite a big lad. I'm going to put you into the boxing team for *H.M.S. Dryad.*" I exclaimed, "Sir, I don't know how to box! I could handle myself in a street fight but in a boxing ring I wouldn't stand a chance."

He was unconvinced, so I was registered to be entered into the Royal Navy novices' championships.

Dryad had a small gymnasium built of the World War Two Nissen Hut construction. Wall bars were

CHAPTER FOUR

provided, vaulting horses, rush mats, stepping benches, a speed ball, and a punch bag that was an old kit bag filled with sand.

This was to be my training and fitness emporium. There was a P.T.I. who would be available to give coaching in the noble art. However, I needed a sparring partner; this came in the form of able seaman Mick Meleaney. Mick was a Cockney Italian, and a damned good boxer! I didn't know at the time that he had been semi-professional, going around with a travelling boxing booth at fair grounds.

Anyway, we got into a training routine, exercising on the wall bars, jumping over the vaulting horses, knocking hell out of the sand-filled kitbag and the speed ball. Then it came to sparing! Being an awkward sod, I was a south paw—this meant that I led with my right whereas conventional boxers led with their left.

There was no boxing ring in the gym at *Dryad* so we would spar in the centre of the gym, wearing sixteen-ounce gloves; these were twice the weight of the gloves worn in a contest. In those days no protective headgear was required or even heard of. Mick and I battled it out, and my long reach helped me from letting him get within my guard. The plan was that one fist was for protection while the other was to jab and punch through your adversary's defence. Mick was getting frustrated and said, "You long-armed bugger, I can't get close to you!" I laughed! His response was an all-out attack, bringing together his skills as a boxing booth contender.

CHAPTER FOUR

I landed outside the gym, having been knocked through the open doors!

The evening of the Novices' Individual Championships arrived and I was nervous as hell. I had a mate at *Dryad* who came from Oxford and lived not far from where I did. His name was Nigel Hatton and he lived on Cowley Road. Nigel volunteered to be one of my seconds alongside with our P.T.I.

The boxing contests were being held at Victory Barracks. Nigel and I caught the bus in Southwick and got off in Commercial Road in Portsmouth. Nigel asked how I felt and I replied that I was bloody nervous! We were walking towards Victory Barracks; the Trafalgar Club was on the same road and next to it was a pub. Nigel grabbed my arm and said, "Come in here!" In we went and he ordered two double whiskies. After getting them down us we proceeded to Victory Barracks.

We were shown into the changing room. I was not supplied with any fancy boxing gear. I had a pair of my issued gym shoes, a pair of white socks, a vest and a pair of white shorts, carried in my small Navy-issued attaché case.

The P.T.I. had arrived before us and was waiting for me to get ready for my bout.

With hands bandaged and the eight-ounce gloves fitted to my hands, I hardly felt prepared. Draped around my shoulders was a red woollen cape and emblazoned on the back in white lettering was Nore Command.

CHAPTER FOUR

A great crowd of people were assembled to watch and cheer on their respective preferred combatants; many of the assembled spectators were senior officers and local dignitaries along with a majority of lower deck ratings.

Getting into the ring, the master of ceremonies introduced us to the audience; in a very refined voice he came out with my introduction: "In the red corner is cook Burgess representing *H.M.S. Dryad*; in the blue corner is naval airman Luck!

A lot of applause and a general ballyhoo took place. Eying up my opponent from my corner I could see that he had a boxer's nose and was wearing proper boxing gear, like boxing boots and shorts. I looked like something out of a charity shop in comparison!

Naval Airman Luck had been brought over from a naval air station in Northern Ireland. My thoughts were that he must be good to have been transported to Portsmouth for this contest.

The referee called us into the centre of the ring and gave us his instructions, emphasizing that when he said 'break' we break and that he wanted a good clean fight under the Marques of Queensbury rules. We were instructed to return to our corners. Through the corner of my mouth I said to the P.T.I., "What shall I do?" He replied, "Stay away from him!"

The bell rang and out we both came, fists at the ready to land the first blow. Being a south paw, I was dominating the progression of the direction of the fight.

CHAPTER FOUR

The referee intervened and instructed me to reverse my direction; this was not natural to me but I had to comply. My opponent landed a couple of good blows on to me, but he was not quite as good as he looked. Although he had better gear than me, he lacked stamina. A boxing ring is the loneliest place on earth for combatants, surrounded by spectators cheering and shouting encouragement for their chosen competitor. In the ring concentration is the key, to the extent that the noise from the spectators is not heard.

The bell to end the first round rang and I went to my corner. The match was three rounds at three minutes per round; these nine minutes would be some of the longest in my life.

Round Two started and with fists flying we got into it. I was hit a low blow below the belt; my adversary was cautioned by the referee, and we continued; another low blow was delivered with another caution to my opponent—and Round Two was over.

My P.T.I. and Nigel were confident that I could win and gave me encouragement; it was alright for them—they weren't out there taking the punishment!

Round Three started and I was pissed off that I had been fouled three times by this guy. It was time for recompense! During the round he went low on me again and without hesitation I brought my right fist from behind and gave him a rabbit punch to the back of his neck. He didn't go down but when he unfolded I forced him into a corner and knocked seven bells of shit

CHAPTER FOUR

out of him. I had a twinge of conscience and let him off the hook. I stood back to let him regain some composure.

The final bell rang and I returned to my corner and sat down on the stool. Nigel and the P.T.I. put towels around me to mop up the sweat and spots of blood. I don't know if they were mine or my opponents.

The referee collected the results from the judges, and announced me the winner! In the centre of the ring my hand was held high. The applause was overwhelming! I felt very humble and went to my opponent's corner to congratulate him on also giving a good performance.

On returning to *H.M.S. Dryad* Nigel and I were confronted by Lieutenant Erwin who was officer of the watch; this was the reason why he was not available to be in attendance at the boxing match. He was eager to hear how I had got on. After informing him that I had won, he was over the moon and invited us into the wardroom for a celebration drink, saying that he would inform the Captain of my success.

The outcome from this was that I received a presentation of the ship's colours presented to me by the Captain who would become Lord Fieldhouse. The ship's colours were in the form of a blazer badge bearing the ship's emblem with its motto written in Latin, *Nobis Tutus Ibis*, which loosely translated means, 'For those who seek we shall guide.'

The presentation took place on a Friday division's parade. I always tried to avoid these ceremonial parades,

CHAPTER FOUR

but on this occasion I had no chance. I was fell in with the rest of the S.&S. division with Lieutenant Erwin being our divisional officer, who was responsible for our smartness; after being inspected to make sure we were properly dressed and ready for the parade, he marched off to the Captain's dais to report the division's readiness for the parade. With his best uniform bearing a number of medals, and his sword in its scabbard, he looked the perfect Naval Officer—very smart and efficient! Unfortunately a shite hawk, better known as a seagull, was flying over the parade ground at the time and decided to relieve itself of the contents of its bowels; these were ejected from its backside and with the aid of gravity fell on our Divisional Officer. He stopped in mid-stride, looked down on his lapel where the shite hawk had left its deposit, pulled out a handkerchief and did his best to wipe away the offending excrement, leaving a whitish, grey-green smudge. Continuing to the dais, he reported our division. The Captain and the senior officers were doing their best to control their laughter as were the rest of the Divisions. After reporting, the Captain remarked, "I see you have received a promotion, Lieutenant Erwin!"

Finally I was called to the dais and marched smartly towards the Captain. I was fortunate—I didn't have a shite hawk flying over me! The Captain shook my hand and congratulated me on my achievement and handed me my ship's colours. I saluted, about turned and marched back to my Division.

CHAPTER FOUR

After the parade we returned to the mess.

I had weekend leave and decided to hitchhike home. Hitchhiking was sometimes faster than traveling by train. There was one train a month that went direct to Oxford and returned, and this was not that time of the month.

Getting home early evening, Mum and Ernie were pleased to see me along with my youngest sister Valerie.

After having a wash and brush up I was off into town. I met up with a bunch of my old mates. A few of them were also serving in the Navy and happened to be on leave at the same time. One of the lads had joined the Marines and had just completed his course as a Royal Marine Commando.

We had a good few pints in the Nag's Head and decided that the next day, being Saturday, we would go down to the river at Eynesham, and have a get-together.

Our mate Sid lived in Cumnor Village, not far from Eynesham.

Sid arranged with the farmer to allow us to use his field, on condition that we cleaned up before we left. Sid also had an old Ford car that he used to ferry us to the field. Some of the lads had girlfriends who volunteered to bring some food along, such as sausages, bread rolls and things; we lads would supply the drinks.

It was early evening when we got started with Sid ferrying four or five of us at a time from a pick-up point in Oxford.

We had gathered a load of dead wood and made a

CHAPTER FOUR

bonfire, the girls using it to cook the sausages and other things they had brought along.

None of us had bathing suits but we didn't care—we had a swim in the river and dried off with what we had around the heat from the bonfire; the food and drinks started to flow, and one of the boys had a guitar; songs were sung, party pieces were given, we Navy chaps giving more bawdy versions of old songs such as Maggie Mai.

It was about 10.30 when things started to slow down. The bonfire was burnt down to a few glowing embers and a few of the lads were a few sheets to the wind, including me and Nobby! Nobby was a good mate of mine who was in the Navy and lived not far from me on Oxford Road.

However, Sid had stayed sober and started to ferry our friends back to Oxford; he made his final trip and returned to pick up Nobby and me. In a blurred look around the site, we could see that it hadn't been cleaned up; our promise to the farmer was that it would be.

Nobby and I let Sid know that we would stay overnight in the field and clean up our mess when it got light in the morning. Sid left, promising to return in the morning to take us home.

We found some wood and got the fire livened up. I had a warm jerking and so did Nobby; we had a chat for a while, and then found a place to sleep under a bush.

The alcohol we had consumed put us into a fitful slumber.

Dawn was breaking. I started to stir as a damp

CHAPTER FOUR

creeping mist was about to envelope us, coming from the direction of the river. I got closer to the still hot embers of the fire, pulling my jerking closer to me; it had got quite chilly during the night.

My mouth felt like it had been cleaned out with sandpaper! Nobby started to move; at first he wondered where I was, for the mist was so thick he couldn't see me. I shouted to him and he joined me by the dying embers of the fire.

Eventually the sun broke out and the mist disappeared. In the distance we heard a car engine—it was Sid coming as promised to pick us up. We cleaned up the field and Sid took us home.

My weekend leave came to an end, but I still had a raging sore throat. I decided not to hitchhike back to *Dryad*, but to catch a coach ride. Southdown Coaches provided a service from Portsmouth to Birmingham, Manchester, Liverpool and major Towns and Cities along the route; the coach's return journey would pass through Oxford at about 3.30 on Monday morning. I made sure I was there. Carfax was the pickup point. Huddling in the doorway of the Chanel fashion shop, a bunch of us would await the arrival of the coaches that would return us to our respective ships and establishments. I didn't have a ticket but if you slipped the driver a few bob he wouldn't leave you behind; if there was no seat available you could crash out on the floor, making sure that you moved when someone was getting off so you didn't get trod on.

CHAPTER FOUR

Back at *Dryad* my throat was giving me hell! Sleeping under a bush with a swirling mist hadn't helped; I decided to go to the sick bay.

The sick bay Petty Officer checked me out and informed the Quack, a term of endearment for the ship's doctor. The Doc checked me out and ordered me to be put into a ward for observation; this meant that my kit had to be packed and put into storage—a duty that fell to one of my mess mates. Archie was nominated for this job; he was a Scots lad and a character in his own right that I will explain later in this chapter.

However, I was in the sick bay for three days with temperature, blood pressure, and all the other things taken to ensure my wellbeing.

I was discharged back to duty; my throat was still very sore but with medication I was assured it would return to normal.

I retrieved my kit from storage and reported to the Chief Cook at the Galley to let him know I had been released from the sick bay and returned to duty.

Returning to duty wouldn't last long. Walking from the galley to the mess I nearly flaked out! I stumbled and came out in a sweat. I made my way back to the sick bay where the sick bay Petty Officer was typing up medical notes. I stood in front of his desk and he said impatiently, "What do you want, Burgess?" I explained how I felt, which was bloody awful; his reply was, "Bugger off! You've been loafing in the sick bay for three days!" I said, "Will you take my temperature?" He said,

CHAPTER FOUR

"Take it yourself." I did—a thermometer was close by in a sterilized container; I took it out and gave it a shake like they do in the films when nurses are involved. I put it in my mouth under the tongue, leaving it there for about a minute. I took it out and looked at it. It registered a temperature close to 105 degrees! The P.O. was still engrossed with his typing. I said to him, "Read this," and stuffed the thermometer under his nose. He reluctantly took it from me and read it; then the shit hit the fan!

He ordered me to lie down and not to move. He was going to get the M.O. Things were happening fast: my kit had to be gathered up and put into storage once again, this job falling to my mate Archie. The Doc carried out various tests on my person and deemed it necessary to have me transported by ambulance to the Royal Navy Hospital Haslar in Gosport.

By this time I was in La-La land. I was put into a ward and had all sorts of needles stuck into me to take blood and administer all sorts of other stuff that alchemists and doctors do.

One diagnosis indicated that I had contracted viral meningitis. A lumber punch was ordered and was not very comfortable when executed.

Fortunately, my ordeal came to an end, and with the expertise of the Haslar medical staff I was able to return to duty.

Returning to Dryad, I had to go through the joining routine and retrieved my kit from storage. I met with

CHAPTER FOUR

Archie and thanked him for taking care of things for me.

I asked him what had been going on during my absence, and he replied, "Not much"—although he explained what had happened to his cook's whites. "Did they get nicked?" I asked, and he shook his head, explaining that he had brought a packet of the New Blue Daz laundry powder that had just come on the market, and one evening, being duty watch, decided to do his dohbeying; taking one of the larger galley pots, he filled it with water, and added the Blue Daz laundry powder that was supposed to make whites whiter than white. He put his whites into the pot and brought them to the boil on the galley range, giving them an occasional stir with a ladle; after a while he removed the pot from the range to cool down before taking his clothes out to be rinsed off in cold water.

When the pot had cooled down, Archie tipped the contents into a galley sink to drain off the soapy water. Horror of horrors, his cook's whites had turned into a bluish grey colour! He said he rinsed them several times in fresh cold water to no avail—the stubborn dye or impregnated washing powder was not going to be shifted.

Archie had written a letter to the manufacturers to complain about their product, remarking that "your new Blue Daz product lived up to its name, turning my cook's whites blue!" As far as I know he is still waiting for a reply.

A couple of other mess mates were officer cooks. Jock and Terry had motorbikes and on weekends when not

CHAPTER FOUR

on duty would take off to Brighton. One weekend I was at a loose end so they invited me and Hughie, another mess mate, to go along with them as pillion passengers. We arrived in Brighton in the early afternoon. The motorbikes were parked and we set off to visit a couple of pubs.

I can remember two of them—one was called the Belvedere, which was close to the sea front; the other was Harrison's, which was closer to the town. Both places were very lively and of course ladies of ill repute frequented them.

Hughie and I were unaware that Jock and Terry were acquainted with a number of them. Introductions were made and one of these ladies took a fancy to me and we had a great time; her name was Sadie. Hughie also got fixed up. Jock and Terry didn't need fixing up since they already had their girlfriends.

All of them were prostitutes; this was not surprising as ladies of this oldest of the world's professions went hand-in-hand with sailors all over the world; perhaps hand-in-hand is not the correct term, but I'm sure you understand what I am saying!

After all, Jesus was friendly with Mary Magdalene, who was of the same profession. It's written in the Bible so they can't be bad. I must say that throughout my time in the Navy I met many of these girls and not one of them was the hard-faced scheming women depicted in films and novels, or how the press sometimes promoted them.

CHAPTER FOUR

I made a number of trips to Brighton with Jock and Terry, always meeting up with Sadie; the accommodation these girls lived in were not ramshackle hovels, but very comfortable apartments in a very respectable part of Brighton. None of us were ever charged a penny for our accommodation or for anything that went with it.

On a couple of occasions Sadie would see that I was a bit skint and would slip me a couple of quid before leaving. I would be embarrassed and would refuse to take her money, yet somehow it always turned up in my pocket.

I still went home to Oxford for main leaves; I had bought a B.S.A. Bantam from one of the civilian employees, and this became my mode of transport from *Dryad* to Oxford.

Christmas leave was over and I had to ride my trusty B.S.A. motorbike back to *Dryad*. I left home about 3 o'clock in the afternoon. I was wearing my uniform under my Black Knight motorcycle gear, and I wore a crash helmet and large leather gauntlets.

By the time I got to Carfax to turn into St Aldates making my way to get to the A34 Trunk road that would take me towards Hampshire, the sun started to disappear; during my Christmas leave the weather had been a mixture of frost, a dusting of snow, some winter sunshine and very cold temperatures.

I connected with the A34 and made my way through Abingdon and proceeded on my journey towards

CHAPTER FOUR

Newbury. Snow was banked up on the roadside and I was on the Drayton Road when I felt the Bike slip. I slowed down and took my feet off the footrests. I had no chance—I was about to have the bike go under me and I aimed for the snow-covered bank; this helped to cushion my fall, and the bike was saved from being laid down. After gathering my composure I slid my foot on the road surface; what had looked like a shiny wetness was in fact black ice! I had no choice than to continue my journey.

By this time it was dark. The moonlight helped to illuminate the icy road and the snow-covered embankments and fields. My progress was slow but so far safe. I had travelled about another fifteen miles and was close to Newbury when the bike slipped from under me. Down I went! My Black Knight riding suit cushioned me from any serious injury. The bike was not damaged, so I got going again. The roads in Newbury were clear. The next stage of my journey was to get to Winchester and connect to the A333 trunk road. Passing through Newbury and the Greenham Common turn off, I was at Highclere when the bike and me parted company once again!

This was one too many. I picked myself up and the bike was still undamaged. I looked around and a house was nearby. I rode my bike down the drive and knocked on the door. A lady answered and I explained my predicament.

She was very kind and allowed me to park the bike

CHAPTER FOUR

in her garage. I told her I would return and collect it as soon as the weather improved.

My next problem was that I had to hitchhike the rest of the way to Southwick or close enough to catch a bus; being a Sunday, you had to take pot luck if a bus came along.

I was back on the A34, walking in the direction of Winchester. I had changed out of my motorcycle gear and was back in uniform. My Burberry along with my cap had been packed in a small hold so all that I had was tied on the bike.

I had been walking for about ten minutes when I heard a lorry approaching. I stopped and looked in its direction, sticking out my arm with a raised thumb protruding from my hand. The lorry came to a halt and the passenger door opened. A young lad spoke to me saying, "Where are you going?" I informed him I was heading to Southwick. He replied, "Hop in, we're going to Southampton and can drop you off at Fareham." This was good news! The good Lord or somebody was watching over me that night.

The lorry cab was warm, much more comfortable than riding my motor bike on icy roads and freezing weather.

The driver of the lorry was not very talkative; mainly, he was concentrating on the adverse road conditions. The young lad however was giving a nonstop commentary over a walkie-talkie radio, talking to, as I ascertained, his dad; the conversation was about the

CHAPTER FOUR

progress the lorry was making on its journey. When the transmission ended I enquired as to what the cargo was that was being transported; without hesitation he replied, "Two Elephants." I was amazed! My Christmas leave had certainly ended on a high note, what with falling off a motorbike three times on icy roads and then sharing a ride with two elephants in a Chipperfields Circus lorry! I was dropped off before we got to Fareham as Wickham was closer to Southwick, and *H.M.S. Dryad*.

I arrived back in the mess tired, bruised and sore, and was ever thankful to find my bunk, taking up my nightly duty of squeezing big Geordie's nose.

My time at *Dryad* would last another few months. Draft chits were being issued and mine arrived. *H.M.S. Albion* was crewing up and getting ready for a general service commission to the Far East.

H.M.S. Albion, being an aircraft carrier, required a large crew to operate her, and I was to become part of that crew.

CHAPTER FIVE

A SHIP in the process of commissioning was a nightmare. Each crew member had to be allocated a mess, depending on the branch they belonged to. Joining routine had to be carried out; kit lockers and keys had to be issued, this task falling into the hands of the Regulating branch. With a crew of close to two thousand men, this was no mean task.

Eventually things sorted themselves out; the ship's cooks of leading hand rank and below were accommodated in 37 mess next to the seaman's 37 A mess, both of them below deck in the bow of the ship.

Other branch crew members were accommodated in various parts of the ship. The officers' wardroom and captains' cabins were aft, and the Royal Marine quarters were close by; this was a Navy tradition, as marines were not only sea soldiers but were provided to protect the officers; this was from the time when seamen were pressganged and dragged off the streets of Portsmouth and other Navy towns to crew undermanned ships.

Albion was coming to life; a ship is just a hulk until it becomes a vessel full of life made up of its captain, officers and crew.

CHAPTER FIVE

It would take a few weeks before *Albion* would be ready for her shake down trials—a Navy term, to make sure that every department was functioning, each divisional officer overseeing his department, reporting to the Captain of the progress on a daily basis.

We did get some time off when not on duty. Portsmouth dockyard had a shore-side canteen that also contained a bar.

One evening after visiting the bar I was walking along the jetty towards the ship when a voice called out, "Do you want a lift?" I looked around and in the dimness of the dockyard lights I saw a large tricycle, with racing bike handlebars; the rider was a member of *Albion*'s crew. I said, "How are you going to give me lift on that contraption?" He replied, "It's easy, climb on the rear frame, hold onto my shoulders and we'll get off!" I did and off we went.

The dockyard was crisscrossed with railway lines imbedded in the roadway, some of them coming close to the jetty; we could see *Albion*'s silhouette in the distance illuminated by the dim dockyard lights and a shrouded moon. Concentrating on our direction of travel, my new-found rider was not aware that a dockyard police vehicle was approaching us. It stopped and a booming voice yelled out at us: "Where's your lights?" My new-found friend yelled back: "Bollocks!" He started to peddle like hell with me hanging on for dear life to his shoulders. The Dockyard copper had turned his car around and was in hot pursuit; the front wheel of the trike got caught in one of the railway lines, which caused us to go in a different direction that was intended! We were close to the edge of the jetty and were getting splashed by the spray from the incoming tide; fortunately this diversion worked to our advantage: we were able to escape from the Dockyard constabulary, and arrived back at the ship in one piece.

After dodging Dockyard coppers and nearly landing in Portsmouth Harbour, I found out my compatriot's name was Riley; he would get into a lot of trouble before the end of *H.M.S. Albion*'s commission; this episode was only the beginning!

H.M.S. Albion was a capital ship; because of her size and the complement of her crew, a number of her officers were of the rank of Commander, three of which had purchased an old London taxi cab with the Captain's permission. They were allowed to store it in a hangar. This taxi would become a part of my mate Riley's altercation with the skipper later in the commission.

Prior to commissioning we were allowed shore leave. With such a large ship's crew the Portsmouth pubs were doing a heck of a trade; if any of us were under the influence and found it difficult to return to the ship, Agnes Weston, affectionately called Aggie Weston's, or the Trafalgar Club, were available; they both provided a restaurant and overnight accommodation. This service was provided every day all year round, a small charge being required for overnight stays; these varied to whether you slept in the dormitory or in a private cabin.

CHAPTER FIVE

The restaurant food wasn't fancy, but it was very nourishing and fairly priced.

After many weeks of preparation, *Albion* was ready for sea. We eased off the jetty and slowly, with the aid of a couple of Admiralty tugs, the ship was nudged into the outer waters of Portsmouth Harbour. The crew standing to attention on the flight deck carried out the ritual for leaving harbour; as we moved towards the harbour mouth, crowds of people were there to cheer us off and to wish us Godspeed; this could be an emotional time for some of the crew who were married with young children or wives that were pregnant. We would be away for many months, not knowing what we were to be confronted with.

As for me, this was what I had joined the Navy for and I was very happy to be going to sea.

Our first task was to de-gauss the ship to neutralize the ship's magnetism; this was carried out by sailing a measured course around Weymouth and Portland bay. This took four or five days to accomplish. Looking at the twinkling lights of Weymouth at night time brought back memories of many happy holidays spent there.

This done, we continued down the English Chanel. Our complement of air squadrons were about to embark, flying from various Naval air stations around the country.

Sea Hawks, Sea Venoms, Sky Raiders, and Westland Helicopters all landed safely and were parked in their allotted places in the hangar.

CHAPTER FIVE

A carrier never sails on its own. A number of ships are employed to support it; these ships consisted of Frigates for anti-aircraft and anti-submarine protection,

Supply ships were known as R.F.A's, short for Royal Fleet Auxiliary. The *Tideflow* was one of them, carrying aviation fuel for the aircraft and oil fuel for the ship's boilers.

Other supply ships carried victuals and ammunition, all necessary to maintain a carrier at sea.

With our squadrons on board and safely secured, we headed into the Atlantic Ocean. Our first port of call would be Gibraltar.

We had sailed through the Bay of Biscay. This stretch of water is notorious for roughness; on this occasion Mother Nature had been kind to us, and the sea had been relatively calm.

Gibraltar is a rocky peninsular at the foot of Spain; opposite is Morocco: this span of sea is where the Atlantic Ocean flows into the Mediterranean Sea.

Gibraltar for many years has been famous for its rock apes. Legend has it that when the apes leave, Britain will give up sovereignty of this very strategic base and harbour.

On our arrival we were nudged into our berth by a couple of tugs. When the ship was secured alongside the jetty, gangways were put in place and mail was delivered. I must say that the British Forces Postal Service did a good job in getting the mail to all servicemen and women wherever they may be serving throughout the world.

CHAPTER FIVE

The carrier was a large ship, but mess deck accommodation was cramped. Three-tiered bunks were supplied constructed of a tubular steel frame. Each rating was issued with two bunk canvases, one in use that was lashed to the frame of the bunk, while the other spare one was stowed in your locker along with your other kit.

The bunks were secured to stanchions and were held in place by chains and could be folded up during the day to allow movement around the mess. A mess table was supplied—this is where the rum would be issued; it was the centre of the mess where mail would be distributed, letters home or to girlfriends would be written, and where games would be played; the favourite was known as Uckers, the navy term for Ludo. Card games were popular; crib was the most popular.

Rum issue was the highlight of the day. "Up spirits" would be piped over the tannoy system and the duty messmen would take their respective mess rum fanny to the main dining room where under the watchful eye of the victualing officer and a member of the Regulating branch the rum was issued, the allocation being determined by the amount of men who were registered for grog in each mess.

Back in the mess the ritual would begin; the rum bos'un, as he was affectionately called, would arrive with the precious supply; a ticker off was another mess member, who had a tally board with each name on it of those who were registered for grog. A measuring beaker

CHAPTER FIVE

was supplied to each mess to give the exact measure of rum that each person was allowed; this in most cases was tampered with, a small 'V' being cut into the edge of the beaker so that the leakage would flow back into the fanny. Another trick was for the rum bos'un to put a couple of fingers or a thumb into the beaker; the overflow was called 'ullage' and after tot time the overspill was shared between the rum bos'un and the ticker offer; this was an acceptable practice as all of us took it in turns to be the rum bos'un or ticker off.

Rum was a great bargaining tool; for example, if you were on duty watch and wanted a run ashore, you could get a mate to stand your watch; his reward would be to come round at tot time for a gulpers, meaning he got a good gulp of your tot; sippers were given for small favours. Birthdays were a great celebration in any mess; if it was your birthday you would draw your tot and pass it around the mess so everyone would share it; the outcome would be that when all the other lads received their tot they would put a splash of theirs back into the fanny at the end of tot time; what was left in the fanny was yours.

I must add that a measure of rum for leading hands and below was known as two & one, meaning one part rum and two parts water; that, when measured, was close to a quarter of a pint. Chief and Petty Officers had one & one, a little stronger than ours; it was the finest Jamaican rum and close as you could get to 100% proof.

CHAPTER FIVE

Other entertainment was Tombola; in today's world that would be called Bingo. The Navy did allow games for monetary gains under strict rules. Films were always popular, provided by the Royal Navy Film Service. These activities took place in the main dining room of the ship.

All this shipboard entertainment was no substitute for what could be supplied ashore. We were in Gibraltar and ready to go; leave was granted and we were more interested in the bars than the scenic views and rock apes. I found myself in the Trocadero, which was humming with activity. Those of us that were experiencing our first time abroad were mesmerized by the activity; wine was flowing like a river, fan dancers were cavorting on a stage, and through the fug of cigarette smoke I saw a table supplying a variety of cheese. I made my way towards it: a very polite gentleman was in charge of the display. In broken English he invited me to take whatever I wanted; being a cheese advocate, I took a few samples which helped to maintain my equilibrium as I was imbibing a bottle of Malaga wine.

This was so different from the last time I had sailed away from England, when Mum and Ernie had taken us to the Isle of White for a holiday!

Malaga wine is stronger than one can imagine; its sweet taste can lure you into intoxication without you knowing it.

Somehow I returned to *Albion* and suffered a three-

CHAPTER FIVE

day hangover. I was not alone for many of my mess mates were in the same condition.

Albion's stay in Gibraltar was a short time, about four or five days, but enough to give each watch a run ashore.

We were now off to continue our commission. Malta, the George Cross Island, was another gem of a strategic base that had given so much during World War Two, and was still very supportive and important to ships of the Royal Navy.

We sailed into Grand Harbour. Valletta is the capital city of Malta and was very welcoming, possibly because we were such a big ship with a large crew; we would certainly have a favourable impact on the local economy.

Valetta is a beautiful city with many fine buildings including many impressive churches. Of course, the majority of our ship's company was more interested in the local bars than the architecture. Wherever one may go within the British Empire or beyond you will always find a pub or bar with the name of the Union Jack! Valetta had one, which drew us in like a magnet. Another popular bar was Beagie Mary's where the beer and wine were in abundance; the local wine, given our translation of Ambete and Marzavin, are both very potent with the same result—a raging hangover the next morning!

On arrival in Malta the Commanders had their vintage London taxi lifted from its domicile in the hangar and deposited by the ship's crane onto the jetty;

they drove it around Malta visiting the sights that the Island had to offer.

In Valetta one mode of public transport was by horse and Garry. The Garry was a small four-wheeled coach that could accommodate four people, but when our lot was ashore the driver would try and squeeze six of us in to transport us from one bar to another. Malta, being an Island poking out of the sea, had some hilly areas and the poor horse had its work cut out; and the roads were not much help, for they were like a blue grey shiny granite and very smooth.

My mate Riley, who had given me the ride of my life on the back of his tricycle back in Portsmouth Dockyard, took a fancy to a horse and Garry and wanted to buy one; he put in a request to see the Captain to get permission to bring them onboard.

The Captain was intrigued by Riley's request and questioned him how he would be able to accommodate a horse on board one of Her Majesty's aircraft carriers. Riley said, "Well sir, I would get the ship's chippie (ship's carpenter) to build a stable in a corner of the hangar; I would get straw and hay at each port of call and muck it out every day; when no flying was taking place I would exercise it around the flight deck."

Unfortunately the Captain was unable to grant Riley's request to accommodate the horse but was prepared to make a provision to accommodate the Garry. Riley's response was one of indignation. "Sir," he said, "I don't think that's fair!" The Captain replied,

CHAPTER FIVE

"Why's that?" Riley replied, "Well sir, the Commanders have a taxi that's powered by ten horses. I have only one horse that I want to bring on board!" Nevertheless, Riley's request was refused; his final argument that a Garry without a horse wasn't worth having fell on deaf ears and so he gave up the idea of buying a horse and Garry.

I should add that Riley came from a wealthy family that paid him a handsome amount of money per month to stay in the Navy; they didn't want him at home, clearly, and this enabled him to afford exotic purchases such as a horse and Garry.

Our stay in Malta came to an end and we set sail into the Mediterranean, our aircraft squadrons carrying out flying exercises and the crew being molded into an efficient and cohesive ship's company.

The Supply and Secretariat branch would carry out other activities outside of their normal duties; these included damage control, first aid, and fire parties. I was to be seconded as first aider along with a number of my other branch mates; we underwent an intensive training course conducted by the senior ship's surgeon and sick bay staff. On completion of the course and having passed the required examination, we were allocated our action station.

We were dispersed throughout the ship in groups of four and issued with a satchel containing a complete first aid kit; for our own protection we were issued with anti-flash gear.

CHAPTER FIVE

When this extra training was completed we took up our usual duties; showing the flag as it was known would take the ship to various countries.

Messina in Sicily was our next port of call. Messina was in the shadow of Mount Etna, one of the world's most active volcanoes. Thankfully it was not active during our stay.

Arriving in Messina was a lot different than Malta. When the ship was berthed alongside the jetty a crowd of people congregated to view her. Gangways were put in place and shore leave was granted to the off-duty watches; the ship's paymaster and his staff were kept busy exchanging our pound notes for the local currency, which was the lira.

Sicily, being the home of the Mafia, was a place where one had to be aware of one's surroundings. On stepping ashore we would be met by a bunch of street urchins of various ages, most of them in the age bracket of eight to twelve, all of them trying to relieve you of any loose change and as many cigarettes as you could spare. Jibber-jabbering in their own lingo with arms and hands gesticulating, you were left in no doubt of what they were after.

Prostitution was always a good earner for the Mafia. A blue-painted Fiat would make its rounds slowly, coming to a halt alongside a prospective customer. With the crew of the *Albion* in town, they were not hard to find.

The occupants of the car were two ladies of the profession; the driver was Mafiosi—he was tall and slim

CHAPTER FIVE

with a chiselled face, with hard piercing eyes; his hair was jet black, combed back and held in place by some sort of hair dressing. He was wearing a white shirt, black tie, dark suit and shoes to match. Other parts of what appeared to be a uniform were out of site; it could be a safe bet that what was hidden were the accessories, being a flick knife and a Berretta.

Back on board you could always find out who the customers and partakers of the forbidden fruit were; they would be in a queue outside the sick bay waiting for their daily cocktail of "MIS POT SIT", and a jab in the bum of penicillin, streptomycin, aureomycin, or any other medication required to bring about a cure.

Other Navy requirements for the afflicted to reduce the spread of disease were to impose the stoppage of shore leave and their daily rum issue. This was more painful than the daily dose of medication; any cook or steward found to be squeezing up, as venereal disease is commonly known on the lower deck, would be removed from normal duty and relegated to the spud locker and food prep areas; the cooking process would kill off any bacteria or infected food they had handled.

Of course, officers are not immune, but they had another name for it known as a social disease.

One evening Jock (who was a P.O. cook) and I decided to have a run ashore. After navigating the usual hoard of street urchins, we made it to a bar; we had a couple of beers and because it was quiet we decided to find a livelier place; it had got dark, and being in a strange place we were not quite sure in which direction we should go. We made a decision and took a back street. We hadn't gone far when two blokes started to follow us. They started to jibber-jabber at us with hands and arms gesticulating, just like the street urchins; they were becoming a nuisance, and Jock gave me a nudge. We had ignored them as much as possible and Jock stopped in his tracks, turned around and in his best Scottish brogue said, "Why don't ye piss off!" The next thing Jock had been sat on his arse by a right hook to the jaw. I said, "Oh shit, here we go!" I was able to let go a flat handed chop with my right hand that caught Jock's assailant in the throat that made him take off running. I grabbed his mate around his neck with my left arm, holding him in a head lock and pummelled the hell out of him with my right fist. Looking around, Jock was still flat on his back. I let matey go and he took off running and screaming as he went. I bent down and helped Jock to his feet. He was still a bit wobbly and I could have flattened him when the first words out of his mouth were "WE GOT 'EM, DIDN'T WE!" We had time to stand and around us the shadows seemed to be moving; our thoughts were maybe our assailants had gone for reinforcements, and we legged it! We came across a bar and on entering it we were relieved to find a lot of our shipmates in attendance. For Jock and me safety in numbers was the order of the day!

We got a beer and found a table. After about five minutes the door opened and in swept a very

CHAPTER FIVE

distinguished looking man. He was immaculately dressed with a camel hair coat draped across his shoulders. He was escorted by four henchmen. Jock and I looked at each other and were thinking the same thing—that our two punch-up buddies had got their reinforcements and we were about to be escorted out and be dumped off some fishing boat in the Messina Straights between Sicily and Italy.

On this gentleman's entry the bar staff froze. The bar became very quiet. As for Jock and I, we were doing our best to look insignificant, lowering ourselves further into our chairs.

All of a sudden he burst into song, giving a performance as good as any opera singer: "*Arriva Delchi Roma*" was his song and he was enthusiastically applauded, on completion. After the applause, the bar became hushed again, waiting for another song that never came. The Mafia works in mysterious ways. Jock and I were wondering if the machine guns would come out and we would be blasted away. We didn't have to worry—our singer pointed to the bar staff and in broken English ordered drinks all round! The door was opened by one of the bodyguards—and they disappeared as swiftly as they had entered.

After things in the bar had returned to normal we plucked up courage to ask one of the barmen who could speak some English if these visitors were Mafiosi. He put his finger to his lip and whispered, "*Si*, they are very important people."

CHAPTER FIVE

We returned to the ship, Jock with a bruise on his chin and a sore backside, me with a couple of bruised knuckles; this would be our last run ashore in Messina.

Setting sail out into the Mediterranean Sea and leaving Sicily behind us, we wondered where our travels would take us next. We knew we were making our way towards the Suez Canal, carrying out flying duties and action station drills on the way.

We had one port of call before forming a convoy at Port Said, Egypt. This was Piraus, the port for Athens in Greece. At the time of our stay the film 'Never on a Sunday' was being made staring Melina Mercouri. When the film was released there was a great shot of *Albion*'s bows where she was tied up to the jetty.

Going ashore in Athens was different, the magnificent architecture stretching back thousands of years. The Acropolis was the dominant feature of the city, and the busy metropolis went about its daily tasks.

I went ashore with Paddy. Needless to say he was Irish! It was said that he had hypnotized himself in a mirror and hadn't quite come out of it; he would always walk around with a slight glazed look in his eyes. He was a soft spoken, gentle soul.

We found a street-side café and bought a bottle of the local hooch, this being ouzo. We were approached by a gentleman wearing a large badge on the lapel of his jacket, stating he was an official guide; he could speak very good English, and we sat down at a table and had

CHAPTER FIVE

a chat. We weren't too interested in touring ancient ruins, but more in the local night life.

Since we were in Greece, instructions had been given not to mention anything about the Elgin Marbles. This was a sensitive subject that the Greeks could get very touchy about.

Our new-found friend persuaded us to try one of the local delicacies, which turned out to be fish eggs smothered in a very sweet syrup; it was very good and helped to make the ouzo more palatable.

We parted company on good terms, Paddy and I looking for pastures anew, taking turns to have a swig from our bottle of Ouzo. Across the street was a bus stop and all of the people in the queue were waving their arms at us and shouting! We waved back, saying to each other that they were certainly a friendly lot! Little did we know that drinking in the street was against the law and they were trying to warn us that if we were caught drinking in the street we could be thrown in jail.

We found a bar called The Black Cat where we stayed for the rest of our run ashore. We left later in the day, Paddy and I holding each other up, me with blurred vision and Paddy looking through his hypnotic glazed eyes. We managed to return on board to nurse what was going to be one hell of a hangover.

★ ★ ★

CHAPTER FIVE

Leaving Greece behind us, we sailed to Port Said in Egypt. On arrival we dropped anchor in the assembly area where ships would gather to make up the convoy for the passage through the Suez Canal.

No shore leave was granted, probably because our relationship with Egypt was still a bit fraught from the invasion in 1956 when British and French troops invaded to repossess the canal when Nasser decided to grab it for himself.

Although no shore leave was given, permission was given for traders to come aboard to barter and sell their wares. For entertainment, a Gully Gully man, the local name for a magician, came aboard and gave a good performance. You might say that the flight deck had been transformed into a Middle Eastern bazaar!

After riding at anchor for a few days the convoy was assembled, each ship with a pilot conversant with the canal's depths and shallows and various contours.

Albion, being a large ship, was limited in how much space she had to manoeuvre; this would become apparent as we slowly made our way to the Red Sea. In the galley some metal trays fell off there rack; potatoes and other vegetables in the process of being cooked started to slop around, and a shudder went through the ship: we had collided with the bank! As previously stated, a large ship of some 22,000 tons does not have much room to manoeuvre in a narrow waterway.

The damage and repair party were piped to report

CHAPTER FIVE

to the Bo's'n at the fo'c'sle. On inspection it was found that damage had been caused to the bow plates that had been buckled; gaps in the bow were in places 18ft long.

The damaged plates were shored up and temporary repairs were made. Why the ship collided with the bank was because a small ship was coming in the opposite direction and was in danger of being run down; the pilot gave the instruction to take avoidance action. The other ship was therefore the cause of the incident and I understand was flying the Egyptian flag. The avoidance action probably saved an international incident.

Exiting the canal and sailing into the Red Sea, we made for the port of Aden and shore leave was granted. Shore leave in Aden was a culture shock: goats roamed the streets unattended, old men smoked hooka pipes in doorways wearing turbans and other headwear that was very different to what we were used to; women were dressed in black robes from head to toe, not unlike nuns, the only difference being that their faces were obscured by a mesh veil, some coloured, red or green.

Aden was a duty free port so buying a camera or wristwatch could be profitable; the art of bartering was born in this part of the world and they were good at it.

There were many small shops and bazaars selling everything from cigarette lighters to miniature stuffed camels; some stalls would seem unattended and one of our mates found out to his cost that this was not so! Slinger found himself outside a shop that sold many things and he called out for assistance. When no one responded he decided to help himself. A stand was close by from which a number of cameras were hanging and he slipped his arm through the straps of the camera cases and started to walk away taking about a half dozen cameras with him; he had only gone a few steps when he was surrounded by an angry mob with knives drawn, one at his throat! He gave up his contraband and to smooth things over purchased a number of items.

After a short stay in Aden we sailed through the Gulf of Aden into the Indian Ocean, gradually making our way down the east coast of Africa to the port of Mombasa in Kenya. This was to prepare the ship for the long voyage across the Indian Ocean to Singapore.

Mombasa was a lively place. The town itself with its paved roads and architecture sported a strong British influence. The main road through the town was embellished with an archway of giant imitation elephant tusks that had been dedicated to the town by Princess Margaret during one of the Royal visits some years before.

One restaurant that some of the lads and I liked to frequent during our stay was called The Five Halls Inn; it was a replica of an old Georgian dining room with its dark oak wooden panelling around the walls enhanced with coats of arms painted on shields of mediaeval times.

One thing struck me as funny: the girls wore makeup and dressed in European clothes. High heeled shoes were in fashion. The only thing was that these Kenyan ladies had rather large feet! They seemed to overflow outside the shoe; in some extreme cases they appeared

CHAPTER FIVE

to stagger rather than walk. Nevertheless they were fun to be with—that was, until one evening when my mate Chalky and I were enticed to go just out of town to a Kraal. There were about a half dozen round thatched roofed huts within the walled compound. Chalky disappeared into one of them with his escort, while I was ushered into another one. When inside, the door was locked by my female escort; she sat down and put the door key in the cleavage of her breasts, and with hardened eyes she glared at me and said, "MY BROTHERS ARE MAU-MAU, they will kill you!" (The Mau-Mau was a terrorist group that had caused problems for the Kenyan people and the British government over a period of time in the fifties.)

I was gobsmacked! Chalky and I had been separated, a cardinal sin in these circumstances. I had never threatened a woman in my life, and going against all of my education to treat women with dignity and respect, I blurted out, "If you don't give me that key by the time I count to three, I'll wrap this stool around your head." When I got to two, she reached between her breasts and flung the key onto the floor! I didn't hesitate—I picked it up, unlocked the door and got out of there as quickly as possible, locking the door behind me. I ran across the compound and found the hut where Chalky was. I banged on the door, yelling to Chalky to get the hell out of there! Chalky got the message and came tumbling out with one leg in his bellbottoms, the other one trying to find its partner! We got ourselves together and ran like hell back towards town. I still had the key in my closed fist. I threw it away into the brush and never looked back.

Albion's stay in Mombasa came to an end and we made our way out into the Indian Ocean. We had already crossed the equator and had held the traditional crossing the line ceremony, with King Neptune holding court on the flight deck. A pool had been erected using wooden spars held together with rope, a large tarpaulin being secured within the frame and filled with water; this would be where those rounded up by the bears with their knotted ropes would meet their destiny if so desired by King Neptune. It was a lot of fun, for all ranks, and was a good morale booster.

Sailing so close to the equator made life unbearable at times with the extreme heat reaching up to 132 degrees Fahrenheit in the galley. The engine room branch also had to suffer the same. One day to prove a point we fried an egg on the flight deck (sunny side up!).

Lime juice was in abundance, made in 40-gallon tubs with tons of ice cubes to keep it cool. A large ladle was provided so that mess hands could fill their fannies and distribute it to their respective mess decks. This was one of the reasons our American cousins called us Limeys! Large high speed fans called Typhoons were also installed to help make life more bearable.

Besides the regular crew *Albion* had others to make up her complement. There was an Army liaison party headed up by Major Compton Bishop , with a Sergeant

CHAPTER FIVE

and two Corporals; we also had a number of civilians. The ship's N.A.A.F.I. was administered by two of their employees, a Chinese tailor and staff also sailed with us. The ship had a laundry staffed by Chinese civilians; we cooks had a good working relationship with the Chinese contingent.

For myself I had a new uniform made by the tailor, the cost of which was a supply of used tea leaves!

Let me explain how this came about! Tea was made and served in ten-gallon insulated containers. To make the tea an infuser was filled with five cups of tea leaves and the same amount of sugar; it was then placed into the tea urn and boiling water was poured into it.

After the serving I would take out the used tea leaves, spread them out on a sheet of parchment paper and dry them off in the oven; this was done when I was on duty watch after the last meal of the day. I would then put the dried tea leaves into a brown paper bag and pass it over to the little Chinaman who was the designated cook for our Chinese shipmates.

He was allocated a small stove in the corner of the galley and worked his magic on a daily basis; he would use his own ingredients and recipes unknown to anybody else except him.

We were now on our way to Singapore crossing the vast expanse of the Indian Ocean. The sea was like a millpond, as calm as it could be. The wake of the ship and the bow wave with porpoises playing in it was the only distraction. Occasionally in the distance a shark fin would break the surface and disappear very quickly as it stalked its prey.

At night there was no relief from the incessant heat. Below decks it could become very uncomfortable. Some of the lads took it upon themselves to sleep in the open air on the goofing deck. The fo'c'sle was still out of bounds because of the damaged bows. Night time would provide us with some of nature's entertainment in the form of phosphorous that danced along the bow wave; it was like a sea-born firework display, without the fizz and bang.

We were about halfway to Singapore when the ship's radar picked up a squall a few miles from us. The Skipper changed course and headed straight for it. Sailing into the wind and rain cooled the ship down by a number of degrees that made life more tolerable.

Sumatra came into view; we made our way down the Strait of Malacca which took us into Singapore dockyard.

Admiralty inspectors came aboard to check the damaged bows. It was decided that the repair work would take up to three weeks; the squadrons had already left and were dispersed to R.A.F. stations such as Seletar within the Singapore peninsular; the rest of the crew would be billeted in shore-side accommodation.

CHAPTER SIX

THERE WAS ANOTHER SHIP docked alongside. This was the Cruiser *H.M.S. Gambia*. My mate Nobby from Oxford was serving on her and we were able to meet up and had a good couple of runs ashore.

The distance from the dockyard to the centre of Singapore City was about 15 miles.

The Navy provided a bus service to take anyone with shore leave from the dockyard into Singapore. Taxis were also in abundance; the taxi fares were reasonable but you took your life in your own hands to ride in one! Once in the cab and the driver was given the destination he would drive flat out to get you there taking no notice of road or traffic conditions. The best thing as a passenger was to curl up in the back seat and close your eyes.

I'm not sure if it was true, but story has it that under the Japanese occupation the road had to be repaired, British and Australian prisoners of war being forced to do the repairs. This gave the P.O.W.'s a chance to cause some disruption to the Japanese war machine; they did this by changing the camber of the road, which could cause steering problems for vehicles travelling at speed. The hope was that they would run off the road and crash.

CHAPTER SIX

The road from the dockyard passed through a couple of small villages carved out of the jungle. One was Sembawang; a military barracks was established there accommodating troops from the Ghurkha regiment and a contingent of Royal Marines. The other village was Nee Soon; this was about halfway between the dockyard and Singapore City.

Nee Soon was popular as it had a hostelry called the London Bar. The bar was just that, a wooden hut with a palm leaf thatched roof; tables and chairs were supplied outside in a beer garden.

To get to the bar and beer garden you had to enter by going over the small bridge that spanned the monsoon ditch. The ditch was about 3ft wide and 5ft deep, so that being in the bar or garden was like being on a small island. During the monsoon season the ditch would be full of water; during the dry season the bottom of the ditch would always contain some muddy residue.

On this occasion I decided to visit the London bar to have a couple of pints of the refreshing Tiger beer that was the local brew around the Far East. I must add that we had been joined by another aircraft carrier; she was the Australian Navy's 16000 ton *Melbourne*. Our Australian cousins could be a bit volatile on occasion if their descendants were called into question. I would find out about this in due course.

I walked over the bridge, went to the bar and got a pint of Tiger. Going back into the garden to find a table, I noticed a number of *Albion*'s crew had taken up

CHAPTER SIX

residence on a number of tables. I found an empty one and sat down. I took a sip of my refreshing pint of Tiger when a very pretty Malaysian girl came and sat down beside me.

She could speak very good English and we fell into conversation, just talking about things in general. We were interrupted by a Chief Petty Officer from *H.M.A.S. Melbourne*, who plonked himself down next to the young lady that I had been talking to.

Our conversation went flat! The Chief was half pissed and my new-found girlfriend got into a confrontation with the interloper. Soon a full-fledged argument erupted! Things were getting a bit out of hand, I thought, and I did my best to stay out of it. The girl said something like, "Why don't you like the British?" His reply was, "We do like the Pommie bastards!" She replied, "No you don't, you're nothing more than a load of criminals!" His reply was, "What for? Just pinching a loaf of bread and getting deported to a penal colony!" The argument continued until the Aussie said to the girl, "If you don't shut your gob I'll give you a back hander!" It was time to step in. I said to him, "If you hit her I'll hit you." The argument continued and the next thing happened very quickly: the Aussie took a swipe at her and missed; she was too quick for him and dodged the blow, throwing her glass at him.

I stood up ready to give him a bunch of fives, but before I had a chance to deliver a punch, a Marine, who was sitting at an adjacent table with my new-found

CHAPTER SIX

girlfriend's sister, intervened and knocked the Aussie Chief Petty Officer into the monsoon ditch!

During the mêlée the table and chairs had been knocked over along with our drinks.

I was in the process of putting the table and chairs back together, when another Aussie came up to me. I said, "What's your problem?" and he replied, "Your mate hit my mate! I'm going to hit you!" He was staggering and I told him it was all over and to go away and sit down. He took a swipe at me anyway. I dodged the blow and he reiterated, "Your mate hit my mate so I'm going to hit you!" Again he took a swipe at me and missed. I was getting fed up with this! He came at me again and this time I put my left arm around his waist and shoved my right arm into his throat. I walked him backwards and dropped him into the monsoon ditch.

Looking around, I saw Albert. He came from Witney in Oxfordshire and was with a bunch of his mates who sat at one of the other tables; he too was one of the *Albion*'s crew. I called out to him, "You weren't much help!" He shouted back, "You were doing okay on your own!"

The table and chairs were put back in place; my new girlfriend had been to the bar and got fresh drinks.

I was unaware that the bar owner had called the shore patrol and had informed them of the punch-up; fortunately for me I had regained my composure and was seated at the table having a quiet drink with my new-found girlfriend when the patrol arrived. The officer in charge took in the view; everything looked peaceful except for two dishevelled and rather muddy Australian sailors climbing out of the monsoon ditch. They were both escorted off the premises and we never saw them again. It was assumed that the two Aussies had been fighting between themselves, so my new-found girlfriend and I continued to enjoy a pleasant evening!

Singapore was a multi-cultural city with a Chinese, European and Eurasian influence. Britain was a dominant factor in its culture and before and after World War Two maintained a strong military presence, which was instrumental in defeating a communist insurgency in the 1950's.

One afternoon I went into the City to have a beer and a swim at the Nuffield Club. I would like to explain that the club was founded by Lord Nuffield who had been instrumental in building the British motorcar industry, from his factory in Cowley, Oxford. There were a number of clubs around the world where British forces were stationed, and of course there was one in London that sported a theatre where variety shows were performed and televised to the nation.

However, on this occasion I got diverted. I was about to cross the road at a traffic light when a voice interrupted my concentration on crossing the road. The voice said, "Where are you going, darling?" I was gobsmacked and looked around to see where the voice was coming from. I crossed the road and was followed by a very pretty young lady; she caught up with me and said again, "Where are you going?" I stopped walking

CHAPTER SIX

and replied that I was going to the Nuffield Club. "What will you do there?" she asked. I replied that I was going to have a swim, a pint of beer and maybe a snack in the restaurant. Her reply was, "Why don't you come home with me?" I said, "What can we do there?" Her reply was, "We can have a drink and dance a little, then we will see what happens."

Who could refuse such an offer? I said, "How do we get to your place?" She waved down a taxi and we were off. I never gave up a challenge and this was one. After my experience with the Kenya Mau-Mau I wondered if I was putting myself in jeopardy again!

The taxi pulled up outside a villa that was part of a vast plantation with perfectly cut and manicured lawns. My new girlfriend paid for the taxi and we entered the villa. It was like a miniature palace, with cool marble floors and drapes of silk with teak furniture upholstered in velvet of various colours.

Yes, we had a few drinks from the well-stocked bar and we danced to music played from a record player. I will leave it up to your own imagination as to what completed a wonderful afternoon.

A taxi was called and I found myself outside the Nuffield Club. I had a swim and a few drinks too many, and decided to return to the ship. I was standing at a bus stop where I thought the bus to the dockyard would come.

After a while a bus came along and I got on it. By this time it was dark and in my fuzzy head I thought I was on the bus to the dockyard. I was wrong! The bus made a few stops and people were getting on laden with various baggage including cages containing chickens, which were taken by the driver and put on the luggage rack on the roof of the bus.

Singapore is connected to Malaya via a causeway that connects with Johor Bahru, and little did I know that the bus was en route to Kuala Lumpur! This was in the opposite direction that I should have been going in.

I started to come to my senses. After talking to a few of my fellow passengers that could speak a smattering of the English language I was convinced I was on the wrong bus. I staggered down between the seats to the driver and asked him to stop the bus so that I could get off; he was a bit miffed at having to make an unscheduled stop, but he complied.

Getting off the bus I found myself on a road surrounded by jungle and many weird noises! The local wild life was about its business of hunting and killing its prey, and I got concerned for my own safety. Cobras and other venomous snakes are in abundance, along with a variety of carnivorous animals that would like me for supper or dinner.

I got lucky, for walking back towards Singapore, I heard a car coming; turning round, I saw the headlights. I stopped and put out my arm with the thumb raised on my hand. This was like hitchhiking in the U.K., only this time I was more desperate.

The car stopped. It was driven by an English doctor

CHAPTER SIX

who had stayed in the Malayan Peninsular after World War Two. He was on his way to Singapore and was surprised to come across a British sailor hitchhiking on a road in the middle of a jungle! I explained what had happened and he laughed, and reiterated my thoughts that the jungle can be a very dangerous place.

The doctor asked where I would like to be dropped off and I replied that the Nuffield Club would be a good place if it was not inconvenient for him; the doctor was very kind and dropped me off at the Club. I found my bearings and caught the Royal Navy bus back to the dockyard.

Singapore in those days was evolving like so many cities from the atrocities of World War Two. The Raffles Hotel was famous for its opulence, and on the other side of the spectrum was Bugis Street, the red light district where brothels were plentiful; the street itself was a dirt road with wooden elevated walkways that could be used during the monsoon season when the road would become a sea of mud.

With so many sailors ashore, Bugis Street became a magnet. The vice squad had their hands full keeping things in hand. I happened to be there one evening frequenting one of the sleazy bars when a raid took place. The raid was carried out by a mixture of Military and Civilian police. The brothels were emptied out along with the bars—there were probably fifty of us, all gathered in the street. The officer in charge, using his very well trained vocal cords, proceeded to berate us, saying that the only thing we could expect to get from this place was a dose of pox, or a knife in our backs, concluding, "We will escort you out of here to a safer place, and we don't want to see you back here again!"

Albion had the damage to her bows repaired and was ready to continue with her commission. We sailed into the South China Sea carrying out exercises and providing humanitarian services to any ship of whatever flag it flew when help was needed. On one such occasion a distress signal was picked up from a merchant ship.

She was the *Twin Horse* registered in London and flying the British red ensign flag; one of her crew had fallen down a ladder and broken his leg. One of our helicopters was dispatched with a medical crew to give assistance.

On another not so friendly occasion we were alerted to intercept a Chinese Junk that was carrying out piratical activities. Piracy in the South China Seas was very active. I was detailed to be one of the boarding party, along with a contingent of our marines. My mate Tony who came from Oxford was one of the marine contingent, so I was in good company. I asked the officer in charge of the operation if I could have a gun. This was refused. My duty would be to take over the galley and feed the boarding crew and captives.

For some reason unknown to me the raid was called off, probably because of some diplomatic reason. Diplomacy is a very weird world. As a humble ship's

CHAPTER SIX

cook I was not privy to the higher echelon's decisions.

We continued with our tasks, and eventually arrived in Hong Kong; this would be another revelation in my worldly education.

Arriving in Hong Kong, and being secured to the jetty, we were met by Jennie and her side party.

Jennie was a legend in her own time. She had an agreement with the Navy to paint the ship's side. If we were tied up with the port side to the jetty, that would be the side to be painted; on our next visit the ship would be secured with the starboard side to the jetty, so that it could be painted.

Jennie was also allowed on board to take away all the waste food from the galley, and to sell soft drinks to the crew from the fo'c'sle whereby she would be supplied with a forty-gallon container filled with ice.

Of course she could not be expected to carry out this work on her own; she was custodian and Mama San to a multitude of orphan children.

The children assisted her in carrying out the various tasks that she was contracted to do.

The waste food was collected by the children in five-gallon containers and taken to some kitchen hidden within the confines of the roof tops of Wanchai. This was where a subculture survived! The waste food was made with Chinese ingenuity into a nourishing and palatable soup and sold for 5 cents a bowl. During my time in the region, the pound was worth 20 Hong Kong dollars.

Hong Kong was known as a free port. No customs

CHAPTER SIX

duty or taxes were applied to the purchase of what could be called luxury goods. Omega and Bulova watches were treasured, along with exotic jewellery; unfortunately all that glitters is not gold, and a lot of the lads got 'seen off'—a navy term for being fiddled. Fakes were in abundance! We had been warned about this prior to entering Hong Kong but sailors, being sailors, didn't take much notice of such warnings.

Two occasions in Hong Kong come to mind, one when I was ashore with Jock Christie. We were in this bar and the usual bar girls were there wearing their Cheongsam dresses with splits up to their hips showing a lot of leg and leaving nothing to the imagination; a juke box was available, and Jock was a bit tiddled and decided to put on a record. The bar was a bit crowded with sailors from a number of countries, including Brits, Aussies, and Americans. Jock found his favourite song, which was called 'I Remember a Hillside in Scotland'. The background noise from the hubbub of the people in the bar was too much for Jock to enjoy his chosen record, so he stood up on a bar stool and yelled out in his loudest voice, "SHITNIT!" I took this for a Scottish sailor's request to please be quiet. A hush duly fell within the bar, so Jock's vocal cords had achieved the desired effect.

I buried my head and nursed my pint of beer, and the next thing I heard was a thud. Jock had fallen off his stool and was laid spark out on the bar floor with his head resting against the juke box. The record was still playing and he had a smile on his face.

CHAPTER SIX

The other occasion was when I met up with Tony, my Royal Marine mate from Oxford. We decided to go and get a tattoo. I already had a couple, put on in the U.K., but this was different: two world-famous tattoo artists resided in the Far East. One was known as Two Thumbs, who had his studio in Singapore. I had some of his artwork put on me, and on this occasion Tony and I were going to Pinky's tattoo parlour in Wanchai.

Looking through the catalogue of the many designs that we could have our skin impregnated with, I chose one to go on my chest; this depicted a sinking ship with a guardian angel taking care of things. Tony decided to be more flamboyant and was going to have an eye tattooed to each cheek of his bum!

The two chairs were next to each other. I was seated in mine with my chest bared, while Tony was kneeling on his, his trousers and underpants at half-mast. Looking over, I said, "You better not fart or else we'll get kicked out!" Anyone who says that tattoos are painless tells lies—it's like being cut with a razor blade! However, Pinky got to work and my chest was shaved and prepared for the procedure. Tony's bum was smooth and didn't need shaving. Pinky put the outline of my tattoo onto my chest then deftly moved over to Tony's bum and proceeded to ink in the outline of the eyes; my thoughts were that one of them should be winking!

We both had what we had paid for; these tattoos would be part of us for the rest of our lives.

CHAPTER SIX

Albion's time in Hong Kong was over. We would return eventually, but for now her far eastern commission had to continue.

We would sail the South Pacific Ocean, the Yellow Sea, South China Sea, the Formosa Straights, and any stretch of water hither and yon.

Manila in the Philippines was where I celebrated my 19th birthday. Mum had sent me a birthday cake that she had baked herself. It was a wonderful gesture on her behalf, but unfortunately when I received it, it was a bit squashed. Nevertheless I shared the remnants with my mess mates. Although it was bent out of shape and a bit crumbly, it tasted good, the lads using their forefingers to scrape the icing off the inside of the box that it had been sent in.

A run ashore was organized and we were anchored offshore along with our Australian cousins' ship, *H.M.A.S. Melbourne*. The Filipino Navy provided a liberty boat to take us from ship to shore. A liberty boat was a landing craft, left over from World War Two, but served us very well. I must add that the United States Navy had a very strong presence in the Philippines based at Subic Bay.

The liberty boat would come to *Albion*, take us on board then head to the *Melbourne* to pick up her liberty men.

Once ashore the world became our oyster! Bars were plentiful, as were the girls. My mates and I found ourselves in one establishment that sported a brothel on

CHAPTER SIX

the upper floor; stairs led to a balcony where rooms were accessed, and the girl of your dreams, or nightmare, would be waiting.

Of course my mate Jock Christie was with us, so trouble wouldn't be far away! A dance floor was provided, but before you could have a dance you had to buy a ticket and give it to the girl you were going to dance with; this would be her wages when her tickets were cashed in at the end of the night.

One of the girls took off her frilly petticoat and hung it on the bannister rail that supported the staircase that led to the rooms above. Being up for a laugh and being egged on by my compatriots, I nicked it and put it on! I was rather inebriated and did my best to do a hula-hula dance; unfortunately the shore patrol happened to turn up and the silly tart complained to them.

The officer in charge of the patrol was an Aussie lieutenant. He wanted to arrest me for ungentlemanly conduct, but fortunately one of the patrols was from the *H.M.S. Crane*, who persuaded the Officer to allow me to return the petticoat to its rightful owner with a small compensation.

One of the lads had disappeared. We had an idea where he had gone to and it didn't take us long to ferret him out! He was on the upper floor in one of the rooms having a bunk up. We burst in to find his bum was in the air with legs all around him. Without missing a stroke he looked over his shoulder and yelled at us to "F**k off!"

CHAPTER SIX

Time goes fast when you're enjoying yourself, and it was soon time for us to return to our respective ships. The landing craft arrived and the deck was full of British and Australian sailors of various ranks. As for my mate Jock and me, we stood on the stern deck where the cox'n controlled the speed and direction of the boat; we were headed to the *Melbourne* to let the Aussies off first.

I don't know how it started, but it did—a punch-up began, fists flying, among other things; Jock and I were watching from the stern deck when this shit bag shoved me in the middle of my back and I went flying into the middle of the mêlée, fists and feet flying everywhere! I rolled myself into a ball and hoped for the best. With the intervention of some Chief and Petty Officers, the altercation came to an end. I was able to unravel myself, although my best white tropical uniform had footmarks on it along with the odd spot of blood.

I returned to the steering deck and bollicked Jock for shoving me into the punch-up! The bugger couldn't stop laughing! We eventually arrived at the *Melbourne* and the Aussies disembarked. The last one had his foot on the first step of the ladder that would take them onto the ship when it happened: one of our guys shouted out, "HEY AUSSIE!" He shouted back: "WHAT?" Our guy yelled out, "You forgot something!" The Aussie said, "What's that?" and our guy yelled in answer, "YOUR BALL AND CHAIN!" The Aussies stopped in mid-step, turned around on the ladder and tried to get back on board the liberty boat to continue the punch-up! Fortunately the cox'n put the landing craft into reverse and backed away from the *Melbourne* before her upset crewmembers could board her.

Although we had our little skirmishes we had a lot of respect for our Australian cousins and I think they had some for us although they affectionately called us 'Pommie Bastards'.

However, after some more sea time we returned to the Philippines. This time we entered Subic Bay and tied up to a jetty.

This was the American Navy's largest base in the Pacific region. Manila was close by Subic Bay; from what I can recall it was a very small town in comparison.

I was ashore one afternoon and visited a roadside café. I ordered a hot dog and started a conversation with the girl that was serving the food. She could speak good English. I was standing at the counter when two chaps appeared, one on each side of me. The girl I was talking to introduced them as her brothers. I was polite and shook their hands; then one of them said, "Look at this." Within a flash a large knife was produced and laid on the counter; the other one produced a revolver and placed it on the counter.

Although they appeared friendly, I got the message: eating the hot dog in record time, I bade them farewell and went off to find pastures anew.

This came in the way of a welcoming bar. On entering it, I took in the ambience; there were no customers except for a girl seated on a bar stool next to

CHAPTER SIX

an American Navy lieutenant. I walked up to the bar and ordered a beer. The barman complied and I sat down on a bar stool. I was served my drink and the girl who was sitting next to the lieutenant, and who had heard me order my drink, exclaimed, "He can speak English!" I said, "I hope so, I *am* English." The American lieutenant said to the girl, "Yeah, we f**ked up a good language!"

The lieutenant was a bit tipsy and decided to leave. As for me, I was just about to get started; after a few beers, my new-found girlfriend who didn't have brothers armed to the teeth with knives and guns became very friendly towards me.

I responded to her invitation and we went to her apartment. For the rest you can use your imagination, and it won't be far wrong! As an appreciation we went to a local market and I bought her some material that she wanted to make a dress from.

Albion's time in Subic Bay came to an end, and our next port of call was Yokohama, Japan.

We were met by a welcoming party of very pretty Japanese girls who performed a traditional dance on the jetty. They were wearing Kimono's and held parasols in their hands; the dance was very gentle and performed with perfection and grace.

Going ashore with a bunch of the lads, we ferretted out a few bars; one in particular was very friendly: girls were in abundance and were supervised by a Mama

CHAPTER SIX

San, who explained to us that if we went to two other bars that she owned we could return to this one at 11 o'clock and drink for free. Who could refuse such an offer? She gave us the names of her other bars, saying in broken English, "You show this to taxi driver, he will take you there." The names of the bars were written down on a piece of paper that she handed to me.

We complied and were aware that one of her male staff followed us to check that we visited her other establishments.

Bang on 11 o'clock, we were back in her bar and true to her word, we never paid for another drink for the rest of the night.

We danced with the girls and had a great time. One girl in particular took a fancy to me; her name was Noriko, and she could speak a smattering of English. She asked me if I would like to visit her at home at the weekend—an offer that I could not refuse!

Weekend shore leave was granted, and off I went. I got a taxi and gave the driver the piece of paper with Noriko's address. On arrival Noriko was outside, tidying her small garden. She greeted me with a warm smile and invited me in. The little house was constructed of cedar wood, and on the inside were wooden floors, the rooms divided by wooden framed paper screens that were delicately decorated in pastel shades.

The house construction was typical of many in Japan because of the ever-present threat of earthquakes, the idea being that the lightly constructed houses would

CHAPTER SIX

reduce the severity of injury in the event of a quake happening.

The house was sparsely furnished but comfortable. A small low table was the centrepiece with large velvet covered cushions around it. Noriko made a pot of the famous Japanese green tea. I was being introduced into the Japanese culture in a very seductive way, and I had no complaints.

After the tea I sampled a couple of glasses of Saki. Noriko then suggested that we go to the local bath house.

I should explain that some houses were not provided with bathrooms as we know them. Washbasins and toilets of a very different kind were installed and were very basic, hence the local bath house provided a more hygienic way to carry out one's ablutions.

After the Saki I was game for anything, so off to the bath house we went. On arrival, Noriko said, "Take off your shoes and put them in the box." A framework containing multiple boxes was positioned at the entrance to the building. I complied and Noriko did the same.

She disappeared through the ladies' entrance, and I went through the gents' entrance. I couldn't believe it! We came together again in the same building, only we were separated by a booth containing a wizened old Mama San. Noriko spoke to her in her own language and handed over a few Yen.

The Mama San produced a large wicker basket and indicated that I should strip off and put my clothes in it.

I took a moment or two to take in the scene: a wall

divided the women from the men, but Mama San could look both sides. The area I was standing in was the changing room. A glass partition with a door opened up to the bathroom area, where a row of low-level washbasins provided with little blue plastic seats were in evidence; next to the washbasins was a row of showers, not in cubicles; this was all open plan. Looking further down I noticed three large tiled bathtubs that were provided, each about ten foot square and two to three feet deep; each one had a different shade of blue water. Light blue water was the nearest to the showers; the next one was mid-blue, while the furthest one was dark blue.

I stripped off and put my clothes into the wicker basket, which stayed on the floor as there was nowhere else to put it.

I entered the bathing area. A couple of young lads were seated at the washbasins throwing water and soap suds at each other. I didn't want to spoil their fun so I went to the showers. The Japanese people being short in stature, the shower heads were a bit low to get my 6ft frame under them; however, I persevered and managed to get wet all over. After the shower I looked at the tempting blue watered bathing tubs; one chap was soaking in the dark blue one. I thought I would be friendly and get in and join him although he was reading a newspaper.

I got in and immediately got out—the water was boiling! Also, I forgot to mention that the bathroom

CHAPTER SIX

interior was like a hall of mirrors, and getting a glimpse of my bum I thought it looked like a boiled lobster!

I'd had enough so I went and dried off and got dressed. Fortunately Noriko was doing the same thing in the ladies' changing room.

On the way back to Noriko's house we stopped at a street vendor's barrow to get some takeaway food, which consisted of savoury rice and fried squid; it wasn't too bad although the squid took a bit of chewing, since it had the texture of rubber.

My weekend with Noriko was a pleasant relief. My scalded bum was not so sore, and we parted on good terms, both wondering if we would ever see each other again. Sadly, this would not be so.

Trouble was brewing; the communist Chinese were flexing their military muscles, with spasmodic shelling from the Chinese mainland to the poorly defended Quemoy and Matsu Islands which were south of Formosa.

Albion with her escorts was ordered to sail to Inchon, in South Korea; we were to be part of a S.E.A.T.O. navy task force. S.E.A.T.O was an abbreviation for the South East Asia Treaty Organization, and our task force would include many ships from a number of countries, including our Australian cousins on the *Melbourne*. The American Navy provided the largest contribution.

Inchon itself was like a shanty town. One could sense the devastation and trauma it had suffered during the Korean War.

I met up with a couple of American sergeants who

CHAPTER SIX

had access to a Jeep. If anyone could get you into trouble they could. These guys were part of the standing American army based in Inchon; after all, the 38th parallel was only a few miles north where the North Korean army was amassed. A fragile peace was achieved by the armistice agreement, but technically the North and South were still at war.

One of my new-found American friends offered to take me on a trip to town. The Jeep would be our means of transport, and driving through the small villages and Inchon itself reminded me of England during the blitz. The resilience of the South Korean people was of those who had to endure severe hardships during times of conflict.

We found a bar and ordered a couple of beers. A brothel was just around the corner and my new-found friend suggested we go and try out what was on offer. I had no option than to go along with him as he was the one with the transport!

We entered the establishment and were confronted with about half a dozen girls, all giggling and gesturing for us to pick one of them for our gratification. One grabbed me by the arm and escorted me into an upstairs room. My new buddy said, "Don't worry, I'll take care of the bill."

About halfway through the cavorting, there was the sound of what could be called a bit of a riot: the door burst open and my new-found friend came into the room! Looking over my shoulder, I said, "What the

CHAPTER SIX

hell's going on?" He replied, "I ain't paying!" He grabbed a chair and put it against the door and sat down, keeping the door shut with the chair and the weight of his body.

With all this interruption I lost concentration in what I was doing. I said, "How the hell are we going to get out of here?" He said, "Out the window!" I hopped around trying to get dressed with two feet in one leg of my bellbottoms! My concubine was laughing at the situation. We got the window open and climbed out hanging by our fingertips, and we dropped to the ground, some eight to ten feet, falling in a heap. We got up and ran like heck to the Jeep!

All of the ships forming the task force were assembled. The Americans put on a U.S.O. show for us, with free beer; we had a great night, and it was a great feeling that we were united in being successful in the task ahead.

It must have been a formidable sight for the people on the shore to see such a gathering of ships, the aircraft carriers being the centrepiece with their escorts of frigates, destroyers and supply ships.

We were at our stations for leaving harbour, all knowing that we were sailing into dangerous waters.

The galley on *Albion* was a hive of activity striving to feed some two thousand sailors for a duration of who knew how long on unfriendly seas.

Other ships in the task force would be doing the

CHAPTER SIX

same; the crew would be fed at their action stations, with the mainstay of nutrition being the Ogee, otherwise known to civilians as a Cornish pasty, made up from diced potatoes, minced beef, diced carrots and onions, put together in a short crust pastry.

This was the staple that Cornish tin miners took with them on a daily basis and was an ideal food adopted by the Navy for the situation we were entering.

As for me, I was at my action station, being part of the first aid and fire party; we were located close to the damage control H.Q. The anti-flash gear we had to wear was not very comfortable, and consisted of a hood over your head to protect your face, neck and ears; long sleeve gloves were provided to protect your hands and arms.

The task force sailed through the Yellow Sea and the Formosa Straights. The aircraft from the carriers flew alternately for twenty-four hours around the clock; this lasted for a number of days.

The Communists got the message and ceased the shelling of the Quemoy and Matsu Islands. Our task force had been a success; the task force was stood down and the ships dispersed to various ports.

Albion was ordered back to Japan where Yokosuka was our destination. Our stay would not be long, but long enough for the Padre to organize a trip to the Kamakura gardens. The gardens were close to the magnificent view of Mount Fuji. We were escorted on our trip by two very sweet Japanese tour girls who could speak impeccable English.

CHAPTER SIX

The gardens were adorned with Lotus trees and many exotic plants and shrubs. The centrepiece was the imposing statue of Buda overlooking all that he beheld. It was a good trip, and educational.

For one of our lads, the international conviviality became a bit serious. He got married to a Japanese girl, in a Shinto ceremony. He let his Mum know about it and she went berserk and told him that he would never be able to set foot in her house again! "So what," he replied, "I'll stay at Aggie Weston's." His Mum's reply was, "Is this another of your dirty women?" His Mum was not aware that Aggie Weston's was a charitable hostelry in Portsmouth! Anyway, I think the ship's Padre got involved and the marriage got dissolved, to the relief of his Mum.

Again *Albion* was on her travels. We would carry out our operational commitments interspersed with visits to remote Islands that were under the British protectorate.

Pulau Tioman was one of them. This small Island was in the South China Sea. Its main industry was growing and harvesting coconuts.

At the time of our visit there were only 12 inhabitants, who harvested the coconuts, not for the nut part that would be used on the coconut shy at fairgrounds, but for the more lucrative part, the fibre that was encased within the smooth shell, which could be processed into a fine oil.

CHAPTER SIX

The *Melbourne* was with us, and fortunately there was no trouble. I think that our task force intervention against the communist Chinese had bonded us closer together.

Our ship's boats transported us to the pure white sandy beach. Funnily enough, the Army Service Corps brought in a landing craft providing us with boxes of canned beer.

I helped a mate who was a Naval Airman to secure a box that contained a dozen cans. We buried it in the sand to protect it from the scorching sun. We had a swim in the clear blue sea, wearing plimsolls (canvas shoes) to protect our feet from the razor sharp coral that was below the surface. The Aussies set up a life guard station; these chaps were in their element, carrying out their duty as though they were on Bondi Beach back in Australia.

Before going ashore we were instructed not to remove any coconuts that had been harvested.

After having a swim and a couple of beers, we decided to do a little bit of exploring. We found a track that led us through thickly overgrown brush and came across a narrow stream. From the bank to the stream was about a 3ft drop. We entered the stream and it was freezing cold! Climbing out of the stream, we continued on our trek through the brush. The track led us to a clearing. Looking around, we were confronted with a mountain of coconuts! Within the clearing was a hut made of palm wood and dried palm leaves. Nobody appeared to be around; my mate and I looked at each

CHAPTER SIX

other and we decided that they wouldn't miss one or two! We slowly crept up to the mountain and helped ourselves to a couple of coconuts.

Then it happened! The shutters on the hut opened and this old shrew of a women started screaming at us. We took off running in the direction where we had come from, holding onto our coconuts for dear life. Looking over my shoulder I saw that we were being chased by half of the inhabitants of the island, all carrying and waving machetes, yelling and shouting at us in a language that was foreign to us! My mate got to the stream before me and was standing on the opposite bank. I got into the stream and slipped up on the rock bed, freezing water cascading over me from the fast flowing water. My coconut went flying out of my hands and floated away downstream. Our assailants had caught up with us: standing on the bank, they started pointing at me, and started to laugh! My mate reached down and I was able to grab hold of his hand and he helped pull me out of the stream.

The villagers let us go with a smile on their faces and a friendly wave. We went on our different ways, returning to the beach where we finished off our beer.

Leaving Pulau Tioman, *Albion* headed to Hong Kong. Jenny and her side party were waiting for us and completed painting the ship's side.

H.M.S. Gambia had completed her Far East commission and was returning to the U.K., taking my

CHAPTER SIX

mate Nobby with her. We would meet up again when *Albion* returned home. *Gambia* was replaced by *H.M.S. Belfast*, a very famous cruiser that is now a floating museum and tourist attraction in the Port of London.

After a brief stay in Hong Kong we carried out exercises with the *Belfast* and our escorts; we did a R.A.S.—this is an abbreviation for Replenishment At Sea, one of the most hazardous operations especially for a carrier taking on aviation fuel from a tanker; sailing side-by-side in unpredictable seas, the skill and seamanship of the vessels' captains was paramount in carrying out a successful transfer. Thankfully we had no mishaps. We would R.A.S. with other ships taking on board food supplies. During these operations all available hands were required to assist in the operation.

It was hard work but necessary to keep the ship fully operational and ready to respond to any international emergency.

We did have one incident that could have had dire consequences for the ship. The bomb hoist, which went from the magazine to the hangar where the planes were armed, caught fire; a link in the hoist broke, but fortunately it wasn't loaded with bombs, otherwise I don't think I would be writing this book. The hoist was undergoing a maintenance run when the link broke; as it unwound at rapid speed, the friction created terrific heat and ignited the lubricating grease. I must add that the hoist shaft passed through the ship's main dining hall. The response to the fire was very quick and affective, although smoke did seep into the dining room.

CHAPTER SIX

A large ship has a large crew, and discipline has to be maintained. The Royal Navy as previously mentioned has a disciplinary code to follow; anyone breaking the code is subject to punishment. The Captain of any ship has the authority to administer punishment in accordance with Admiralty instructions.

A ship at sea is different from a shore establishment. *Albion* was provided with a half dozen cells, deep down in the bowls of the ship, close to the bows. Anyone who was found guilty of a crime that warranted incarceration was subjected to this dim and dismal place; they would not only be locked up, but would be given a daily task to do; this was oakum pulling: five shanks of old rope some two inches in diameter and about a foot long were supplied on a daily basis, and these had to be unwound and teased out; each fibre had to be broken down to about two-inch long strands; no tools were provided and every strand was broken down using fingers and nails.

Another part of the punishment was that the prisoner's mess mates had to collect his meals from the galley and be escorted by one of the Regulating branch three times a day to feed him; this was an inconvenience to his mess mates as this duty was done in their time, so the prisoner had to face them after his time in cells was over; this could be for a maximum of 14 days.

My mate Riley got his share. We had the Commander in Chief Far East on board and the Admiral was being dined in the wardroom; this meant that all officer stewards were required to be on duty. Riley would

CHAPTER SIX

normally have been off duty. During the height of the service, Riley slipped away and reported a man overboard. Being night-time, searchlights were rigged and all off-duty seamen were piped to stand by the ship's boats. Helicopters were launched for search and rescue and signals were sent off to any ships in the area; in all, some twenty something ships were looking for someone who wasn't there!

When Riley was put under arrest and placed on the Captain's report, he was asked his reason for reporting a man overboard. His reply didn't endear him to anyone! He said, "Well sir, I had to be on duty, so why shouldn't everyone else be?"

Another time Riley was in trouble, although not quite as serious as the man overboard incident, was when he was carrying a pile of dinner plates. The Chief Steward said to him, "Drop what you're doing, Riley, and give a hand over here!" He did just that! One almighty crash and broken china plates were everywhere. For Riley there was more punishment to come, and in his defence he said to the Captain, "I was told to drop what I was doing, so I did. I was carrying out orders, sir." The Captain failed to accept the excuse and Riley again became a man under punishment.

Albion continued on her commission and after several weeks at sea returned to Singapore.

A Banyan was organized. (A Banyan was the name given for a camping trip or other recreational activity.)

CHAPTER SIX

On this occasion a number of us with our chief and divisional officer were taken by a ship's pinnace up a river to a small beach where we would camp for a few days.

On putting the bows of the pinnace as close to the beach as possible our divisional officer, Sub-lieutenant Nash, jumped overboard and landed up to his knees in the brownish coloured water. He gave out a yell, thinking he had been bitten by a water snake! Fortunately it wasn't a snake bite, but a sharp root from the surrounding jungle brush.

It was common knowledge that crocodiles were also known to be in this river that flowed into the Straits of Malacca.

After getting our kit ashore we made camp in a shore side clearing. We had two-man tents and I shared mine with a mess mate called Tubby May. He was from the West Country and his nickname explains his build; he wasn't however worried about being called Tubby.

Because of the wildlife that inhabited the river it was decided not to use it for any swimming; fortunately we were not far from Seletar Royal Air Force Base.

The Air Force Base was accessed through a gate in the perimeter fence, and a track from our campsite winding through a part of the jungle was used to reach it. The base provided a N.A.A.F.I. where the bar became the most popular venue, although the swimming pool was a close second.

One evening after a session in the N.A.A.F.I. bar, Tubby and I with a couple of lads were making our way

CHAPTER SIX

back to our campsite and we had to pass by the swimming pool that was close to the perimeter fence. Tubby gave me a challenge, saying, "If you can swim the length of the pool before I can walk it I'll give you half me tot!" I accepted the challenge and I dived in fully clothed; all I was wearing was a shirt, shorts and plimsolls.

I won the challenge; the only thing was that my pay book was in my back pocket and was soaking wet! I did manage to dry it out without any harm done.

Arriving back at camp we turned in for the night. Tubby was a bit pissed off for losing the challenge.

We both went into a deep alcoholic induced sleep, until about one in the morning when Tubby let out a loud yell. Whatever caused it made him shoot out his right leg that hit the tent pole, causing the tent to collapse on top of us!

After waking up the rest of our mates and creating some chaos, things settled down and we put our tent together again. I asked Tubby what had caused him to yell out and wreck our tent. He said something furry had run over his face and disappeared out of the tent; this could have been a rat, or part of a bad dream—whatever it was, we will never know.

However, later in the morning I was suffering with severe pains in the right side of my upper chest and shoulder. I checked to see if I had any puncture wounds to my skin that may have been caused by a spider, or any other insect bite, but if I had they were not visible.

CHAPTER SIX

Anyway, it was decided that I should go to the sick bay at the Seletar Air Base.

I made my way through the patch of jungle leading to the gate that we used to enter the base; this was not a social call to go to the N.A.A.F.I. bar or to use the swimming pool. I finally found the sick bay and was met by a sick bay tiffy, Air Force style. I explained to him what my problem was; he was sympathetic and informed the M.O. of my medical condition. After a few minutes I was ushered into the consulting room. The Doc asked me a few questions, then went around with the stethoscope checking all the relevant areas; after checking for any puncture wounds or swelling, he came to his diagnoses.

He wrote something down on a pad. Handing it to me, he said, "Give that to my medical assistant." I thanked him and left the room.

I handed the piece of paper to the medic who read it and said, "Wait there." I did as I was told and before long he returned with a glass of fizzy foaming liquid. I was ordered to drink it down in one. I obeyed and a moment later thought I was going to explode! I burped, I belched, and, yes, I farted! Embarrassed? Yes, but much relieved!

On leaving, the medic enquired where I was camped. I replied that I was camping on the beach the other side of the jungle from the perimeter fence, and he let out an expletive: "Bloody hell, that place is infested with Cobras!" I made my way back to the camp, very wary of where I was treading.

CHAPTER SIX

Our Banyan came to an end and we returned to *Albion* like children home to their mother.

Off to sea again and plying the Indian Ocean, we made our way to Ceylon. We arrived at Trincomalee, on the north-eastern side of the island. Shore leave was granted and I went ashore to explore the local environment. I met a local chap who called himself Brooklyn. He had what could be called a bric-à-brac stall in the town; he also ran a taxi that was an old Morris Minor, probably one that I had worked on when I worked for Morris Motors back in Oxford.

Anyway we sort of got on together, and he offered to give me a tour for a few rupees of the local places of interest. We drove around for a while and landed up outside a Buddhist Temple. It had a walled garden with ornamental iron gates at the entrance. We got out of the car and I looked around. Suddenly I was confronted by a Buddhist monk who had a shaven bald head and who was dressed in golden robes from head to foot except he didn't wear any shoes. In perfect English he offered me a tour of the gardens. I accepted the offer, though Brooklyn didn't. The Monk informed me that I would have to remove my shoes and I complied, although I did refuse to leave them at the entrance in case they got nicked; instead, I tied the shoelaces together and slung them over my shoulder.

My guide escorted me through the garden. When we came to what could be described as a very long curved

CHAPTER SIX

wall, there were seven large alcoves built into it, all numbered from one to seven.

Starting at number one, it was explained that this was number one heaven; it had statues of people of what could be described as in a state of torment; moving on through each of the alcoves, we finally arrived at the alcove depicting the seventh heaven where utopia was depicted. The Monk explained that Buddhists believe that when they die, they start off in torment in number one heaven and work their way through the heavens until they reach the seventh heaven; the effigies in each heaven were very life-like and the heavens were decorated in colours that reflected which heaven you were in.

It was time to leave and the Monk escorted me to the gates. I thanked him for his hospitality, at which point he asked if I had alms, meaning, could I give him a few Rupees? I complied, after which he asked if I could give him a cigarette; again, I complied. I offered him a light which he refused, saying he was not allowed to smoke in public.

After putting my shoes on I returned to Brooklyn who was having a doze in the back of the car. After waking him up we drove off and finished the day in the sand dunes drinking a bottle of Arak (a potent local brew); needless to say, Brooklyn had rounded up a couple of dusky maidens to accompany us.

Before *Albion* departed from Ceylon we had another

CHAPTER SIX

Banyan; this was within a jungle clearing inland from the coast. We were transported and accompanied by the Army Liaison contingent that had sailed with us throughout our commission.

Major Compton Bishop was the officer in charge. We travelled down mud roads and jungle tracks using Land Rovers. The vehicles traversed the difficult terrain very well.

We made camp and one of the lads decided to sling a hammock between two trees, the rest of us happy to sleep in tents. We turned in for the night and after a few cans of beer we fell into a pleasant slumber. We weren't aware that our campsite had been visited by a herd of elephants during the night.

When we were awake and compos mentis, the Major gathered us together and informed us of the elephants' visit. One of our lads was missing from the gathering, this being the one that had decided to sleep in his hammock slung between two trees. We found him still in his hammock. He had a snake curled up on top of his mosquito net that he had put up as a canopy above him. He was shit scared of moving! Realizing this, we were able to get the snake to shift by prodding it with sticks. It got the message and it fell off the mosquito net and slithered off into the undergrowth.

We reassembled and the Major again addressed us, saying, to prevent any other intrusion into our camp by the elephants we should carry out our bodily functions around the perimeter of the camp; he explained that the

CHAPTER SIX

elephants don't like the smell of it, but we replied, "We don't either, sir!" Nevertheless, it worked and we weren't bothered again.

Our camp was not far from a native village. Unfortunately one of our crew decided to check it out. He was an old hand and was probably stoned on Arak. A messenger arrived from the village to inform us that he was trying to force himself on one of the chief's daughters. The chief, understandably, was very displeased. A Land Rover was dispatched with a couple of army corporals and the Major. The miscreant was apprehended and apologies given. On arrival back at camp, the silly sod wouldn't calm down so we had to restrain him by lashing him to a camp bed, putting him into the back of the Land Rover and transporting him back to the ship where he could recover in a cell.

Time was up for our stay in Ceylon and the *Albion* slipped away into the Indian Ocean. Our next port of call would be Karachi, a coastal port on the Pakistan shore of the Arabian Sea.

What a dump! Sacred cows were permitted to wander the streets unhindered, taking anything that took their fancy from the street vendors' stalls that sold farm produce.

A couple of things happened during our visit. One was that a Polio epidemic was rearing its ugly head. A United Nations medical team came aboard to administer a squirt in the mouth of the Salk serum. I

CHAPTER SIX

had a strong reaction to it and landed up in the sick bay for a couple of days. I was put under observation. Fortunately I was found to have a strong resistance to the disease.

Albion was anchored someway offshore. The ship's boats were employed to take liberty men to Karachi. I had been ashore and caught the liberty boat back to the ship. It was nightfall and the ship's boat had a searchlight mounted on the bows; we were about halfway back to *Albion* when the sea erupted and we found ourselves in the middle of a large shoal of flying fish attracted by the beam of the searchlight. Their outstretched fins and scales shone in the moonlight and the searchlight's beam. They were flying into the boat as fast as we could throw them back into the sea! This was a marvellous experience and one I will never forget.

Another incident that was not so pleasant was when a tannoy message was piped throughout the ship, for everyone to take cover as we were being shot at! We carried out this order without hesitation.

Our Far East general service commission was coming to an end and another carrier was on her way to relieve us. We made way sailing across the Indian Ocean, through the Gulf of Aden into the Red Sea, heading towards the Suez Canal.

Exiting the Suez Canal, we were back in the Mediterranean Sea. The Med, as she was affectionately called, was normally a tranquil sea, but not on this

CHAPTER SIX

occasion when she decided with Mother Nature to show us how angry she could become.

Within hours of our entry into the Med, the sea started to get choppy; white-crested waves started to form—the sailors' name for these were sea horses, or white caps; it didn't matter what you called them, they were a foreboding warning for what was to come.

The weather deteriorated rapidly and the ship ploughed through mountainous, heaving waves, her 22,000 tons tossed around like a cork.

A ship's galley is a hazardous place at the best of times, but when you get a heaving deck below your feet, with boiling water around, and water flowing back through the scuppers, it can become bloody dangerous. Trying to keep your feet was one thing; the other one was trying to dodge cooking utensils, and metal galley dishes that could come flying off their storage racks! On one occasion it took four of us to remove trays of meat from an oven, one holding onto a stanchion with one hand, the other hand gripping hold of one of the other cooks, the rest supporting each other as though we were a human chain.

No matter what the weather we had to provide meals for the crew; that was our job and we succeeded under very difficult conditions.

We weathered the storm that lasted for a number of days. The majority of the ship's crew was happy to be homeward bound, especially those that were married.

As for myself, I was looking forward to seeing the

CHAPTER SIX

family and my mates again. Sailing through the Bay of Biscay, we made our way towards the English Chanel. The first to leave us were our aircraft squadrons, flying off to their respective Royal Naval air stations. We knew when we were close to home, with the Long Ship's Lighthouse on the tip of Cornwall throwing out her light that had helped to keep mariners safe for many, many years. The Isle of White came into view as we entered the Solent. The Nab Tower was the next milestone that brought us closer to our home port of Portsmouth.

All off-duty men were called to divisions to be in position on the flight deck for entering harbour.

After sailing many thousands of miles, visiting many countries, carrying out our duties to help keep the free world free, there is nothing like coming home!

A welcoming home party of the crews' family members and friends, along with a number of Portsmouth's fine citizens, were gathered to observe *Albion*'s return. I was in my division, standing on the flight deck, feeling rather humbled by the turn out of those who greeted us. Union Jacks were in abundance, waved by the people ashore as we passed by Sally port, and Portsmouth's power station; this was close to the entrance to the harbour.

With harbour tugboats escorting us we were gently nudged into our berth. After being secured to the jetty, we were dismissed from our divisions and allowed to go ashore to meet our loved ones. Lots of hugs and kisses were taking place. As for me and a few of the other lads, no one was there to greet us.

Two weeks' leave was granted to each watch. Although the ship was going to be decommissioned, a skeleton crew would still be required and I was part of that crew.

CHAPTER SEVEN

MY TURN CAME for leave. I had my travel warrant and leave pass, and made my way home by train.

Oxford hadn't changed much—it never did. However, it was good to be home. I was warmly greeted by Mum, my stepdad Ernie and my younger sister Valerie. Auntie Evelyne and Uncle Tom lived next door and were equally happy to see me.

I had managed to pass my driving test and had saved some money. Scanning the *Oxford Mail* newspaper advertisement section I came across an advert for a car for sale, and I answered the advert.

The car was being sold by the landlord of the Chester Arms pub in Chester Street that was off the Iffley Road. The car was a 1936 Vauxhall, painted blue with blue leather upholstery; it had four scoop-you-in doors, and a 14 hp six-cylinder engine. It was not unlike the cars that Al Capone was driven around in! The price being asked for it was 50 pounds or nearest offer. I could afford 40 pounds and after some haggling I was able to clinch the deal.

Mum was quite impressed with my deal, and she herself would drive it. I customized it a little bit by

CHAPTER SEVEN

applying whitewall tyre paint that made it a little bit more individual.

This was going to be a leave to remember. Fortunately two of my other mates were home on leave and we met up at Vi's pub, The Jolly Farmers. The pub was in the shadows of Oxford Castle, which had been built in Norman times and now was part of Oxford jail.

We all had driving licenses, and needed some way to augment our Navy leave allowance. I may add that after our first week's leave we were getting short of cash.

We had another week to go before we had to return to our respective ships.

Don came up with an idea. He had seen an advert for taxi drivers in the *Oxford Mail* and he suggested that we apply for positions on a part-time basis. It was his idea so we decided he should be the one to apply for a job. He did and was successful. Nobby and I followed and we were also successful. Our shifts were mornings and afternoons; night shifts were out of the question—they were reserved for us to continue our revelry! Of course, the good citizens of Oxford would be three taxis short come noontime as we would be parked outside The Jolly Farmers pub partaking of a liquid lunch.

Our pay from Luxicars, the cab company, was two shillings an hour; the rest we made up in tips.

One morning I got a radio call to go to Iffley Village and pick up a fare to take to London Heathrow airport. On arrival at the address I was met by an American gentleman surrounded by luggage; his wife and three

CHAPTER SEVEN

children of various ages were also in attendance. There was no way that my cab would be able to accommodate five passengers and the amount of luggage they had; the gentleman saw the anguish on my face and put me at ease by explaining that his wife and children were going to be driven to Heathrow by friends in their car. I let out a sigh of relief and proceeded to put as many suitcases as would fit into the boot. When it was full I secured the lid; there were still a lot left over and I asked the gentleman where he would prefer to sit, front or back; he replied that he would sit in the back. The front seat was occupied with small luggage, the back seat with larger suitcases, leaving a space for my passenger.

We set off and had an uneventful journey to Heathrow, although we had a very interesting conversation on the way. My passenger had been in England for a couple of years and was a professor whose subject was the American Civil War; he had been a lecturer at Oxford University during this time. I informed him I was a member of Her Majesty's Royal Navy and was making a few bob on the side to eke out my leave pay.

On arrival at the Airport I let him out of the cab. I unloaded the luggage so that he was once again surrounded by luggage; this time porters descended on him as his wife and children arrived. He asked what the fare was and I checked the meter, which read seven pounds fourteen shillings & sixpence. He handed me a five-pound note, two one pound notes and the

CHAPTER SEVEN

appropriate change. I thanked him and he then said, "Hold out your hands." I did as I was asked, he delved into his pockets and shovelled all of his loose change into my cupped hands! His lady wife also gave me a ten bob note.

Again I thanked them and wished them a safe journey home to Austin in Texas.

On leaving the airport I headed onto the A4 trunk road, stopping at the Peggy Bedford pub for a pint and a pie. I also checked my tip that came to a couple of quid; this had been a profitable trip.

Christmas leave was always a fun time. One I remember well was when a whole bunch of us were on leave together—Tony, our Royal Marine buddy, Don, Nobby, Mick, who was in the Irish Guards, and a couple more of us. It was Christmas Eve and we were all wearing our respective uniforms. We decided to have a pub crawl, starting on the outskirts of Oxford. We had heard of a new pub in Kennington called the Scholar Gypsy and we descended upon it like a swarm of locusts! It was my turn to get a round in and I paid the barmaid. Unfortunately some of my change fell on the floor and I bent down to pick it up—and there was a tearing sound: my bellbottom trousers had split, the stitching coming apart under my crotch.

The Landlady was also behind the bar. I cautiously asked her if she had any needle and thread and she produced a small tin box that contained thread, but no needle, although there were a number of safety pins. I explained what I wanted it for and she was very gracious. "Come through here," she said. I did and went into an alcove between the bar and the lounge. I dropped my trousers and she proceeded to pin the split part together. "You've made my Christmas Eve a time to remember!" she laughed.

Our pub crawl continued and we visited many of the Oxford pubs. I stood up all the time not taking a chance sitting down in case one of the safety pins holding my bellbottoms should open and cause another embarrassing situation.

Feeling a bit religious, for the occasion was Christmas after all, we decided to make our way back to Cowley. The pubs were shut and St Luke's church was providing a midnight mass. We duly attended and there were a good many of the people of Cowley in attendance; we increased the congregation by a few and at least contributed a very good support to the carol singing; a good sing-song always went down well with sailors!

Father Whye was in charge of the service and noting that some of his congregation had already imbibed liquid refreshment, namely us, he no doubt considered we would be better off not partaking in the communion. We, and a few others, abstained, in any case. I was very cautious when sitting down on the hard wooden pews in case one of the safety pins holding my bellbottom trousers opened up!

The mass came to an end and the congregation dispersed, everyone going home with spirits uplifted, my mates and I in particular to greet the coming of Christmas.

CHAPTER SEVEN

All good things come to an end. My Christmas leave was over and I made my way back to Portsmouth. Looking around on the jetty where *Albion* was moored, I wondered where my next draft would be.

It wasn't long before I was notified. I was going to be part of the ship's company of *H.M.S. St. Vincent*. This was a boy seaman's training establishment in Gosport; it would be a month before I took up my duties at *St. Vincent*, and I managed to get in a couple of weekend leaves before being drafted.

On one weekend leave I took my mate, Mickey Haloran, home with me. He came from Belfast in Ireland. Mum was very welcoming to both of us and made it a pleasant weekend.

I took Mickey into Oxford and introduced him to some of my mates. It goes without saying that we visited a few of the Oxfords pubs; we were both in uniform and this had a certain attraction for the local girls. However, I found out that a dance was being held at the Carfax Assembly rooms, and we decided to go along.

We had imbibed a few pints of Oxford's best ale before we arrived at the dance hall, and proceeded to go through the two glass doors at the entrance where the admission fee would be taken. A policeman was standing by the entrance. Mickey and I went to where our admission fee would be taken and entry tickets would be issued. We had got this far in our endeavour when, unfortunately, a little chap dressed in what could be described as fancy dress, came running towards us,

CHAPTER SEVEN

waving his arms and hands in all directions above his head, saying in a loud voice, "You can't come in here!" I asked why not and he replied, "This is a private function—it's an Old Time Dance, for members only." I got the message and said to Mickey, "Come on, we've been chucked out of better places than this!" The policeman overheard the altercation and was finding it hard not to laugh. We left peaceably and found other places in Oxford to be entertained.

I must say that Mickey was a gentle soul. As I mentioned before, it was said that he had hypnotized himself in a mirror and had never recovered. He did have a slightly glazed look in his eyes! Nevertheless he was a good mate.

Our weekend leave came to an end and we returned to *Albion*. My draft to *H.M.S. St.Vincent* was imminent.

I said farewell to *H.M.S. Albion*, which was destined to join her sister ship *H.M.S. Bulwark* and be transformed into a commando carrier.

St.Vincent, being a shore establishment, enabled me to use my car to get around.

I was employed in the main galley; this lasted a few weeks when the Chief Cook decided to put me in charge of the Chief and Petty Officers' galley. This was a plum job for there were between fifteen and twenty Chiefs and P.O.s that were catered for at dinner time. Most of them were married and lived ashore, and went home at the end of the day.

This left about half a dozen that were accommodated

CHAPTER SEVEN

within the establishment. I had two civilian mess men to work with who served the meals and kept the dining room and lounge area clean; they were decent chaps albeit one was as queer as a nine bob note! However, that was his way and not mine. I had a few perks: one was that I was given the privilege of having a neat tot of rum; another was that I had the use of the bar.

I knew a few of the other lads in the main galley. Stutch was one of them; we had met in Chatham when we were under training.

Stutch was a Yorkshire lad from Sheffield. He was no different from any of us and enjoyed his pint of beer. We used the Black Swan pub which was local; of cause, we had our own name for it and called it the Mucky Duck.

However, one evening, Stutch had been drinking at the pub and was getting short of cash. He enquired of the landlord if he would like a chicken and how much he would pay for it; the landlord agreed to pay twenty-five bob for it. Stutch disappeared and returned to *St. Vincent*; he managed to get hold of the main galley keys, let himself in and helped himself to a chicken from the fridge.

Stutch was wearing his uniform. Being winter he was wearing his overcoat and had hidden the chicken inside it, hanging from a hook under his right armpit. He was heading towards the main gate when he was confronted by the officer of the watch and his escorts, which consisted of my old mate and sparring partner from *H.M.S. Dryad*—Mick Meleaney and a Royal Marine.

CHAPTER SEVEN

Stutch came to attention. If he had just stood to attention until the Officer and his escort had passed by he would have got away with it, but the silly sod tried to give a salute, raising his right arm with his hand ready to touch his forehead. His arm got stuck halfway and the hook with the chicken hanging on it impeded his arm's motion, allowing him to give only half of a salute.

The officer came to an abrupt halt. Looking Stutch up and down, he said to the Marine, "Search him, Royal." The marine carried out the order and did his best to conceal the offending chicken, replying, "Nothing there sir." The officer pushed the marine aside and said, "What the hell is this then?"—pulling the chicken from the inside of Stutch's coat.

Needless to say, Stutch got arrested and charged with misappropriation of Naval stores. Punishment for this crime was severe and he was subjected to 60 days in D,Q.'s—short for Detention Quarters.

This was not a very nice place. The discipline exercised was very harsh, overseen by a Navy legend who was generally known as Tiny Short, who was the Master at Arms responsible to the Provost Marshal.

Later in my career I would be part of an escort to deliver a shipmate to the dreaded D.Q.'s.

During my time at *St. Vincent* I made contact with my Aunt Alice, one of my Dad's sisters who was married to Perce Twidle; they lived in Cuthbert Road, which was within the district of Fratton, an area of Portsmouth. I would visit them on a Sunday and go for a lunchtime

CHAPTER SEVEN

drink. Their favourite pub was called The Battle of Minden—well, it was, until they got barred for some reason. I never found out what the reason was. They were both certainly a couple of characters!

Uncle Perce had been in the Navy during World War Two. He was part of the crew of *H.M.S. Cornwall*. He had been adrift (a navy term for being late) in returning to his ship; she had already set sail to the Far East. Unfortunately she was sunk by Japanese aircraft in the Indian Ocean. This was very lucky for Uncle Perce as he was incarcerated in Portsmouth jail until another ship required a crew.

Aunt Alice had been in service as a young girl to very wealthy people. She spoke with great eloquence, and in many ways could be very refined, until sitting opposite her in the pub. She always wore a hat held together with a hat pin as long as a spear. Her olive green coat had smudges of powdered snuff down the front of it. Uncle Perce wasn't very happy with Auntie's snuff taking, saying to me on many occasions, "I don't know why she takes that stuff! All it is, is the root of a tobacco plant ground up with some scent added." Of course, Aunt Alice had her complaints about Perce; with his cigarette roll ups, they nevertheless complemented each other, with Aunt Alice being the housewife who had the ability to conjure up a meal from nothing, and Perce operating a crane in the Navy dockyard.

I called round one afternoon. Aunt Alice was in, on her own, and I asked, "Where's Perce?" She replied that

CHAPTER SEVEN

he was in hospital. I asked what for, and she said, "He took a hot water bottle to bed. He sat on it and it burst, giving a big blister on his bum! He popped it with a pin and it turned septic."

We went to visit him in St. Mary's Hospital and he was lying on his stomach with a frame holding the covers up over his bum. I called him a stupid sod for doing such a thing! He laughed and agreed with me.

Back at *St. Vincent* I was developing a problem of my own. My right foot was playing up. I noticed something that looked like an overgrown blackhead growing on the sole of my foot. I went to the sick bay. To reach it meant that you had to leave through the main gate, cross the road and walk a couple of hundred yards on the public road to access the building.

On examination, the Doc told me that I had a verruca. It was like an ingrowing wart and would have to be cut out as they were very contagious. He instructed me to return to the sick bay at 2 o'clock that afternoon, and I obeyed. I was ushered into the treatment room and instructed to lie down on the examination table. I had been instructed to bring slippers with me.

Lying on the table with my right trouser leg rolled up, shoe and sock removed, my foot and lower leg supported on a couple of pillows, the Doc proceeded to prepare me for the removal of the offending verruca. A local anaesthetic was injected into my foot in a number of places, and Iodine was liberally applied to the same area.

CHAPTER SEVEN

The Doc was in a good mood saying he hadn't done one of these operations in a long time. He had probably had a couple of pink gins in the wardroom at lunchtime! The scalpel came into play, and along with a pair of tweezers, the incisions were made with the scalpel paring away at the skin, assisted with the use of the tweezers to pull out the offending bits.

I felt a certain amount of tugging, but no real pain—that would come later! The pillow that my foot had rested on was blood soaked in places. The Doc filled in the hole he had made in my foot with sterile dressings.

I was unable to get my slipper on my foot and the sick bay Tiffy bound it on with a bandage. I asked the Doc if I could be excused duties, and his reply was, "If you want a weekend leave pass, the answer is no!" I got the message and I hobbled back to the mess, turned into my bunk and waited for the anaesthetic to wear off and the pain to begin.

It did! This was one of the most uncomfortable nights of my life. However, I got through it. I carried out my duties, and made my daily trek to the sick bay to get the dressings changed on my foot. Eventually the swelling on my foot went down and I was able to get my galley boots on.

A couple of the lads had found out that there was a W.A.C.S. camp not too far away near Liphook. I had the transport, being my old Vauxhall; they bribed me into taking them there. I gave in and drove to Liphook.

After parking the car we went off to find the local

CHAPTER SEVEN

pubs. (I must add that their estimation about Liphook not being far away was a slight underestimation; they had to cough up a few more bob to cover the petrol cost!)

However, the trip was not uneventful; we found a pub that some of the girl soldiers frequented and being sailors in uniform we were a bit of a novelty.

We got talking to a few of the girls and shared a few drinks together, although I had to back off a bit as I was driving.

Closing time came, the pub emptied out, and I offered the girls a lift back to their barracks. We found the car and, climbing in with six of us, things were a bit cramped; none of us were going to complain, however, even when my hand fell off the gear stick and found the knee of the lady soldier sitting next to me.

Fog had descended so driving was a bit hazardous. My new girlfriend was a good navigator, and before long we arrived at the main gate of the barracks; after showing our identification, and explaining that we were just giving the young ladies a lift, we were allowed to enter.

Being foggy, it was difficult to know where the car park was. We thought we were in it. We were saying our goodbyes in a very friendly manner, and with the car's windows steamed up and a foggy night outside, we thought that we would not be noticed. WRONG! A tapping on the car's window alerted me to the fact that someone wanted our attention. Everyone untangled themselves and I opened the car door—to be confronted by the sight of the female equivalent of an

CHAPTER SEVEN

army Sergeant Major! She bellowed at me: "Where do you think you are!" I replied, "In the car park." I thought she was going to explode! "No, you are not!" she shouted. "You have parked in the middle of the parade ground!" My unspoken response was, *Oh shit*.

Needless to say, we were escorted from the camp. Our female companions were directed to return to their barracks and we returned to *St. Vincent*.

Every ship and establishment at some time has to undergo an Admiral's inspection, and *H.M.S. St. Vincent* was no exception. Every department would be inspected by the Admiral and his staff.

My humble galley, including the Chief and Petty Officers' mess would also come under scrutiny. Along with my two civilian mess men we worked our backsides off, scrubbing all the galley utensils, the galley range and ovens. The food storage cupboards and refrigerator were always clean but still needed to be made exceptionally clean. Last but not least was the galley deck; this was constructed of a mosaic of black and white ceramic tiles which we scrubbed with strongers until it shone.

After finishing our hard work, the Chief Cook came over to check it out. (He had been busy overseeing the main galley's preparations for the oncoming inspection.) He was satisfied with our effort and said we had done a good job. On the day of the inspection the trainees and ship's company were called to divisions. The guard of honour was inspected along with the inspections of the divisions; this was always a stressful time, the reason

CHAPTER SEVEN

being that the Admiral's aide de camp at random would single out a rating to be subjected to a kit inspection.

I was excused the main divisional parade because I was required to report my galley ready for inspection.

The Admiral and his staff arrived and I came to attention, saluted and reported, in strict Naval fashion, "Chief and Petty Officers' galley ready for inspection, sir!"

Commander S., my big boss, along with the Captain of *H.M.S. St. Vincent,* were all part of the Admiral's entourage. The inspection was going well, until Commander S. got my attention by grabbing my arm. Without saying a word, he looked up and pointed to a lampshade. I got the message: the lampshade had been missed during the cleaning process, but fortunately nobody else noticed it.

After the Admiral's inspection *H.M.S. St. Vincent* returned to a normal routine; that is, until some of the trainees started to suffer from stomach pains associated with diarrhoea and vomiting.

The sick bay was overloaded; food poisoning was the main suspect. A Pathology team was sent for to investigate the problem. Fortunately none of the Chief, or Petty Officers were affected, so my galley was off the hook.

Swabs were taken from all who worked in the Main Galley, and scrapings were taken from galley equipment—all sent for analysis; the result was that one of the cooks in the main galley had been infected with

CHAPTER SEVEN

a bacterial infection that he unknowingly had spread through coughing or sneezing around food in the preparation stage.

He was put into isolation; the main galley was sanitized and inspected to make sure no traces of the bacteria were left.

As for me, my time at *H.M.S. St.Vincent* was coming to an end and I was summoned to the office of Commander S. On entering, I stood to attention, saying, "You wished to speak to me, sir?" I wondered whether I was about to get a bollocking for having a dirty lampshade in my galley during the Admiral's inspection, but the Commander put me at ease; he went on to explain that one of the cooks was a bright lad and was wanting to remain serving in *H.M.S. St.Vincent* so that he could continue his academic studies to enable him to become an officer.

I said, "How does that concern me, sir?" and he replied, "Well, he has a draft chit." I asked where to, and the Commander went on to explain it was to a frigate, *H.M.S. Blackwood*; she was employed on home sea service and was based at Gareloch Head in Scotland. He then continued, saying, "Would you be prepared to do a swap draft with him?" I thought about it for a few seconds and then I agreed. After all was said and done, I had joined the Navy to go to sea.

The Commander thanked me for my decision, informing me that I would be notified within a couple of weeks as to when my draft would take place.

CHAPTER SEVEN

Word got out that I was going to be drafted, so there was some jockeying by the lads to take over my job as the Chief and Petty Officers' chef.

My old sparring partner Mick Meleaney also started to hound me; he wanted to buy my car but I refused to sell it. I was still entitled to have a couple of weekend leaves, and needed it for my transport to get me home to Oxford.

On one of these leaves I met up with two of my mates. Don was serving on *H.M.S. Puma*—a frigate based in Simon's Town, South Africa; the silly sod had fallen down a dry dock and broken his leg. He had been sent back to the U.K. to recuperate. My other mate, Nobby, had been on leave, in Oxford, when he had got struck down with appendicitis. He was in the Radcliffe Infirmary, the same hospital where I had my appendix removed some years previously.

Don and I went to visit him. We were both wearing our uniforms. Don's leg was still in a plaster cast. Bellbottom trousers were quite roomy and could accommodate the plastered leg, although he still had to use crutches to get around.

We took Nobby the usual things—a packet of fags and a bunch of grapes. During our visit an old gentleman called Don over to his bedside. Don responded and the old gentleman asked Don how he managed his crutches. Don's reply was that you get used to them after a while. The old gentleman thanked him and said, "Why I asked is because I have gangrene in my lower right leg caused by an ingrowing toenail; they're going to chop it off, so I'll be on crutches for the rest of my life."

My draft to *H.M.S. Blackwood* was drawing closer. Meleaney was becoming more persistent in his resolve to buy my car; one night after a night out with the lads down at the Mucky Duck, he made his move. I had turned in my bunk half stewed. It must have been about one in the morning. He was doing his rounds as quartermaster and he gave me a nudge. In my fog I awoke. His torch was in my face and I said, "Turn that bloody thing off!" He lowered it and said, "Take this for your car." He tucked a bunch of money under my pillow. I knew that my days at *H.M.S. St. Vincent* were numbered and that sea time was beckoning; also, I was aware that a car parked on a jetty for weeks or months on end, without being run and exposed to salt laden air and other elements, would not last long. I agreed to the sale and told him I would sort the handing over of the keys and log book in the morning.

My car was gone, and my draft orders came through; this heralded another mishmash of my life.

CHAPTER EIGHT

WITH MY KIT PACKED AWAY in my kit bag and pusser's suitcase, I was ready to leave. Transport was provided to take me to the Gosport Ferry that plied between Gosport and Portsmouth Harbour.

I made my way to Portsmouth Harbour train station, boarded the train to London's Waterloo station, and on arrival had to transfer to King's Cross station to catch the overnight train to Helensburgh, the nearest station to Garelochhead. The train's final destination would be Fort William in the Highlands.

Travelling through the night I fell into a fitful sleep, woken occasionally by the ticket conductor to check my ticket; these conductors changed throughout the journey and had to check the passengers' verification to travel.

This was a tedious journey that spanned many hours, but it had its compensations. The morning sunlight peeked through the carriage window providing a wonderful view of the Scottish countryside.

On arrival at Helensburgh, I was met by a Navy transport driver who would take me to Garelochhead. The road took us past the Ballentines whisky bond; what struck me most was the security system that consisted of a large flock of geese!

CHAPTER EIGHT

On arrival at Garelochhead I was informed that *H.M.S. Blackwood* was at sea and was expected to arrive at Rothesay on the Isle of Bute, in the Firth of Clyde; her estimated time of arrival would be late afternoon.

For me this would be a two and something hours of travel on an M.F.V. These boats were small navy vessels operated by civilians to service ships with mail, and various stores. If anyone was prone to seasickness these would not be the best vessels to sail on. However, I was not of the seasick type and enjoyed the trip. The Isle of Bute came into sight and I was put ashore on Rothesay's pier.

Sitting on my kit bag, looking out to sea waiting for *Blackwood*'s arrival, I had time to reflect on the past forty-eight hours. I had travelled by road, rail, and sea, and had not yet reached my destination!

At last *Blackwood* came into view, the late afternoon sun reflecting off her hull. She dropped anchor and one of the ship's boats was launched and made its way to the pier where I was waiting to be transported to her.

The boats cox'n expertly put the boat alongside the pier and a couple of lads jumped onto the pier to hold it steady with bow and stern ropes. This allowed me to get my kit aboard and we set off heading towards my new ship.

Once on board I had to carry out the usual joining instructions. This didn't take too long as *H.M.S. Blackwood* was not a large ship.

I was issued with a hammock, hammock mattress, a

CHAPTER EIGHT

pillow and a couple of blankets. The leading hand of the mess issued me with a key for a locker. The accommodation was a bit cramped, so strict rules were applied; hammocks could not be slung until after the evening inspection by the officer of the watch; they had to be unslung and secured before 0800hrs in the morning, and stored in the mess hammock rack.

We used to have a joke that if you slept in a hammock long enough you became shaped like a banana. However, the lowly hammock did have some advantages over fixed bunks which I will explain later. After stowing my kit, I was introduced to my new mess mates.

After close to two days of travelling with very little sleep, I couldn't wait for the officer of the watch rounds to be over; all I wanted to do was to sling my hammock and climb into it.

On her Majesty's ships no trees are available to which hammocks can be attached, so hammock bars were built into the ship's construction; these were designed in such a way that each hammock would not bump into the one next to it during rough weather; they were positioned athwart ship: when the hammock was slung it faced stem to stern.

My first night aboard we were at anchor within a sheltered bay. At 0700, reveille was called, when a rush to the bathroom was made to have a wash, clean teeth and perform other ablutions.

I found the galley and was introduced to the Petty Officer cook who was in charge. I had already met with

CHAPTER EIGHT

the leading cook called Dinger Bell, and my compatriot Buck Taylor. (It was a long standing tradition in the navy for shipmates to have nicknames.) The P.O. was in my opinion a bit dour; being a Scot it wasn't surprising, perhaps. However, I did have a bunch of Scots mates who were a lot of fun.

Dinger and Buck came from Manchester, and had a bit of rivalry in respect of the football teams they supported. Dinger was for Manchester City whereas Buck was for Manchester United.

Blackwood up anchored and we set sail to carry out our operational duties. This was known as perisher running and involved working with submarines that were used to train and test future submarine captains.

H.M.S. Blackwood was an anti-submarine frigate designed and built to hunt down and kill submarines. She was armed with triple-barrelled mortars for submarine attacks and three single barrel Bofors guns for anti-aircraft defence.

My primary job was that of a ship's cook, but for action stations I had to be trained in other skills; for anti-aircraft action stations, I was a member of the starboard side Bofors gun crew; alternately for anti-submarine action stations I was detailed to be in the magazine assisting in loading the mortar bombs into the mortar barrels.

I was being gradually introduced to my various duties, as part of *Blackwood*'s ships company.

CHAPTER EIGHT

One evening after a hard day's work lying in my hammock I dosed off into a fitful never-never land.

My mind slipped back to my time at *H.M.S. St. Vincent*. I had met a girl when on leave; her name was Belinda and we had met at a party held in one of our mate's house. John was in the navy and we had both attended Temple Cowley School. John had joined the Navy after leaving school at the age of fifteen; his training was carried out at *H.M.S. Raleigh*, a tough training establishment.

At the time of the party John was serving on *H.M.S. Dainty*, a destroyer.

John's mum was a good sport and would allow us to have a party in the basement of their large house on the Iffley Road in Oxford.

Belinda and I had a few dates and decided to get engaged. I had my old Vauxhall car and with another mate and his girlfriend we went to London for a night out. I presented Belinda with the engagement ring that I had bought her. (This engagement ring was going to prove to be more costly than I thought!) However at the time we enjoyed ourselves.

I had to return to *St. Vincent* a couple of weeks later. I received information from one of my Oxford mates that a bunch of them were going on a day trip to Brighton on one of Tappin's coaches, and I contacted Belinda who agreed to join the gang on the trip.

They were due to arrive in Brighton at about 11 o clock on the Saturday morning. I had a weekend pass

CHAPTER EIGHT

and drove to Brighton on Friday afternoon. I parked my car and took a walk around some of the old haunts that I had come to know when I was at *H.M.S. Dryad*.

I met up with this bloke who was a ventriloquist, who carried his dummy in a battered old suitcase; apparently he was going to be part of the variety show at the Butlin's Holiday Hotel and he had been given a time to report to the hotel—at 10 o'clock on Saturday morning.

Come Friday evening, we found ourselves in Harrison's bar. It was crowded with the Friday night revellers. My newfound friend and dummy got permission to do a performance, which was a success although no payment was given. We didn't pay for a drink all night, although the dummy was wearing my sailor's cap. At closing time we went back to my car which was parked in a side street not far from the pub.

Having no other place to stay, I offered my new mate the opportunity to sleep in the car. He jumped at the offer and I crawled into the back seat; he had the two front seats, having to deal with the steering wheel and gear stick. Before nodding off I told him to keep his dummy quiet!

Come the morning, awakening with mouths feeling like the bottom of a bird cage, we left the dummy in the car and set off to find the public toilets to get a wash and brush up.

After our ablutions we returned to the car and I drove my accomplice to Butlin's Hotel. After dropping

CHAPTER EIGHT

him off along with his dummy, I drove along the Brighton sea front; the sea was calm and shimmering in the early morning sunshine.

I noticed a chap walking along the promenade. He looked around and, seeing me driving towards him, he started waving his arms in the air, gesticulating for me to stop. I pulled up alongside him and he opened the front passenger door. "What's up?" I asked, and he asked if I could drive him along the sea front. I had no immediate plans as the coach from Oxford wasn't due for another hour.

He got in and then went on to explain that his brother had run away with his wife! Alarm bells started to sound in my head. I didn't want to be witness to a domestic altercation; however, I was already committed by giving him a lift. We had travelled a few hundred yards when he shouted out for me to stop, and I responded. He had spotted his wife and brother walking along the shoreline. Getting out of the car, he said, "Thanks mate," and pushed some money into my hand. The last I saw of him was running down the pebble beach towards his wayward wife and his brother. I didn't hang around to see what happened next.

Looking at the cash that had been thrust into my hand, I discovered that it was a five-pound note, a tidy sum in those days. Needless to say, Belinda and I along with my mates from Oxford had a great day out in Brighton.

CHAPTER EIGHT

That was in the past. Now was the present, and I was engaged, serving on a ship where the only communication was by mail. I wrote to Belinda frequently. The B.F.P.O. was very efficient; our mail would be collected and delivered from shore bases, dockyards, and anywhere else in between.

Blackwood was employed sailing and exercising between Londonderry in Ulster, Northern Ireland, and the North Western approaches of the Atlantic to the west coast of Scotland.

I had not received any mail from Belinda for many weeks. The ship was due a maintenance period, and sailed to Rosyth Naval Dockyard in Fife, Scotland.

During this time I tried to contact Belinda but without success. I was getting frustrated and wondered what to do; receiving mail from loved ones was always a morale booster, no matter what armed service you belonged to.

It was a Friday night and I was ashore with one of my mates. We were in Edinburgh, and Fairlies was the attraction on Leith Walk. We had partaken of a few pints of heavy (the Scots name for a good pint of beer); however, Dave, my mate, could see that I was upset about something and he coaxed it out of me. I told him about not receiving any mail from my fiancée, and went on to add that I was going to hitchhike to Oxford to find out what was going on.

He persuaded me to wait until the next day—at least until the mail was delivered—and followed up with the

CHAPTER EIGHT

remark, "You silly sod, you can hardly stand up let alone try to hitchhike four hundred miles!"

Saturday came and as usual I didn't receive any mail. The other lads in the mess were avidly reading theirs and I was pissed off! There and then I decided to take off and hitchhike to Oxford.

I told my mate Dave that I had had enough and needed to go to Oxford to find out the reason why I was not receiving any letters from Belinda.

I had enough money to get me to Edinburgh, by train, but not enough for a return journey from Edinburgh to Oxford.

Getting off the train at Waverley station, I made my way through Edinburgh to the A1 trunk road that connected Edinburgh to London. I would have to deviate from this route to get to Oxford. Wearing my uniform with my small attaché case containing my toothbrush, toothpaste, a bar of soap, and clean underwear, I started my hitchhiking journey.

My first lift was from a lorry driver going to Newcastle. This brought me a hundred miles nearer to Oxford. The driver dropped me off on the outskirts of Newcastle. I had no clue where I was, for it was dark, but fortunately there were still a few people about. I asked a couple for directions that would reconnect me to the A1. The Geordie accent can be difficult to understand, but fortunately I had a few Geordie shipmates and was able to interpret the lingo! Walking through Newcastle, I found the A1 and continued my journey south.

CHAPTER EIGHT

With a thumb out, the recognized signal that the owner wanted a lift, a car stopped and the driver asked where I was going to. I said I was going to Oxford and he said, "Get in, I'm going to Leicester." This was a good lift and got me another 150 miles closer to Oxford.

I thanked the driver for the lift. It was now close to 5 o'clock in the morning. Being Sunday, the church bells would soon be ringing to summon the faithful to the morning service. As for me, I had another 65 miles to travel.

Dawn was breaking. I was walking along on the outskirts of Leicester with my thumb stretched out waiting for any compassionate driver to give me a lift when a vehicle came to a halt alongside me. It was a converted Morris Ten van, and the driver asked me where I was going. I informed him I was making my way to Oxford and he said he and his family were on their way to High Wycombe. I said, "Fine, when you get to Oxford I can give you directions."

I got into the back of the van and made myself as comfortable as I could. Being surrounded by four young children was rather difficult; nevertheless I was very grateful to the gentleman who offered me the lift.

Entering Oxford, I directed the driver to the Plain. After crossing over Magdalen Bridge the road splits into three—one goes to St Clements, one goes to Cowley, the third one to Iffley. I got out of the van and directed the driver to continue up St Clements and through Headington to the Green Road roundabout where he

CHAPTER EIGHT

would see the signs to connect him to the A40; this would put him on the road to High Wycombe.

As for me, no busses were available at this time of the morning and I had to walk to wherever I was going. Walking up the Cowley Road, I started to think about where I should go to. It was too early in the morning to go home—if I did my reception would have been less than welcome! I decided to go to my sister Cynthia's place; she and her husband Pete had a council house on the Airfield estate.

I arrived at No.10 Lockhart Crescent, knocked on the door and got no response. I didn't want to awake the whole neighbourhood so I got some small pebbles out of the garden and threw them at a bedroom window.

Unbeknown to me, Cynth had taken in a lodger. He answered the door and enquired who I was and I explained that I was Cynth's brother. He let me in and returned upstairs to his room; as for me, I crashed out on the settee and promptly fell asleep. After travelling 400 miles by lorry, car, van, and shank's pony, I was worn out!

Cynth was the first to get up to get breakfast ready for Pete and her children. She startled me as much as I startled her, lying on the settee looking up at her! "What the heck are you doing here!" she exclaimed, and I explained my situation, saying I had come to find out what was going on with Belinda. She made breakfast which was very welcome. After having a wash and brush up, and it now being a reasonable hour (about 10

CHAPTER EIGHT

o'clock in the morning), I decided to leave and make my way to Belinda's house.

I walked up the pathway to the front door and gave it a knock. It was opened by Belinda's Mum who was a bit taken aback to see me standing there. She invited me in and I asked if Belinda was home. She invited me to sit down and explained that Belinda had gone out on Saturday night and had not yet returned.

I got the message! I went on to explain the reason for my visit. Her Mum was a very gracious lady and explained that things were different in her day. Not wanting to upset her, I took my leave.

What to do now? I decided to go home to Hendred Street. Mum was glad to see me but was concerned that I had not let her know beforehand that I was coming home. I explained the situation and stayed the night in a comfortable bed.

Leaving home on Monday morning, I made my way to the bus stop on Oxford Road. My thoughts were in turmoil with the realisation that my engagement was over, and that by now the Navy would have me reported to the local constabulary as being absent without leave.

I was not wrong. I had enough money for my return journey to Scotland, by train. As I got on the bus that would take me to the station I noticed a policeman on his bicycle turning into Hendred Street. I had no doubt that he was going to check up if I was still at home. Mum informed him that I had already left and was returning to my ship.

CHAPTER EIGHT

My train journey took me from Oxford to Banbury where I changed trains; to get to Birmingham, not only did I have to change trains, but also stations; when my train from Banbury pulled into New Street Station, I had to get to Snow Hill station to make my connection to Edinburgh. On arrival at Edinburgh's Waverley station I had to find the platform where the train for Inverkeithing would leave from.

Arriving at Inverkeithing, I left the station and boarded a bus to Rosyth Dockyard. After showing my Identification to the Ministry of Defence policeman at the dockyard gates I made my way to my ship.

When on board I reported to the cox'n who obviously wanted to know my story. He recorded my time of arrival back on board and I was placed on open arrest; this meant that I could move around the ship but was not allowed to go ashore.

The cox'n advised me to have Lieutenant Commander Seamarks as my defending officer, as I would be on Captain's report the following morning.

I took his advice. After consulting with the Lieutenant Commander he agreed to be my defending officer.

I had been charged with being 45hrs and 49min's adrift. After the charge was read out, the Captain enquired who my defending officer was. Lieutenant Commander Seamarks stepped forward. He started off by saying, "Burgess is a victim of his own actions." (Well, I knew that already, I thought to myself.) He then

CHAPTER EIGHT

went on to explain that I should have confided in my Divisional officer about the lack of mail from my fiancée, and should have applied for a leave pass. He continued, stating that thus far I had been of good conduct and had carried out my duties in an exemplary manner.

Turning to me, the Captain asked if there was anything that I would wish to say in my defence. I responded by apologizing for my absence and intimated that I concurred with Lieutenant Commander Seamarks' report, adding that I wasn't absenting myself from the Navy and took a calculated risk that my action could incur punishment.

I must say that the Captain, who is all powerful and Lord and Master over every member of his crew, was very fair in his deliberations to me.

Before meting out my punishment, he said he understood my predicament and told me that if I should encounter any future domestic problems I must go through the proper channels to obtain leave. He went on to say that after due consideration he would give me the minimum punishment for my offence allowed under the Navy code of discipline, which would be 'seven days scale', meaning that I will have seven days stoppage of leave and pay.

During my confinement to the ship I did a few favours to the lads by standing their watch so they could go ashore for a night out; this was always complemented by being asked round for a whet of their tot at up spirits.

CHAPTER EIGHT

Blackwood's maintenance was going to be more extensive than first thought; the ship's company were moved to a shore base that was an annex to *H.M.S. Cochrane*; this was in a place called Donibristle.

We were billeted here for a couple of months. Not much happened, except that our P.O. cook was sent off to hospital; he had developed an ulcer, which was possibly the reason why he was such a miserable bastard!

Blackwood was ready for sea again. It was like returning home! We had a replacement Petty Officer cook join us, who was very fair and capable; our galley crew was complete and ready to face the challenges that would face us.

We set sail for Londonderry in Northern Ireland, sporting the Red Hand of Ulster mounted on each side of the funnel. It was mid-afternoon as we sailed under the Forth Railway Bridge, always an awesome sight. Completed in 1890 this colossus of a bridge stands as a monument and tribute to British engineering and the men who built it; however, we were being met by white crested waves, which could mean one thing only—that after leaving the calm waters of the Forth estuary and heading into the North Sea, it was going to get choppy.

I was not wrong; we carried out shake down trials, which is what all ships do after undergoing maintenance and refits, to make sure that everything on board was functioning correctly. Although the sea was choppy, it would be nothing compared to what lay ahead of us in the not too far distant future.

CHAPTER EIGHT

We arrived in Londonderry, sailing through Lough Foyle. This is a treacherous stretch of water as it is in a tidal race that surges from the North Atlantic; ships had to be made extra secured when tied up to the jetty.

Our operations involved a lot of sea time exercising with submarines, surface ships, the R.A.F. coastal command, and Fleet Air Arm.

This was known as the Cold War although the pot was simmering between the eastern bloc headed by Russia, and the western alliance of N.A.T.O. with America at the helm.

Our job was to help keep the lid on the pot to stop it boiling over. Between our exercises we did get some shore time. On one occasion I was in Londonderry on a Wednesday, around lunchtime, when I noticed a pub and went in for a pint of Porter. I pulled up a stool to sit on next to the bar, and another chap sat next to me. He was very interested, watching the horse racing on the television, as were most of the customers. There was a great cheer when the winner crossed the line! Half the pub emptied including the chap who was sitting next to me, leaving the remains of his pint of Porter on the bar; within a few minutes he was back again taking up residence on his bar stool.

Next to the pub was a betting shop—this is where half the customers had gone to collect their winnings and to place another bet!

I struck up a conversation with this gentleman and during our conversation I asked if he was on holiday.

CHAPTER EIGHT

He looked at me with some disdain and said he was on a permanent holiday; then, with a twinkle in his eye, he explained that he had eleven children, and that he received twelve pounds a week from the British government per week. He went on to say that if he worked he could earn fourteen pounds a week, so why should he work for two pounds a week?

I admired his logic but was repulsed by his ethics.

On the other side of the coin, I met a very nice Irish girl whose name was Margie. She lived with her Mum and five brothers on the Creggan Estate; all had jobs and Margie worked in the local shirt factory. The shirts, bearing the St Michael brand, were distributed throughout the Marks & Spencer chain of shops.

Margie was very generous and purchased a couple of shirts for me at a discount price. Unfortunately sea duty separated us and we drifted apart. Nevertheless there was no animosity between us and I still have fond memories of her and hope she has a full and happy life.

Sea time is what it means. *Blackwood* was involved in an Anti-Aircraft exercise with the Royal Air Force, and the Dutch equivalent; I was part of the starboard guns crew. Butch was the seaman gunner, while the steward and I were the gun loaders and ammunition suppliers.

This exercise was taking part in the North Western approaches. The weather and sea conditions can change very rapidly in this part of the world, and they did; what was a reasonably gentle swell quickly turned into waves that started to churn up to eight to ten feet. A Dutch

CHAPTER EIGHT

plane was flying overhead towing a sleeve target; this is what we were to fire at. We loaded the gun as fast as we could, trying to keep two feet on the deck at the same time. With the ship starting to rock and roll, this was not easy. Butch was doing his best to hit the target. Unfortunately our shells got uncomfortably close to the towing plane and he quickly buggered off.

Because of the deterioration in the weather the exercise was called off and the aircraft returned to their respective bases. As for us, we were to remain at sea to ride out the coming storm.

Seas were becoming mountainous and the wind was reaching force twelve. The height of some waves could be as much as thirty feet. Looking up at a wave cresting with the white spume flying off it could be exhilarating and frightening at the same time.

The ship was hove to, meaning that the bow was headed into the waves and steerage and speed was calibrated to give the ship the maximum stability. The Captain never left the bridge for the duration of this ordeal that would take close to four days before it would subside.

Duties had to be carried out to maintain the ship's operational ability. Unfortunately many crew members had to be watch on stop on. Those of the engine room branch were mostly affected; their mess deck was in the after part of the ship. With the ship being battened down it was too dangerous for them to go on deck to transfer from the mess to the engine room.

CHAPTER EIGHT

The seamen were huddled in the fo'c'sle flat. I must add that we had smuggled a stray dog on board in Londonderry. The Petty Officer steward had been designated the job of dog handler; however, she preferred to sit with the seamen. Trying to keep two feet on a heaving deck is difficult, but with four feet it becomes near impossible.

Some of the crew succumbed to seasickness, among them being my mate Buck and our Petty Officer cook; this left me and Dinger Bell to provide nourishment to any of the crew that wanted to be fed.

Pot mess was the only sustenance that we could provide. Pot mess is akin to a stew that only Navy cooks and provisions can supply. The galley with its heaving deck and galley cooking range going in different directions at the same time made one into a ballet dancer trying to avoid pots, pans and any other missile that could be launched.

The galley range was provided with steel bars that could be put in place to stop the cooking pots from sliding across the range. We were hit by an almighty wave; the pot containing the pot mess was held securely, but unfortunately the contents took off and went airborne, finishing up on the galley deck head—the ceiling, for those not associated with Navy terms.

The ship had moved its position caused by the humongous wave, and gravity played its part; the pot mess stuck to the deck head became unstuck and dropped down onto the hot range, missing the pot

CHAPTER EIGHT

where it had come from; the burning meat, vegetables and gravy caused a hell of a mess and an acrid smell! I managed to get things under control; dinner would be served as usual although the portions would be smaller.

This was one hell of a storm! We lost our ship's boats and life rafts; these had been either washed overboard or smashed to bits by the ever constant waves crashing over the ship. It was a credit to our Captain and crew that we survived such an onslaught.

CHAPTER NINE

MOTHER NATURE had flung everything she had at us and we survived. The mountainous seas had subsided and the calmer waters enabled us to take stock of the damage that *H.M.S. Blackwood* had sustained.

The crew members that had been holed up in their messes and duty stations started to emerge. Dinger and I reassembled the galley, putting pots, pans and galley dishes back into the racks where they belonged. As expected, everyone was hungry; those that had suffered seasickness were now ready to eat.

It was late afternoon. The evening menu as designated to me, being the duty chef, was individual pork pies and baked beans in tomato sauce. (This was a change from the pot mess that was served during the storm!) I could now use the oven. The pork pies were warming through and I was about to put the baked beans into the oven when Buck came into the galley. He asked, what's for scran—another Navy term for food—and I told him what it was. His reply pissed me off: "Is that all!"—followed by other derogatory remarks. I responded by telling him "to f*** off out the galley",

CHAPTER NINE

adding, "You have been lying in your hammock for the past four days while Dinger and I were working watch about, trying to keep the crew fed!" I couldn't help myself; Buck was leaving the galley muttering other things over his shoulder and I still had the galley dish of baked beans in my hands—which I threw at him! Some of the beans hit him and as he ran away they were dripping down his back, the rest landing on the galley deck. "Sod it!" I said to myself as I scraped them up and put them back in the dish. I ditched them and had to get hold of the jack dusty for replacements, explaining that there had been an accident in the galley.

Because of the storm's damage to the ship, we headed for Rosyth. The ship's boats and life rafts that were lost had to be replaced, and bent and broken guard rails had to be repaired.

Calmer waters prevailed and the ship returned to a normal routine. One afternoon, after tot time, I went to see a mate in the steerage compartment, which was below the bridge. My mate was the duty helmsman. The compartment obviously contained the ship's wheel and other navigational aids, the compass and azimuth repeater (a piece of equipment by means of which the helmsman would steer the course set by the navigator and adhered to by the officer of the watch). I was always interested in all aspects of the workings of a ship.

On this occasion I persuaded my mate to let me have a go at steering the ship! He agreed and let me take the wheel. Watching over my shoulder he explained that the set course was what should be maintained: the vertical line on the repeater indicated the ship's position, and I was supposed to keep the ship on its predetermined course.

With the motion of the ship and the swell of the sea I was trying to stay on course; unfortunately, I didn't have the gentle touch that the experienced helmsman had and the ship started to zigzag! The officer of the watch yelled down from the bridge, "WHO THE HELL is on the wheel?" I replied, "Cook Burgess, sir." His response was apoplectic: "Get the f*** off it!" I promptly handed the wheel back to my mate. We were both out of order, since a proper procedure should have been carried out before I took over the wheel—this was to inform the bridge, the name of the person taking over and the course and speed of the ship; we were lucky not to be put on a charge. Leaving the wheel house, I looked aft: the wake of the ship looked like a dog's hind leg!

Arriving in Rosyth without further incident, we berthed alongside the jetty. Dockyard inspectors came aboard to inspect the damage; it was assessed that the repairs would take two to three weeks.

This was a lot different from World War Two when ships coming into Rosyth dockyard had not only had to endure the elements, but had been subjected to torpedoes, aircraft bombing, and shelling from enemy surface ships.

It was a known fact among the dockyard employees

CHAPTER NINE

that during the war many women were employed. Their tasks were very distressing; some of the work included going into ship's compartments that had been shored up, helping to remove dead bodies and limbs that had been severed by shrapnel. Needless to say, they were given a well-deserved tot of rum before carrying out this very important work.

As for us, a long weekend leave was granted and one of my shipmates, Ginger, who came from Oxford, was a leading seaman.

Ginger and I got together to make travel arrangements as we were both going on leave at the same time. Ginger found out that the Talisman would get us to King's Cross station in London in eight hours, the only stop being in Newcastle, to change crews.

This was a special train and travelling on it cost an extra five bob over and above the regular fare. We had travel warrants that covered the expense for normal railway journeys but we had to pay for any other expenses.

Being at sea for long periods allowed us to save our money as we had nowhere to spend it; this enabled us to pay the extra fare for our journey.

Ginger made the arrangements and we got the train from Inverkeithing to Edinburgh, crossing over the Forth Bridge. We arrived at Waverley station in good time to board the Talisman.

Arriving at King's Cross station, we had to get to Paddington to get the train to Oxford; we made it and arrived around 10 o'clock p.m.

CHAPTER NINE

We parted company, Ginger going to Marston, me making my way to Cowley. Ginger said, "Don't forget our train leaves Oxford at 8 o'clock Sunday night to get us back to Rosyth."

I had a good weekend, meeting up with my mates, the family, and some of my girlfriends.

Sunday lunchtime always held good memories. I would go with my Uncle Tom to the Exeter pub where we would meet up with Frank, a retired Major, Chick, who had been a sergeant, and Tommy Stritch, of unknown rank; all had served in the army during World War Two. Uncle Tom had the distinction of being the radio operator and gunner of the tank that made the breakthrough at El Alamein.

As the drink went down the war stories would come out. Tommy had a close escape; he had two weeks to go from being demobbed when he got recalled for the Korean conflict; lucky for him, he was able to convince the powers that be that he had served his time.

Other local characters would converge on the pub. Ivan was a second-hand car dealer; unfortunately he had lost his driving licence for being in charge of a vehicle while under the influence of drink. However, he was very resilient and bought a horse and trap! Sunday lunchtime the horse and trap could be found tethered to the pub sign. The trap was provided with two very ornamental brass paraffin lamps. Ivan would always remove them and take them into the pub with him, not wanting them to be nicked while he was imbibing.

CHAPTER NINE

He always had a couple of friends with him. The lamps would be put on the corner of the bar within full view of the staff and customers. One customer was Johnny, a little Irishman who lived on Oxford Road.

Time was called and the pub had to be emptied out. Uncle Tom, myself, and our friends drank up and were standing outside the pub saying our farewells when Ivan came out a little under the weather, accompanied by a couple of his friends. He unhitched his horse and trap from the pub signpost. The trap had a little door in the rear with a foot step to help one get in. Ivan took the reins and the horse took off at a gentle trot, going up Oxford Road on its way to Horsepath where Ivan lived.

At this point the pub door opened and Johnny came running out with two brightly shining brass ornamental paraffin carriage lamps, one in each hand! He proceeded to chase after the horse and trap with its occupants, yelling out, "Oyvan, Oyvan, you forgot your lamps!" The last we saw of the spectacle was the little door of the trap being opened and four burly hands reaching out grabbing hold of Johnny; they hauled him into the trap as it merrily went on its way. From that time on, Johnny was known as Johnny the lamp!

My weekend leave came to an end. After having tea with the family it was my time to make my way to Oxford railway station.

According to Ginger our train was due to leave at 8 p.m. to take us to London's Paddington station, where we would use the underground railway to travel to

CHAPTER NINE

King's Cross to catch the overnight train to Scotland.

Getting off the bus at Carfax and being early, I strolled down to Vi's pub, The Jolly Farmers. I arrived at opening time, went in and had a chat and a couple of pints. I bade my farewells, and made my way to the station; on arrival I presented my ticket to the ticket inspector. Going through the barrier and entering the platform, I found it empty. I looked around for Ginger who was nowhere in sight. I wondered if he was having a pee in the gent's, but no one appeared; a porter was passing and I asked him when the train for London was due. His reply was that it had already left! I was gobsmacked. I said it was supposed to be the 8 o'clock, and he said, "No way, it left at seven-fifteen."

My next question was, "When's the next one?" The reply didn't endear me to him. He told me it would be a stopping train due at about eight forty-five; this was no express and would be about as slow as a tortoise.

I had no option but to wait for it. Eventually the train arrived and after boarding and settling down in my seat, I had time to reflect on what my options were; this was a slow train and there was no way that I would be able to make my connection at King's Cross to get me back to Scotland and my ship before my leave expired. If I was adrift I would be in the rattle again.

A thought came into my head. Not wanting to be subjected to punishment that was not of my making, I thought of pulling a flanker. (Anyone who has served in the armed forces will understand this term of phrase.)

CHAPTER NINE

Arriving at Paddington station I found a telephone kiosk. I remembered my Uncle Ken's telephone number and gave him a call. If anyone could help me out I was sure he would. He lived at 25 Jeffreys Road in Stockwell. The phone was answered by a lady whose voice I didn't recognize. I explained who I was and she said that Ken was out of town working on a film production. I asked if I could come over and she agreed. I arrived at the flat, and was met by this very attractive lady.

I was welcomed in and after settling down I asked her if she could do me a favour. Her reply was, "What do you want?" I said, "Could you phone my ship for me and say that I am unwell and unable to travel?"

God bless her, she agreed! After the phone call I was able to relax and chatted about things relevant to our lives. Annie was her name, and was a very good artistic window dresser for one of the upmarket high fashion stores in Oxford Street in the West End of London.

It was time to turn in and Annie went to her bedroom. As for me, I made myself comfortable on the couch. Thoughts kept going through my head as I thought what I would do tomorrow.

Monday morning I was awakened with a cup of tea and a couple of slices of toast and marmalade. Annie was a good sport; we had a chat and I said now the ship had been notified that I was unwell and unable to travel, I needed to see a doctor for confirmation.

Annie said that Ken's doctor had his surgery around

CHAPTER NINE

the corner on the Stockwell Road. I made my way there and, entering the building, I was met by a very smart and well-dressed receptionist in full nurse's uniform. I explained to her that I was not a registered patient with the doctor but my uncle Ken was, and that I had taken ill when traveling back to Scotland to join my ship.

I was assured that the doctor would take care of me. A few minutes later I was shown into the consulting room.

This was not the usual doctor one would be confronted with, wearing a tweed jacket and grey flannel trousers. This doctor was wearing a very different attire; a portly man of a very pleasant demeanour, he was dressed in a morning suit with a starched white shirt and black bow tie.

He offered me a chair and enquired about my physical condition. I did the best to explain that I had taken ill on the train between Oxford and London and had suffered stomach cramps followed with a case of the runs, and nausea. He looked at me over his wired rimmed glasses—then instructed me to get onto the examination table. I complied and he pushed and prodded around my abdominal region; when the examination was complete I was invited to get off the examination table and take a seat. His next words were, "When do you feel able to return to your ship?" I said Wednesday. He smiled and wrote a sick note giving me permission to travel on the coming Wednesday. Taking the sick note with gratitude, I got up to leave and the doctor said, "I have also given you a prescription if you feel the need for it."

CHAPTER NINE

I wondered what to do next. A thought came into my head as I remembered meeting a family many years before when on holiday at the Coronation Holiday Camp on Hayling Island. Tony, his Mum and sister Janette were on holiday at the same time and we had struck up a friendship. I fell in love with Janette; we were all about the same age, between twelve and thirteen years old. It was many years ago. I corresponded with Janette frequently by mail, and her address was still fixed in my memory; it was 58 Boundary Road Colliers Wood, London, S.W.19.

I made my way to the address, not knowing who lived there; things can change over the years, but I thought I would give it a try.

I found the house and knocked on the door and to my surprise Janette's Mum answered the door. I was standing there in my Navy uniform, all six foot of me, looking a lot different from a kid of twelve from back in 1953! I explained who I was and a vague recollection came into her eyes; she then embraced me and ushered me into the house.

We had a long chat over a cup of tea. Janette had married a soldier and Tony had graduated Art College and was working as a set designer for the Hughie Green Show on TV. He was still living at home.

Tony arrived home and was surprised to see me sitting there chatting to his Mum! We embraced each other as old friends. I explained what my predicament was, and that I had to return to my ship on Wednesday.

CHAPTER NINE

Tony came up with a plan. "Can you get over here for about 11 o'clock tomorrow morning?" he asked. I replied that I could. It was time for me to leave and I returned to Ken's flat.

Annie was home. We had a bite to eat and watched a bit of telly. I told Annie how my day had gone, informing her that I was going to meet my friend tomorrow and that I would prefer to wear civvies rather than my uniform.

She said that Kenny had a whole wardrobe of suits and shirts and was certain that he wouldn't mind if I borrowed an outfit. I took up the offer.

I met up with Tony as arranged and we made our way to the West End of London. Tony knew his way around. We did a tour of Soho, taking in Old Compton Street, visiting a few bars and strip clubs; one in particular sticks in my mind: a fan dancer was on the stage carrying out her routine, using two large fans, the plumage being ostrich feathers; one bloke in the audience was a bit boisterous and was giving her a hard time and, in mid-stride, she dropped her fans, standing stark naked! She pointed to him and gave him a mouthful, yelling out, "If you can do any better, get up here and have a go!" She got a round of applause! Matey boy was gently escorted out of the building by a couple of burley gorillas—at least that's what they looked like.

All good things come to an end and it was time to return to my ship. Early Wednesday morning found me

CHAPTER NINE

at King's Cross station in uniform catching the train back to Scotland.

H.M.S. Blackwood was tied up to the jetty where I had left her. Approaching the gangplank, I saw Ginger sitting on a bo's'n chair slung over the side of the ship; a paint pot full of battleship grey was in one hand, a paintbrush in the other,

I was a bit peeved that he had given me the wrong time for the train leaving Oxford and I let him know it! His reply was, "I realized my mistake but wasn't going to look in every pub in Oxford to find you."

Reporting back on board I found the cox'n. In his usual way, he said, "Okay, Burgess, what's your story?" I said it as it was, referring to the telephone call made by Annie; he then enquired if I had anything to back it up and I produced the doctor's note. Taking it from me, he scrutinized it and attached it to his report, then dismissed me without any charge. As I was leaving to go to the mess deck, he said, "By the way, we checked every timetable from Oxford to London and no way could you have caught the overnight train to Scotland." This was said with a smile on his face. (This would not be the only time a doctor's sick note would get me out of trouble!)

Blackwood was ready for sea again. We went to harbour stations. The order was given: "Let go forward, let go aft!" The ropes and lines that had secured us to the jetty were let go and we made our way into the Forth

CHAPTER NINE

Estuary heading for the open sea to take up our duties.

This time we made our way into the Irish Sea. We were to exercise with a couple of our submarines. One of them was experimenting with a newly devised indicator buoy; this is part of a submarine's safety equipment; it could be operated from within the boat if it got into difficulty.

This is a nice way of saying that it was knackered and was at the bottom of the sea. The indicator buoy would be released and would make its way to the surface where a radio transmitter would automatically transmit through an antenna that had a light attached to it, giving in Morse Code the boat's identification and location. It was attached to the boat by many fathoms of cable. Unfortunately the cable attaching it to the boat had come adrift and was bobbing about all over the Irish Sea—and it was our job to find and retrieve it.

This we did and continued with our exercises. Our ping bosuns (this was the affectionate name given to the lads that manned the sonar and submarine detection equipment) were very concentrated in their profession. We had two echoes that indicated where our two submarines were. One of the lads picked up a ghost signal and the officer in charge of the division listened in; he reported to the Captain that we were picking up three signals, and through the ship's communication system our two subs were informed to surface; we then continued to monitor the third echo: without a doubt our exercise was being monitored by a submarine of a

CHAPTER NINE

foreign power! This being the Cold War period one could be sure it was Russian.

After exercises were completed and the Russian sub had left our area (they knew we were on to them), we made our way to Douglas in the Isle of Man.

It was Armistice Day weekend and the ship was providing the guard of honour for a ceremony being held at the Villa Marine. This establishment was a couple of miles outside of Douglas.

Leave was granted to the off-duty watch. This being Saturday, leave would expire at 0800 hrs on Sunday morning; the ship's schedule was to sail on the Sunday morning to go to Peel, the capital of the Island, and take the Governor and his wife for a sail around the Island. My mate Geordie and I went ashore together. The pier where *Blackwood* was secured was port side on, her starboard side exposed to the open sea.

We made our way to the end of the pier wearing our No.1 uniforms with our winter raincoats wrapped around us; the wind was brisk, and chilly. At the end of the pier we found what could be described as a soda fountain type café, where a number of soft drinks were available that could be pulled like bar handles in a pub.

Geordie went for a traditional lemonade. I was a bit more adventurous and ordered a sarsaparilla. I wish I hadn't!

Leaving the café we made our way into town. A pub called the Market Inn attracted us. On entering we

CHAPTER NINE

found a couple of seats. The pub was quite busy and Geordie ordered a couple of pints. Bringing them to our table, we took in the surroundings. I had drunk about a quarter of my pint when I felt a distinctive uncomfortable feeling in my stomach! I got out of my chair and made a rapid dash for the door leading to the toilet, with one hand trying to open the door and the other across my mouth trying to subdue what was about to exit from my digestive system. I didn't make it! I did what is known in navy terms as a five-finger spread—vomit forced its way through my fingers and spread itself over the door.

The Landlady was very compassionate; she cleaned up my mess and made me a drink of what I don't know of. She said, "Drink that down in one gulp and you'll be as right as rain!"

I did as I was told and was very apologetic for the inconvenience I had caused; I now know that sarsaparilla and beer don't mix!

Whatever the Landlady gave me worked. Within about five minutes I was as good as gold.

I hadn't noticed a blonde lady sitting in the pub, but she had seen Geordie and me. Looking over in her direction, we made eye contact. She smiled at me and I smiled back. I went over to where she was sitting and apologized for my previous behaviour for throwing up all over the door!

I invited her to have a drink with us and she accepted. We had a good chat, after which she said she

CHAPTER NINE

had to leave; however, before leaving, we made an arrangement that we would meet later in the evening and she would bring a friend with her so we could make up a foursome.

Day turned into night, and after having a bite to eat, both of us caught a bus to the Villa Marine to attend the Armistice Parade. It was not mandatory for us to attend as this was Saturday night. The main event would be on Sunday, after taking the Governor and his wife on a trip around the island.

On arrival everything was over; not knowing when the next bus was due, we decided to hitchhike back to town.

We got lucky—a car stopped and two chaps were in it; they said, "Where you going to?" We said the Market Inn pub, in Douglas, and they invited us to get in, saying they could drop us there. During the drive back to Douglas we overheard a very interesting conversation between our new-found friends; apparently they were professional poachers who also bred Manx cats for export around the world. (Manx cats are highly sought after, being an exotic breed without any tails.) However, this was none of our business; our interest was to get back to the Market Inn to meet with our dates.

Going back into the pub we found Florence, for that was her name, sitting at a table with a girlfriend. After ordering a pint we joined them; we had a very convivial evening.

Pub closing time came and we were escorted by Florence and her friend back to her place. We spent the

CHAPTER NINE

night; after all, our leave didn't expire until 0800hrs, and sex was the predominate activity.

Lying there in a proper bed in a state of euphoria, the latest hit parade song of the day come into my mind: HIT THE ROAD JACK! I looked at the clock—it was 07.30! We had thirty minutes to get dressed and leg it to the ship!

Unknown to Geordie and me, the weather had deteriorated; gale force winds were battering the ship alongside the pier and it was decided that she had to be put to sea to ride out the storm.

Police cars had patrolled the streets of Douglas with loudspeakers, informing any of *H.M.S. Blackwood*'s crew to return to their ship immediately; a message was also broadcast by the local radio station.

Geordie and I were of course not aware of these messages as we were involved in more personal activities.

Running through the streets of Douglas with a biting wind and freezing rain coming down like stair rods, we found our way to the pier. *Blackwood* was in the process of releasing her stern ropes so we ran like hell towards her! On arrival, we had a decision to make; one was to stay on the pier and wait for the ship to return, or to take a running jump onto the quarter deck.

We decided to take a running jump! The quarterdeck crew quickly disassembled the guard rail. The ship's quarterdeck was about six feet below the pier, with something like eight foot of sea water between the ship

CHAPTER NINE

and the pier and angry waves washing over the pier and the ship. With the howling wind and sea spray, we made our run! A gust of wind caught us as we were flying through the air. Any onlookers would have thought we were Batman and Robin! We landed in a crumpled heap on the quarterdeck; we had made it back on board within the leave period so no charges were put against us.

Because of the adverse weather conditions the trip around the Island for the Governor and his wife was cancelled.

If anything could be called a mishmash, this was it! Nevertheless I do have very fond memories of the Isle of Man, especially the good people of Douglas.

Blackwood made her way through rough seas back into the Atlantic; we weathered the storm, and after a couple of weeks exercising with surface ships and submarines, we returned to Rosyth.

It was a Friday night and I went ashore with a couple of mates. We went into Dunfermline and after a couple of pints in a local pub we went to the Kinema Ballroom. The dance was already under way. We found a vacant table close to the dance floor. Sitting down, we looked around at the local talent; one girl took my fancy—she was tall with a proportionate figure; she had a wonderful dark brunette hairstyle and a smile with perfect teeth that could melt your heart.

I made my mind up that I would ask her for a dance. The band started to play and lads with their girlfriends made their way onto the dance floor. I plucked up courage and I approached the brunette and asked for a dance. She accepted my request and for the rest of the evening we stayed together.

During one dance I asked her name; she said it was Elizabeth but everyone called her Betty or Bette. Of course I responded by giving her my name. I didn't elaborate on my other names that my shipmates called me, which included Budge, Budgie, Chef, Slushy, and many others!

This was a very pleasant run ashore. The dance came to an end, and Bette said she had to go to the bus stands to catch the last bus to Cowdenbeath where she lived; this was convenient as my bus back to the dockyard left from the same place.

We made arrangements to meet the following evening; the Kinema Ballroom was part of the Kinema Cinema complex, and the current film being shown was Ben Hur staring Charlton Heston.

One is always apprehensive if a girl will turn up, but as arranged, Bette did; we saw the film and afterwards we went for a drink in one of Dunfermline's pubs where we got to know each other a little better.

This was the beginning of a relationship that would last a little over thirty-one years!

CHAPTER TEN

OUR COURTSHIP spanned about eight months. Bette came from a very impoverished home; her father had been a Japanese prisoner of war and died in a Japanese prisoner of war camp of malnutrition and other related diseases. This was deep inside Java; he died as the camp was being liberated by the Australian army.

Bette's mum had three young children to bring up; Alex was the oldest, Billy was the next oldest, while Bette was the youngest.

However, at the time of our meeting her Mum had gone through a few romances over the years and was mother to another five children; these were George, Eddie, Danny, Christine, and Patsy.

Patsy was the youngest, being three years old. George, Eddie and Danny, being boys, were boisterous. Christine was very demure and shy.

Alex was married and lived with his wife Wilma on a housing estate in Dunfermline. Alex was a miner and worked at the Valley Field pit, in Fife.

Billy was married, serving in the Royal Air Force; he was stationed in Staffordshire. Bette was the oldest living at home, and was the only wage earner in the

CHAPTER TEN

family; she worked as a school meals cook in Cowdenbeath. She was a very hardworking girl and did her best to help keep the extended family together.

The first time I met the family was a Friday night. Bette had given me her address—No.3 Park Avenue, 'doon the brea' from the Woodside. I caught the train from Inverkeithing to Cowdenbeath; it was winter time and the Scottish weather can be brutal.

Getting off the train, I asked the station porter the way to Park Avenue. His reply was, "Aye laddie, you go up the brea to the Woodside, then you'll be at the top of Park Avenue."

I followed his instructions. Leaving the station, I was met with a biting north east wind; hugging my coat around me, I made my way through the dimly lit streets and found the Woodside. No one had told me that it was a pub! I was under the impression that it was the name of a street or a road.

I saw one of the locals heading towards the pub and asked him if he knew where Betty Wilson lived. He pointed across the street, saying she lived there. I thanked him and proceeded in the direction he had pointed. I knocked on the door a couple of times and an upstairs window opened. A head popped out but in the darkness I was unable to see if it was male or female. It was female, as it turned out! Shouting down to me she said, "What do you want?" This was not the Bette Wilson I was looking for! I replied, "I was looking for Bette Wilson's house." She said she lived across the

CHAPTER TEN

street. There were two Bette Wilsons living in the same street, and I had gone to the wrong one!

Arriving at Bette's door I gave it a knock; it was answered by Bette and she introduced me to her Mum, who was affectionately called Chrissie. The house was a derelict miner's cottage probably built in Victorian times; there was one gas lamp above the fireplace; a sink was in the same room with one cold water tap; no bathroom was in evidence. A gas stove was provided with a couple of broken gas rings. The toilet was in the back yard. To get to it one had to go out the front door. (This was the only entrance and exit to the house!) I had to go into the street to enter the back yard through a side gate; the toilet was housed in a brick-built structure with a rickety wooden door for privacy.

Bette's Mum did the best she could with what she had, which was very little; however, my theory is that a house is not a home, it's the people in it that make it a home.

Bette and her Mum did their best to make me welcome. With *Blackwood* being in dock for another few weeks I was able to see Bette more frequently.

We were falling in love and didn't realize it. Bette's Mum had a partner, an Irishman who had also served in the Navy many years before; he was also the father of Bette's sisters Patsy and Christine.

Cowdenbeath was well provided with pubs and did a good trade. Saturday night was the highlight of the week. Friday night was Amami night; this was when the girls and ladies of the town would put their hair in curlers, Amami being the hair setting gel to keep it in place for the Saturday night revelries!

The back of Slauries was a popular place; this was the name of a local club that provided a dance floor, music being provided by a local band or one instrumentalist with his accordion.

Bette's Mum's cousin, Andy Morris, was an accomplished EMCEE. He was a very good singer and had a voice like velvet; he had sung with the Andrews Sisters, Andy Stewart, and a host of Scottish celebrities; he did the rounds of pubs in Cowdenbeath and the surrounding towns and villages.

Andy was an attraction wherever he went, encouraging people to get up from the audience to give a song; some were very good, some were not so good; nevertheless, they all gave of their best and were applauded accordingly.

This was home-grown entertainment and gave a welcome relief from the hardship of everyday life.

As for me, I had to say farewell to Bette. *H.M.S. Blackwood* was ready for sea again and duty called. Sailing once again into the Forth estuary, I reflected on the memories of the last few weeks.

Blackwood made her way to Londonderry; we resumed our duties working with submarines, and surface craft. Bette and I corresponded frequently. Our courtship was carried out by letter writing; of course we had been very sexually involved during my shore time.

CHAPTER TEN

It was a Sunday lunchtime. I was off duty and with a couple of mates went to the dockside canteen; the bar was full of submariners.

I was surprised to meet an old mate, Keith, an Oxford boy. We had been in the scouts together. He was serving on *H.M. Submarine Thermopylea*. After a few pints Keith pulled out a request form and in my alcoholic state I was persuaded by him to put my signature on it. He filled the rest of it in and handed it to one of my mates, whispering in his ear to put it into the request form box, which all ships had.

A couple of days later I was summoned to the Coxn's office. I was informed that I would be on Captain's parade the following morning.

Dressed in my No.1 uniform, I was called to attention; the Captain and the ship's officers were in attendance. The Captain was silently reading my request form; he then looked at me and said, "I understand, Burgess, that you have volunteered to join the submarine service?"

A vague recollection came into my mind involving my lunchtime drinking spree with Chappie. (Keith's surname was Chapman, hence the nickname Chappie.) I drew in a deep breath and a gulp. I said, "Yes sir." He then said, "Depending on your physical examination, your request is granted."

Things happened very fast. The next day I was transported to a Naval Air Station not far from Londonderry. The Doc carried out my examination and declared me fit for submarine service.

CHAPTER TEN

Leaving *Blackwood* and her crew was a bit of a wrench. We had shared many experiences together, not forgetting the time when ashore in Dumbarton when my mate Dave broke his forearm on the dodgems during the fair week; he was bumped from behind and he had one hand on the steering wheel, the other nonchalantly stretched holding onto the pole that supplied the power to the car; the impact forced him to brace himself and he was pushed into the side of the track! Something had to give and his ulna was the victim.

Getting off the ride, Dave was in agony. I had been trained in First Aid when serving on the *Albion*, and my thoughts were to immobilize the limb; a splint was needed and Dumbarton had wooden latticed baskets containing metal litter bins attached to lamp posts. I broke one off; I had a splint, but nothing to attach it to, but a sailor's uniform is very adaptable! I took off my silk to make a sling and so my lanyard was used to strap the splint to his arm; this helped to relieve his pain.

We found the local hospital where Dave would receive professional care. Returning on board I wondered if I would be in the rattle for being improperly dressed as Dave was wearing half my uniform!

These were very fond memories that will stay with me and be part of the Mishmash of my life.

CHAPTER ELEVEN

MY DRAFT CHIT was to report to *H.M.S. Dolphin*. This was the home and training base of the Submarine service, located opposite Portsmouth Harbour on the Gosport side.

I was allocated a mess and informed of the general orders of the establishment. I met up with the rest of the lads that had volunteered for submarine service; these would form the class that I was to join.

Dolphin (2) is where the training school was established. This was known as Haslar creek.

Dolphin (2) was self-sufficient, having its own catering arrangements and dining facilities, although our sleeping arrangements etc., including the N.A.A.F.I., were incorporated within the main establishment.

There were fifteen of us volunteers, made up from various branches. Our instructors were a different breed from the ones I had encountered during my recruit training; these were very experienced men who had served many years below the waves and were about to pass on their knowledge and expertise to us. I was eager to learn.

CHAPTER ELEVEN

The submarine service was a Navy within a Navy, so to speak; our instructors were compassionate and supportive; a number of submarines had dived and had never surfaced, with the loss of their crew. This was after World War Two, when the world was at peace.

To name a few, *H.M. Submarine Truculent* was involved in a collision with a surface ship while diving on the 12th of January 1950. *H.M. Submarine Affray* went down in the English Chanel carrying out a snort exercise; this was on the 17th of April 1951. *H.M. Submarine Sidon* was sunk alongside in Portland harbour with a hot run torpedo that exploded in one of her tubes, killing thirteen souls.

My friends and family (especially my Mum) said I was nuts to have volunteered for submarine service, but it was too late now—I was already committed.

This was a new adventure for me; being a volunteer was a personal decision and I held myself responsible for my actions.

Our introduction to confinement was in the compression and decompression chamber. This would sort out anyone that was claustrophobic—it barely accommodated us! Two wooden benches were provided, encased within the steel tank that had various gauges and valves.

The instructor told us what to expect. He explained that we would hear a loud hissing noise as the pressure increased; other things could happen—any loose tooth

CHAPTER ELEVEN

fillings could pop out, ear drums might burst; nose clips were provided to help equalize the pressure: this would be like the popping of your eardrums when going up a steep hill. We were assured that if an eardrum burst it would repair itself within three weeks; if a tooth filling popped out we had to raise a hand—the pressure would be equalized and the sufferer would be transported to the dentist to have a new one put in.

Our instructor operated the various valves. In theory we were being taking to a depth of 100ft; the pressure on the body at this depth was 50lbs psi. Reaching this depth in a dry run would prepare us for the S.E.T.T.— the Submarine Escape Training Tank.

The tank was housed in a building that was a local landmark; it was over one hundred feet high and was of a rectangular construction with many windows; it's ironic that my Uncle Fred had been involved in its construction a number of years before my acquaintance with it. The company that Uncle Fred worked for was Williams & Williams, who had supplied the glass window frames for the project; being his company's representative, he made frequent visits to make sure that the frames were correctly installed.

The tank itself was circular, like a round peg in a square hole; it was a masterpiece of construction.

Internal staircases took us to various levels where airlocks were installed. As a class we would be introduced to each level where our escapes would be made from.

CHAPTER ELEVEN

We made our way to the top of the tank. A doctor was always in attendance to give assistance in the event of anyone getting into difficulties. (I might add that I had served with Doctor Parsons on board *H.M.S. Albion*. He was now the tank doctor; as another aside, my Mum and stepdad had met his parents while visiting the Ideal Home Exhibition at Earls Court in London.)

However, to continue with the training: it had to be determined as to what buoyancy each individual had, since we are all different.

Attached to the side of the tank was a rope that went to some twenty feet under the water. It had been explained to us that there are three states of buoyancy: positive, neutral, and negative.

To briefly explain what this means: if a person is positive, you will float on the surface as your metabolism is lighter than the water you displace; if neutral, you are equal to the amount of water you displace; if negative, you are heavier than the water you displace.

One at a time we entered a small diving bell with an instructor. The tank swim boys, as they were known, were in position to come to our aid if we got into difficulties. The diving bell was a platform with a domed hood. The hood was pressurized to 10lb psi above water pressure. We descended to 15ft and the instructor told me to take a deep gulp of air. I did as I was told; I then slipped out from the diving bell with the instructor giving me a gentle push on my head. I started to ascend to the surface. I had gone possibly 8ft when I came to a

CHAPTER ELEVEN

halt, so I was classed as neutral buoyant; I swam the rest of the way to the surface escorted by one of the swim boys.

The rest of the class went through the same routine. Those that were deemed negative buoyant, were the ones that the rope had been provided for; when leaving the diving bell they would start to sink and the swim boys would get to them very quickly and put the rope into their hands; they would then pull themselves up the rope to the surface; for the rest of the tank training they would wear red caps for easy recognition.

A body can change its buoyancy. I started off as neutral, yet a few months later I became positive.

After a couple of dives in the diving bell to 15ft., we were taken to the 30ft. air lock. This time we were provided with life jackets that when inflated would assist us to reach the surface; our training was known as free ascent, meaning that no breathing apparatus was used.

I will explain the reason for this in due course. We carried out three escapes form the 30ft. air lock, and then we carried out three escapes from the 50ft. level; on completion we had to prepare for the 100ft. escape.

Back in the training tank classroom we were informed what to expect and were instructed in the operation of the B.I.B. system. (This was an abbreviation for the Built in Breathing System.) Every submarine in the Royal Navy was fitted with it. It consisted of a ring main of pipework in each escape compartment; these were in the fore ends, control room, engine room and after ends. The pipework had Schrader valve connections supplied spaced some 3ft. between them, and the pipework was connected to a high pressure air supply to release the air into the system. A large highly serrated valve wheel painted red would be opened, and the air supply to the system was pressurized to 5,000lbs psi. This had to be reduced. Pressure reducers were installed to achieve this. Escape lockers within the boat contained escape equipment, including an immersion suit, and for want of a better word, a very large adaption of a baby's nappy; also a life jacket, and most important of all, the breathing tube that would connect to the ring main via the Schrader Valve connection. The breathing tube was some 5ft. long, provided with a mouthpiece and diaphragm that was lung operated; on the exhaust side of the mouthpiece an assembly connection was provided to attach to the life jacket; exhaled air would inflate the life jacket prior to the ascent.

At the bottom of the tank an escape chamber had been constructed, identical to what would be found on a submarine. Surrounding the escape hatch was a twill trunk that would be lowered and secured.

On completion of the classroom instruction it was time to put what we had learned into practice. Entering the escape chamber, it was a bit unnerving to think that 100ft. of water was above you; however, we had every faith in our instructors and the training we had gone through.

CHAPTER ELEVEN

In the event of a disaster and time was available, we would first of all put on the oversized nappy, followed by the immersion suit, followed by the life jacket; the breathing tubes were inserted into each of the Schrader Valve connections, and when everyone was ready we stood in line; two instructors were in attendance and we were told to pick up our breathing tubes and put the mouthpiece in our mouths. The high pressure control valve was opened and the hissing sound of compressed air was noticeable as the air entered into the ring main, gradually being reduced to allow us to breathe; with our exhaling breath we were instructed to inflate our life jackets. Nose clips were also provided; the instructors checked and we were ready to go into the compartment. The flood valves were opened, water gushed in and the compartment filled quickly.

When the pressure equalized one of the instructors ducked under the twill trunk, climbed a short ladder and opened the escape hatch; when this happened the compartment was completely submerged.

One at a time we ducked under the twill trunk and made our ascent to the surface.

Being in line, as one chap moved forward he would drop his breathing tube and move on to the next one, and so on.

Ascending 100ft. takes approximately 19 seconds. This may appear to be a short time, but things can happen; one breath of air under pressure at 100ft is equivalent to four breaths of air in normal atmosphere.

CHAPTER ELEVEN

The way to gradually equalize the pressure in your lungs is to exhale during the ascent. This is best achieved by pursing your lips as though you were whistling. During the ascent your posture was very important; the "at attention position" was the best. If you leant too far forward, you could go head first into the side of the tank; leaning backwards, the reverse would happen. The swim boys were expert at observing each individual's ascent, and would quickly intervene to correct one's posture or breathing. For example, anyone exhaling rapidly would be swum to and a hand tapped on the mouth to inform him not to breath out so much. If one of us was not breathing out sufficiently, he would be given a firm punch in the solar plexus region of the anatomy to increase his exhalation.

Not only was exhalation of the lungs important to stop them from bursting, the life jacket also had the same problem. To prevent this from happening a gag was incorporated in its construction. This was a relief valve that would vent the air during the ascent. On reaching the surface the gag would be shut to stop the remaining air from escaping.

On reaching the surface I closed the gag on my life jacket; the next thing to do was to pull the metal ring attached to a cylinder incorporated in the immersion suit. Doing this, the immersion suit inflated; it was like being encased in a rubber dinghy.

The immersion suit was made of a very bright yellow coloured fabric to give optimum visibility to any search craft.

CHAPTER ELEVEN

The nappy came into play; it had been known for many years that cold water coming into contact with the human body can make one pee. The nappy was provided to soak up the liquid to stop it from slopping around in the base of the immersion suit.

Other accessories were provided; a salt-water battery light was attached to the life jacket that automatically would illuminate, and a plastic whistle was in a small pocket in the immersion suit that could be blown to attract a search craft to your position. A pair of waterproof gloves was in another pocket. Attached to the gloves were very long tapes; the tapes would be entwined to each survivor to keep them together. The gloves also had an air seal that was inflated by blowing into the mouthpiece attached to them.

On the surface we completed our S.E.T.T. training, floating around like a bunch of inflated Michelin tyre men.

We all passed. This was a time for celebration, and we went ashore, landing up in the Royal Oak Pub in Portsmouth. We were having a good old time when one of the girls in our company said to me, "What's that coming out of your ear?" I stopped in mid-gulp of my pint, put my free hand up to my right earhole and discovered wax running down my neck! I wiped the yellow muck away with my handkerchief and disappeared to the gents to get rid of any other unmentionable excrement leaking from my body. As previously stated, pressure on the human form can create embarrassing situations.

CHAPTER ELEVEN

Our training continued. Technical drawing was a very important part of it. Other practical instruction involved visits to the model room where failed engine parts were on display: bent engine con rods, along with other components that had failed. *The Tally Ho* was a floating classroom. She was built in 1942, served in World War Two and was now a training boat. Our training was very thorough and rightly so. The training was intense, but we did get some time to relax. Going ashore in Gosport had its moments; we would visit a few pubs, even visiting the local Bingo Hall. There was a café that we would visit on our way back to *Dolphin*, located in a place we called Squeeze Gut Alley. The name says it all! We would get a cheap meal after the pub chucking out time; not to give away any confidences, I think it was supplied by one of my old compatriots from the *H.M.S. Dolphin*. It was easy to chuck stuff over the fence from the back of the galley in *Dolphin* (2)

However, leaving the café late at night could be a problem. There were no public toilets provided within the vicinity. One of the lads was bursting for a pee: he found the doorway of an unlit shop and he was part-way in relieving himself when a light shone in his face. The policeman said, "I hope you're going to wipe them off." Our mate had only pissed over a bobby's boots! We took off running, up and over what was known to us as Pneumonia Bridge that connected Gosport over Haslar Creek to where we could make it back to *Dolphin*. (I might add that a public toilet has now been

CHAPTER ELEVEN

installed next to Pneumonia Bridge.)

The bridge was named by the local residents because of the chill winds that would blow around it during the winter months bringing freezing rain, hail, and snow. Anyone crossing the bridge during this time of year was in danger of contracting the dreaded disease.

CHAPTER TWELVE

OUR TRAINING was completed. We had all passed our final examination and now awaited our draft chits in anticipation as to which submarine we would be drafted to.

The submarine service was a Navy within a Navy, and responsible for allocating submariners to various submarines as required; this was different from the General Service Navy that drafted Officers and Men to ships and Establishments from the central drafting offices near Haslemere.

The submarine drafting office was established within *H.M.S. Dolphin*. I got word that I was being drafted to *H.M. Submarine Astute*; she was operating from *H.M.S. Ambrose* that was part of a Canadian Base named *H.M.C.S. Stadacona*, located in Halifax, Nova Scotia.

My draft to the *Astute* was scheduled for early July; this meant that I would have to spend time in *Dolphin*. I was not very happy about this; however, I got to know the Petty Officer cook serving on *H.M. Submarine Seraph*.

With the help of the P.O. I managed to become a part of *Seraph*'s crew, if only for a two-week period; this would enable me to gain some practical experience in becoming a submarine cook.

Seraph was a wartime submarine that had become famous under the command of her skipper Lieutenant Jewell. When the French had surrendered to Hitler and had many ships and soldiers that could fall into Nazi hands, *Seraph* was designated to transport the American, General Mark Clark, on a clandestine operation to negotiate with the Vichy French commanders, to stop this from happening. (The French would not negotiate with the British, but agreed to talk to the Americans. *Seraph*'s crew were dressed as American sailors and she flew an American flag as part of the deception. A book was written about this called *The Ship with Two Captains*.)

Another part played by *Seraph* was dropping off the body of the fictitious Major Martin near the coast of Spain, bearing information designed to fool the Germans. A film of this was made in the 1950s called 'The Man Who Never Was'.

Seraph had a new profile from her wartime days. She was now a target boat; her conning tower had been streamlined, and armoured steel plates had been attached to her sides to protect the ballast tanks from the hits she could take from practice torpedoes.

We set sail from *Dolphin* late Sunday afternoon, making our way to the Hook of Holland. We had some passengers aboard, namely six Royal Marine commandos, along with their three canvas canoes and

CHAPTER TWELVE

other equipment; they were carrying out a clandestine exercise that we were not privy to. The exercise was to start at midnight.

We had dived some hours before. The Skipper had the Dutch coastline in view on the search scope and the sea was getting choppy; this was about 2300hrs (11 o'clock p.m.); after consulting the officer in charge of the Marine contingent it was agreed to start the exercise a little early. Seraph surfaced, the fore hatch was opened and with the help of our crew our commando friends were launched into the angry waves—and they paddled away to a destination unknown.

As for us, we dived and made our way to West Bay off the Dorset coast. We would exercise for a number of days with the Fleet Air Arm, after which we would make our way to Bristol; this was what was known as a Jolly. Arrangements had been made for *Seraph* to tie up alongside a jetty next to a pub; visits to the local brewery, cigarette factory, and a dance held in our honour at the local nurses' home were all on the agenda.

Helicopters from their base in Portland would come looking for us using dipping sonar. Once found, a torpedo would be released and directed towards us; a slight shudder and a thud would be felt and heard within the boat when a hit was made.

Weather always played a part in this type of exercising; high winds and torrential rain intervened and the exercise was called off because of the inclement weather. *Seraph* surfaced and prepared to make a

CHAPTER TWELVE

surface passage to Bristol. This was Thursday afternoon. The crew were in good spirits as the exercise had ended prematurely! Our visit to Bristol would be earlier than expected—that was, until a signal was received from F.O. S.M. (Flag Officer Submarines), which read, "Stay in position, *Submarine Artemis* is undergoing running up trials, dive to 200ft." The Captain obeyed the orders.

Diving stations were called, master blows were shut (this was my job), main vents were opened and air gushed out of the ballast tanks as water rushed in; the fore and after planesmen adjusted the angle of the dive according to the Captain's orders. We were somewhere between the surface and 200ft. A terrific thud was heard and felt as the first torpedo hit us on the starboard side, followed by another crunching sound as the second torpedo made contact.

We knew that something was seriously wrong. The Captain responded to the situation immediately, ordering the planesmen hard to rise, open all master blows (my job again), shut main vents, blow main ballast, and stand by to surface. We made our way to the surface. The top lid was opened and the order to run the blower was given. The welcome dulcet tone of Johno's voice came over the intercom: "BLOWER RUNNING." We were now safe! The blower would bring us up to full buoyancy.

We were now on the surface but had no propulsion, which meant we were at the mercy of the tide. Fortunately there was an offshore wind that kept us

CHAPTER TWELVE

from being grounded on the Dorset coast.

It was first thought that the A-bracket, stern gland and plummer block had been damaged; whatever it was, we weren't going anywhere until an Admiralty tug turned up to tow us to Devonport Naval Dockyard.

The tug arrived and *Seraph*'s casing party attached the tow lines to her; the slack of the tow lines was taken up and we were now under way heading towards Devonport Dockyard. Our course would take us by Plymouth Ho, where as a young child many years before I had observed ships of the Royal Navy navigating the same waters. This was my time to be a sailor travelling the same seas as our forebears had done—with men of stature like Sir Francis Drake and Sir Walter Raleigh; the main difference was that I was on a crippled submarine under tow.

On arrival at the Dockyard the boat was nudged into a dry dock that could be emptied to allow a full inspection of the damage sustained from the two torpedo hits.

Our Jolly to Bristol was cancelled. The visions of the tour of the brewery, cigarette factory, and the dance at the nurses' home faded. We were stuck in Plymouth.

Bette and I had communicated by mail for months; these were love letters for want of a better word.

I applied for an extended long weekend leave pass and it was granted. I caught the train from Plymouth to Paddington in London. I was able to get the overnight

CHAPTER TWELVE

train from King's Cross to Edinburgh's Waverley station; I then transferred to another train to get to Cowdenbeath.

Bette was pleased to see me. Our time together would be for a few short hours. We made the most of the time we had. I explained to her that I was being drafted to a submarine operating out of a base in Canada. We discussed our options; one was that we could get engaged before I left; the second one was to get married.

Bette's wish was that she would prefer for us to get married before I left for Canada.

My weekend leave was up and I travelled back to *Seraph*. Travelling from one end of the country to the other and back again can be very tiring, especially after being torpedoed!

However, a decision had been made: Bette and I decided to get married. Plans had to be put in place; these arrangements would have to wait until I could confirm my leave prior to my departure to Canada.

Arriving back on board *Seraph*, the information was that the damage to her was not as severe as first thought; the hull was still intact and the A-bracket and plummer block were undamaged; however, the propeller was wrecked and completely bent out of shape. A replacement had been fitted and *Seraph* was ready for sea again.

We made passage back to *Dolphin*. After saying farewell to my shipmates I returned to what was known as spare crew.

CHAPTER TWELVE

I was granted leave, which was normal procedure before being shipped overseas. I made my way to Scotland. Bette and I had a heck of a lot to accomplish within a two-week period.

We had already contacted the Reverend Stevens who was the vicar of the West Parish Church in Cowdenbeath. He agreed to marry us, and the bans of marriage had been read on three consecutive Sundays without any objections.

Our wedding was to take place on the 13th of June 1962. (The number 13 was supposed to be an unlucky number, but for me it wasn't! I will explain later what the number 13 meant to me in the future of my submarine service.)

As for now, arrangements had to be made. Bette had to buy a dress and other complementary items such as a hat, handbag and matching shoes; as for me, my No.1 uniform would suffice decked out with a white ribbon to tie my silk instead of the dark navy blue one.

On the morning of the wedding Bette's Mum wanted us out of the way. Her Mum's partner Alex was going to be my best man, and also to give Bette away, so he had a dual role. Bette's close friend Janette was to be her best maid.

Alex and I went to Slauries club and had a couple of beers. Chick, the club steward, noticing my white ribbons and Alex wearing his carnation flower in the lapel of his jacket, asked what we were all dolled up for.

We explained that I was getting married at 2 o'clock

in the West Parish church. Chick enquired how we were going to get there, and I said we were going to walk. His reply was, "Ye cannae de that lad, ye have to have a car to tak ye!" I did my best to explain that our wedding was on a shoestring budget and hiring cars was out of the question. (Bette and I were far from being Cowdenbeath's wedding of the year!) Chick's response was very kind: "I'll tak ye!" he said, "I have a car, where do ye live?" Alex gave him the address and Chick said, "Don't worry, I'll close up early and pick you up in good time to get ye tae the kirk!"

Chic was as good as his word, arriving on time with his car bedecked with white ribbons. I will always be thankful for his benevolence! Bette, Alex, Janette and I got into the car and we safely arrived at the church. Bette's Mum declined to go to the church ceremony, giving the excuse that she was needed at home to prepare a tea for us when we returned.

We were met by the Reverend Stevens. The church was empty except for a few of Bette's aunties and uncles.

Reverend Stevens proceeded with the wedding ceremony by welcoming the sparse congregation to witness the joining of a young couple in matrimony.

All was going well until the Reverend said, "Do you, Paul, take Janette to be your lawful wedded wife?" Bette intervened, saying, "He's marrying *me*!" The reverend with a cough and a splutter recomposed himself! On the second time round he got the names in the right order. Another hiccup occurred; the wedding ring that I had bought, from Winski's jewellery shop in Cowdenbeath didn't fit Bette's finger! It was a hot day and Bette's finger had swollen; to overcome the problem the Reverend said it would be alright to hold the ring between her forefinger and thumb.

Bette and I were now married! This was the start of a long journey that would last for some thirty-one years, ten months and twenty-nine days. This was a significant part of my Mishmash of Life.

Bette's Mum had put on a reception for us. Alex and I disappeared to the Woodside Pub and bought half a dozen screw-top bottles of McEwan's ale. Bette and I didn't have much time to be with the family, as we had to catch the 4 o'clock train to Edinburgh.

On leaving the house, word had got out that a wedding had taken place. The local kids were outside waiting for the scour oote—a Scottish tradition that should bring good luck to the bride and groom; the groom being me would take all the loose change out of his pocket and scatter it down the street. The kids would then run after the scattered change and pick up as many coins as possible.

Being a serviceman I was able to purchase a concessionary ticket for my wife. I did this at Cowdenbeath station. We changed trains in Edinburgh and boarded the overnight train to London. We would have to change trains at Bletchley to transfer to the local train to get us to Oxford, which was scheduled to arrive in Oxford around about 7 o'clock a.m.

CHAPTER TWELVE

Bette and I were fortunate; we were able to get a compartment to ourselves. I had changed into civilian clothes when the ticket inspector came into the compartment, asking for our tickets in his authoritative manner. I gave him our tickets. After scrutinizing them he said, "Which one of you are in the forces?" I said, "I am." He then said, "Whose this then?" looking at Bette. I replied with some indignation that the lady was my wife. He replied, "Do you have any proof, such as an allotments book?" (This was a book allocated to wives of servicemen to identify them and to receive their family payment from their husbands.) My response was short and sharp. I was starting to get annoyed with this officious oaf! I said, "My wife is not in possession of an allotment book because we were only married today, but I do have our marriage certificate if you would like to peruse it."

The inspector started to perspire; his complexion reddened and he apologized and never returned. Bette and I continued to Bletchley without further interruption.

On arrival in Oxford, Mum was there to meet us with the car; things had changed—the car was a new Hillman Minx.

Ernie my stepdad was at work and Valerie my youngest sister was at school. Mum could see that Bette and I were tired after our journey and she suggested we have a lie down to recuperate. We were grateful; Mum had prepared the back bedroom for us and we lay down

CHAPTER TWELVE

on the bed and had forty winks, as the expression goes.

When Valerie came home from school and Ernie came home from work, I introduced Bette to them; she had become a sister-in-law and daughter-in-law; this was not the end of her trial as I had to introduce her to my Dad and stepmother! Bette was made of stern stuff and took the introductions in her stride; her mother had also been partner to complicated relationships.

Mum had been busy; she had arranged a wedding reception for us to take place on the Saturday. A bunch of my mates had been invited along with my aunties and uncles. My cousin Mona was visiting from America and she was always a joy to see. Mona's lifelong friend Vi was also invited; Vi had been a friend of the family for many years and had babysat me along with Mona many years before.

Our brief honeymoon came to an end. I had to comply with my orders and make my way to Canada to join *H.M. Submarine Astute*. Bette would return to Cowdenbeath in Scotland; this was not the best way to start a marriage, but because of the love we had between us we were confident we would be able to overcome the obstacles that we would have to face for now and in the future.

I gave Bette a big hug and a kiss as we departed to our respective platforms on Oxford station, Bette going north to Scotland, me heading south to Gatwick airport to make my way to Canada.

CHAPTER THIRTEEN

ARRIVING AT GATWICK AIRPORT, I found my way to the booth that was manned by Canadian Air Force personnel. I produced my pay book and travel documents, and I was informed that my flight was scheduled to leave at 1400hrs. This flight would take me to a Canadian Air Force base close to Marville in France. I would stay there overnight, then transfer to a flight to Trenton, another Canadian Air Force base in Ontario.

My flight was announced and I made my way to the departure gate. (This was not the Gatwick Airport as is it is known today.) The departure gate opened up to the runway and I made my way to the awaiting plane; this was a Dakota, a relic left over from World War Two. A ladder was supplied to gain entry into the aircraft.

On boarding, I was ushered into one of the canvas seats by one of the flight crew who was wearing a fur lined leather bomber jacket. The seats were positioned along each side of the plane; in fact, the seating arrangements had not been changed from the days when brave paratroopers used to jump out of it.

My fellow passengers consisted of a couple of

CHAPTER THIRTEEN

Canadian Army lads, some Canadian Airmen and a high ranking American Air Force officer, distinguished by the silver embellishments on the peak of his uniform cap.

Take off was a new experience for me, since I had never flown before! The plane trundled along the runway for what seemed ages, and finally we were airborne. This would be a flight of a couple of hours' duration. I got into a conversation with the two Canadian soldiers, who were returning home after a tour of duty in the U.K. and Europe.

Arriving in Marville, we were taken to the reception area of the accommodation building. The American officer was given preferential treatment as befitted his rank; next in line were the Canadian Airmen, the two Canadian soldiers and me, being the only ones left.

The Sergeant in charge of the reception area came from behind the desk and gave us our respective room keys. He then went on to explain that our flight to Trenton was scheduled to leave at 12.00 noon; we were to report to the reception desk no later than 11.15hrs. He then went into a sermon about the rules and regulations of the facility, such as the dining room times, and that this accommodation building was used by servicemen and their families so he warned us, looking in my direction, that no drunkenness would be tolerated; as an aside he said he had trouble with one British Submariner before. I would eventually find out who it was. We were dismissed and went to our allocated rooms, and made an arrangement to meet in the bar after having a wash and brush up.

CHAPTER THIRTEEN

I found my way to the bar. Through the fug I heard a voice very loudly saying, "Hi buddy! I know that uniform!" Waving at me, he called me over to join him and his mates at their table. After getting a lot of back slapping like old lost friends, I sat down with my new-found friends. My two army compatriots joined us and the beer started to flow. I managed to find out that the Submariner that had caused a bit of a ruckus prior to my arrival was the one that I was relieving on the *Astute*.

Closing time was called at the bar and I made my way back to my room, pleasantly pissed but not inebriated, passing by the reception desk manned by the ever-watchful eye of the desk sergeant.

After a fitful night's sleep, I woke up with a mouth resembling a lavatory brush! I got myself together and went to the dining room and had some breakfast; this done, I returned to my room and got my things together.

By this time it was necessary for me to present myself in the reception area. It was like a zoo! Military families with babies, and kids of all ages, were everywhere; all these people would be my fellow passengers on the flight.

Boarding the plane, I was met by the Canadian Air Force equivalent of an air hostess, smartly dressed in her uniform, very pretty but as hard as nails under the veneer. In the pandemonium of everyone putting luggage into the overhead lockers, shouting kids and crying babies, I was allocated a seat. The plane we were travelling on was a Yukon; as far as I know it was the Canadian version of the Bristol Britannia. It was a four-engine prop job; this was going to be an eleven-hour flight taking us on the polar route over the North Pole.

I did my best to get some shuteye without much success; there was not much to occupy the youngsters—their Mums and Dads did try by giving them colouring books to fill in and comics to read, though without much success; some of the kids argued with each other, babies continued to cry, and mothers made frequent visits to the toilets to change dirty nappies, soiled by the wearers.

It was a relief when the Captain gave the order to put on the safety belts. We were making our approach into Trenton. The landing was a bit skittish. Trenton had been bathed in summer sunshine for a number of weeks; however, not long before our arrival Mother Nature had decided to give Trenton a light shower of rain, the result being the runway we were about to land on was very slick, not unlike a skid pan. On landing with all wheels on the ground, brakes being applied, the plane started its own waltz down the runway; we came to a skidding halt and taxied to the disembarking area.

What with a rather uncomfortable flight, I was looking forward to having accommodation where I could get some peace and quiet along with a good night's sleep.

This was not to be! After retrieving my kit, I went to the reception desk and the desk sergeant looked at me, requesting my identification and travel orders. I produced my pay book and travel documents as

CHAPTER THIRTEEN

requested. After checking them he said, "Sorry buddy, we don't have any accommodation for you; this being a holiday weekend, everything on base is occupied. We didn't know you were coming."

This was Friday evening. I enquired when the next flight would be available to get me to Halifax in Nova Scotia, as I had to join my submarine. His reply was, "Return here on Tuesday." He followed this up with a little compassion in his voice, saying, "You can sleep on one of the reception area benches and eat in the mess hall; you can also use the men's toilet to wash and shave in. You could also go into Trenton and rent a room for a few nights."

This was a joke! When I received my travel documents they were accompanied with an advisory note, one part stating that ten Canadian dollars would be sufficient to cover any out of pocket expenses. Being a bit sceptical, I had taken twenty with me; with my overnight stay in Marville this was now slightly diminished. No way did I have sufficient funds to rent a room in Trenton!

By coincidence I bumped into my two Canadian soldier friends who were going to catch a train from Trenton to their hometowns; they had a few hours to wait for their train. I left my kit at the reception desk and decided to tag along with them. By this time it was dark; the train station was not too far from the Air Base, so we walked along the main road for close to a mile. We noticed a petrol station—these were a lot different to the ones in England. They provided snacks and soft drink machines; we each got a coke and sat down on the chairs provided.

We got into a conversation and unfortunately somehow politics became a topic of discussion; this was a time when Britain had been refused entry into the Common Market, vetoed by the French president De Gaul; one of my new-found friends asked me why, and my reply was that De Gaul was shit scared that Britain would outshine him and that he wanted to be the big chief.

Our stay didn't last long in the petrol station; unbeknown to us, the proprietor was a French Canadian and he was not happy with my remarks about his revered De Gaul, so he chucked us out.

I parted company with the two soldiers and made my way back to the Air Base taking up the offer to sleep on one of the benches in the reception area.

After another uncomfortable night I made my way to the men's washroom; I had some essentials with me such as a tube of toothpaste, toothbrush, a bar of soap, shaving cream and a razor. I cleaned myself up as best I could and enquired at the reception desk if there were any flights leaving for Halifax. I had the same response: "No, come back on Tuesday."

I decided to venture into Trenton where I purchased a couple of post cards, one to send to Bette, the other one to Mum and the family. Finding a tavern open (the Canadian equivalent of a pub), I ordered a beer at the bar. I was instructed to take a seat at one of the tables. I complied and a waiter approached me and took my order. He returned with two half glasses of beer. I said, "I know I ordered a pint but didn't expect it to be served in two half glasses!" The waiter explained that this was the law and that parts of Canada were in a state of semi-prohibition; you were not allowed to walk anywhere in the tavern carrying your beer; if you wished to change tables the waiter had to be summoned to carry the drink for you. Taverns could only sell beer, no wines or spirits.

I borrowed a pen from the waiter and wrote out my post cards, explaining that I was still in transit and was not sure when I would reach my destination.

Leaving the tavern, I found a post office and bought a couple of stamps. I was in the process of posting the cards when a young lad of about fourteen years came up to me, saying, "Where are your Canada flashes?" This took me a bit unawares. The Canadian Navy uniform was styled on the one issued to the Royal Navy, the difference being that the Canadians wore shoulder patches inscribed with Canada in gold braided lettering. (The Australian, New Zealand and South African navies sported the same insignia of their respective countries.)

I explained to the young lad that I was British. We got into a conversation as we walked along the promenade that skirted Lake Ontario. During our chat he asked where I was staying. I explained to him what my situation was and he stopped in his tracks and said,

CHAPTER THIRTEEN

"Why don't you come to my house? My Grandfather lives with us—he was in England during World War Two."

I had nothing to lose so I accepted his offer. On arrival at the house I was greeted like a long lost son! The family were very kind to me and insisted that I stayed with them until my departure on Tuesday. I must add that one of the older brothers was serving in the Royal Canadian Air Force and was stationed at Trenton Air Base.

My hosts treated me like royalty. The family members visiting from Buffalo, New York state from across the border in the United States, also made me feel very welcome.

During my stay with this wonderful family they introduced to me some of life's unforgettable experiences—to name a few: on the drive that the Grandfather took me in his old Chevy car, the steering was so sloppy it drifted all over the road; he assured me that he could master it! He gave me a running commentary on who lived where and what was under the ground that some homes had been built on; one such person was a chap called Lively, he said, explaining to me that there was a large amount uranium on his land; the Canadian government wanted to purchase the land but Lively wasn't selling so a big court battle was going on.

Food was another experience; every meal was cooked to perfection, especially the home-cooked honey baked ham. I have never tasted ham like it before or since—it

CHAPTER THIRTEEN

was fantastic. I was introduced to a game called Piggy; I can remember that it consisted of a pot that pennies were put into; the rudiments of the game are now a bit vague, but I remember it created a lot of family fun and friendly rivalry.

I had never been close to horses; the nearest I ever got to riding one was on a very docile donkey on the sands at Weston Super Mare, as a young child.

My new friends took me to visit a ranch owned by a cousin. On arrival the cousin and his family were taking turns, riding a magnificent looking chestnut brown stallion around in a paddock. I noticed that it had no saddle; it was fitted with a bridle and reigns to control it, all the family taking turns to ride the magnificent animal. I looked on in admiration at their riding skills.

One of the ranch hands noticed me looking on and called me over. He was holding the horse, standing in front of it; holding the bridle, he invited me to have a ride. I was hesitant, but the family encouraged me to take up the offer. How could I refuse! I agreed to have a go and one of the lads came over to give me a leg up. I found out that a horse has a very shiny coat; the lad giving me the leg up cupped his hands and I put my left foot into them as he lifted my left leg. I sprang up with my right leg, passing it over the horse's back. As I said, the horse's coat was like silk, and with the momentum of my spring and the leg up, I slid off the horse's back and landed in a heap on the other side! The horse was getting impatient with this carrying on and stamped its

CHAPTER THIRTEEN

foot, catching the lad that was holding the bridle on his toes. Everyone was having a good laugh at my expense.

I was encouraged to have another try. I took up the challenge, sitting there on a bare back horse in the middle of a paddock wearing a sailor's uniform—not the usual image of a British submariner! I had hold of the reigns and it was now time to get the horse to move. I said the usual things like "Gee up!" but nothing happened. I wondered if in view of my difficulty mounting him he had gone on strike! One of the ranch hands came over. (I looked like Roy Rogers in a sailor's suit.) He said, "You have to give some encouragement by giving a kick in the ribs with your heels and yell at it to giddy up!" My reply was, "Isn't that cruel?" He laughed and said, "No, he's used to it!" I did as I was instructed. I gave him a gentle kick with my heels and said the famous words, "Giddy up!" A slight shudder of recognition went through the horse's body and my appointed instructor said, "Kick him harder!" I did and he took off like a rocket! We were heading towards the white painted rail fence, by which time I was yelling for the horse to stop! I managed to pull on the reigns to turn the horse and stop it from crashing through the paddock fence. The horse came to a sudden halt and I finished up hanging around his neck!

All good things come to an end. Tuesday arrived and I had to say farewell to the wonderful family that had welcomed me into their home with a warmth and friendship I would never forget.

CHAPTER THIRTEEN

Arriving at the Air Base, I enquired if a flight was available to get me to Halifax. The answer was no. The desk sergeant then went on to say that he would issue me with a rail ticket; this would be comprehensive, giving me sleeping accommodation on the overnight train and meals provided in the dining car. He went on to explain that the train from Trenton would take me to Montreal, which would be close to a three-hour journey. I would then transfer to the overnight train to Halifax. He would inform the Naval authorities in Halifax as to my E.T.A. (estimated time of arrival).

I was on the move again! Transport was provided to get me to the railway station and I boarded the train. The gentle swaying of the train enhanced the view I was taking in of the Canadian landscape, which changed from wide open spaces to urban sprawl as the train approached Montreal station.

I disembarked from the train and enquired at the information office as to what time and platform the train to Halifax would leave from.

I had a two-hour wait before departure time. I found the refreshment lounge and took a seat at the bar. My funds were getting low so I ordered a small beer. A gentleman and his wife came in and took seats next to me. They were very friendly and offered to buy me a drink. I explained my situation and declined the offer as I could not afford to reciprocate; they weren't having any excuses and insisted that I should have a drink with them. I had no option than to accept their generous

CHAPTER THIRTEEN

offer; they went on to explain that they were starting a vacation and were delighted to have met someone from the old country (this being me!). I was rather flattered.

It came time for them to leave and the gentleman took out his wallet and pressed a twenty-dollar note into my hand as a parting gift, saying "Have another drink on us!" I was embarrassed and grateful at the same time.

After this very generous couple left I ordered another beer. Unfortunately three or four boisterous lads came in and sat at the other end of the bar; one of the loudmouths shouted in my direction, "Hey, are you a kipper?" (This was a direct insult aimed at me.) My response was not going to be diplomatic. "If you mean two faced with no guts, you're wrong," I said, and added, "However, a kipper beats a banana." He was a bit taken aback by my reply, and said, "Waddya mean by that?" I said, "Green when you're young, yellow when you're old, soft inside and hang around in bunches."

I didn't have time to listen to any other response—it was time for me to leave and board my train to Halifax.

I found my allocated seat. Looking around I noticed that a bunk was suspended and stowed above me. Each seat in the carriage was accommodated in the same way.

The train was about to leave with the conductor shouting out the famous words in a distinctive voice "ALL ABOARD!" as the train gently left Montreal Station. Hopefully this would be the last leg of my journey to Halifax.

I settled down in my seat and looked out of the

CHAPTER THIRTEEN

window, taking in the view of the Canadian landscape.

Time came for me to go to the dining car and I had a meal. After the meal I went to the lounge car and had a couple of drinks. Tiredness came upon me so I made my way back to the accommodation carriage. On entering it, I was surprised to see that all the bunks were lowered and people were turned in for the night with curtains drawn around them for privacy. My bunk was the only one that was not in the vertical position. I took a deep breath, hoping not to disturb anybody, and managed to unhitch the bunk, and was able to get it into the correct position. It was about 5ft off the floor, but in line with the rest of them; my next problem was how to get into it! Thoughts of how I used to get into my hammock on *Blackwood* came back to me: strap hangers were suspended from the ceiling of the coach, so I took hold of a couple of them, pulled myself up and swung my bum onto the bunk, then pulled my legs and feet in. I was used to functioning in confined spaces. I had already taken off my shoes and placed them at the bottom of the bunk. I wriggled out of my bellbottoms and folded them up, tucking them under my pillow; the rest of my uniform was given the same treatment.

With the gentle motion of the train I fell into a welcome slumber. Waking up in the morning, I poked my head out of the curtains surrounding my bunk; to my horror the bunks occupied by my fellow travellers were all put up in their respective stowage places. Some of them had gone to the dining car for breakfast; as for me, I had to wriggle back into my bellbottoms. After getting somewhat decently attired I made my way to the bathroom, carrying my faithful toilet pouch containing a bar of soap, razor, shaving brush, toothbrush and toothpaste.

After my ablutions I returned to the carriage. After completing getting dressed (by this time I didn't care who saw what), I fought with the dratted bunk and got it back to where it belonged, stowed away.

I sat down and took in the passing scenery. Unknown to me a little old lady had been accommodated across the aisle from me and had observed my endeavours to navigate the Canadian Pacific railways system of travel. She was very sweet and informed me that if I had pushed the bell by my seat the porter would have come and lowered my bunk for me and provided a ladder to get into it, and then in the morning would come along to put the bunk away. I thanked her for the information although it was 24hrs too late.

Arriving in Halifax, the train came to a halt. Getting off the train a porter of African descent was standing by the door with his hand out. I shook him by the hand and said, "Thanks for nothing."

Navy transport was waiting to take me to *H.M.S. Ambrose*, this being the establishment responsible for overseeing the operational activities of the 5th submarine squadron. I should make it clear that *Ambrose* was part of *H.M.C.S. Stadacona*, where accommodation was made available to us.

CHAPTER THIRTEEN

This mishmash of life was over, but another was about to begin.

CHAPTER FOURTEEN

I CARRIED OUT the usual joining routine at *Ambrose*. I was then transported to *H.M.C.S. Stadacona*, where the submariners' quarters were allocated.

This was a two-story wooden building tucked away in a corner of the barracks far from any of the main buildings. My allocated guide was a submariner who was in the spare crew pool. He was a good lad and knew the ropes. The accommodation was a lot different to what I was used to in the U.K. My room was provided with four beds, much different from messes that could have fifty bunks or more crammed into them.

Inside the main entrance a desk was provided. A telephone was installed, along with the microphone for giving out any announcements through the tannoy system. A couple of vending machines were conveniently positioned close to the desk; one dispensed cold drinks, the other provided hot canned food like chicken con carne—all designed to tempt a sailor returning after a run ashore or a snack saving him the

CHAPTER FOURTEEN

trek to the main dining hall that was some distance from the block.

Fire regulations were explained to me backed up by posters; one in particular was very descriptive: it showed a bed with a skeleton on it with a cigarette hanging out of its mouth, the caption reading POOR OLD FRED, HE SMOKED IN BED! My guide went on to explain where the main dining hall was located and, most important, where the BIN was. I asked him, "What the hell is that?" He laughed and went on to explain that this was the canteen and bar; it was the name given to it by our lot.

Astute was at sea when I arrived. After settling in and meeting with a few of the lads in spare crew, I found out that I would be entitled to a N.A.T.O. forces liquor licence; to qualify you had to be 21yrs old and have a bona fide address ashore. I replied that I didn't have a bona fide address ashore. "Don't worry," they chorused, "you will get one."

Astute arrived back from her patrol. I was part of the shore side party to help secure her to the jetty. The majority of the crew disembarked and were transported to the barrack block in *Stadacona*, leaving the duty watch on board.

I crossed the gangplank and entered the boat through the fore hatch, making my way into the forward torpedo space. I reported to the cox'n, as I had been instructed. My first impression was that this was a man of confidence and compassion; he sported a beard, his voice was soft but authoritative, and he took me through the boat explaining where my diving station was. My job was to be responsible for shutting the 4.5.6.7. L.P. master blows on diving and to make sure they were open for surfacing, reporting by shouting their condition to the control room. I must add that the master blows were positioned in the passage adjacent to the galley.

H.M. Submarine Astute had been built in early 1945, and had undergone a major refit. In 1958 her conning tower, as it was known in those days, had been transformed into a streamlined fin; improved sonar, radar and other detection equipment had been installed; and the propulsion system had been improved with a more efficient snort mast. Being a diesel electric boat the engines had to breathe; this was a plus for the engine room branch, though for me it would be a curse. I will explain this later in this MISHMASH! One of the refit projects was that a slop tank had been installed; this replaced the previous toilet system where you had to dispense your own excrement through a regime of charging air cylinders and operating various valves to eject it. This system could only operate down to 100ft. If you needed 'to go' below that depth you had to hang on to it!

This improved system could accommodate the waste water from the ablutions, the toilets and the galley; the slop tank would be blown once a day by one of the engine room lads. We all knew when this was carried out

CHAPTER FOURTEEN

as a strong odour would permeate through the boat. A deodorizer was incorporated in the system, but was not very efficient.

After the cox'n had completed his orientation of the boat with me I was left alone to familiarize myself with the galley. *Astute* had a couple of gadgets that I was unfamiliar with; one was a telemotor operated can crusher; its name explains it—empty cans would be put into the receptacle, the lid would be closed, a button pushed, and the ram would then operate and crush the cans into a concertina shape and would be used as weights to sink the bags of garbage through the underwater gash ejector. (Gash being the navy term for garbage!) The bags had to be weighted so as not to float to the surface; if this happened it could give the submarine's position away to any surface ship and put it in jeopardy.

The other piece of equipment that I was unfamiliar with was the gash grinder. This was fitted to the galley sink. It was used for grinding to a pulp things like potato peelings, egg shells, and any other vegetable matter that needed to be discarded; the grinder could only be used with running water. Fresh water in a submarine was a precious commodity and had to be used sparingly. Fortunately sea water was provided through a separate system for flushing toilets; owing to the fact that the sea makes up for something like two thirds of the earth's surface there was plenty available.

My service on the *Astute* was a bit of a mixed bag—

CHAPTER FOURTEEN

excuse the pun—was a MISHMASH! Joining a crew that had started the commission together had its drawbacks; they didn't know me and I didn't know them. However, I was fortunate to have a compatriot called Rubberwasp; he was the boat's Officer's Steward; his real name was Leatherby. Another crewman was Peanuts Whitehorn, otherwise known as Pinktrumpet. I might add that Peanuts served on the Battleship *H.M.S. King George V* during the sinking of the German Battleship *Bismark* during World War Two.

The nicknames of these lads were all carried out in a friendly banter. I gradually bonded with the rest of my shipmates. The crew had just returned from a three-week trip and were out for fun. My introduction to this revelry was that the whole barrack block became a party; booze was coming from all directions! This had been stashed away and was now being freely liberated; every known alcoholic brand was available, from a Bells Whisky ballerina bottle to a bottle of Haig Dimple, followed by Bacardi Rum, Vodka, Brandy and anything else that was in a bartender's vocabulary.

I got talking to a leading stoker, Mickey Lydon. Mickey came from Dublin and I enquired as to how the drinks were so available. Mickey explained that the lads had stowed them away before the trip, bought from their N.A.T.O. Forces liquor licence issue. I said, "Aren't you supposed to have a bona fide address ashore to take it to?" His reply was, "Yes, but the Canook authorities didn't bother them as the barrack block was so far away from the main barracks." My next question was, "How do I get hold of a licence?"

Mickey went on to explain that I had to get an application form from the Admin Office, fill it in and get a signature from the owner of the bona fide address and then submit it to be sanctioned. I explained that I had just arrived and didn't know anyone ashore. He replied by saying, "See Billy, he's married to a Canadian girl. Her Mum's a sort of part-time bootlegger."

I found Billy and asked if he could supply me with a shore-side address so that I could get a liquor licence; he was very accommodating and told me to get the form, fill my part in and he would take care of the rest. He was as good as his word! I submitted my filled-in application form and was issued with my N.A.T.O. Forces liquor licence.

It was a known fact that half the crew shared Billy's mother-in-law's address to legitimise their applications.

To explain how the bootleg business worked is as follows: due to the strict Canadian licencing laws, Taverns were not allowed to open on Sundays. Lounges could open but food had to be purchased. The bootleg fraternity had regular jobs, and on payday a portion of the family income would go to buying some crates of beer; this would be sold from the house on Sunday when the Taverns were shut. If the beer was purchased and taken away, a 5-cent charge was made per bottle; if it was drunk on the premises (a room was set aside for this) a 10-cent charge per bottle was applied; the local

CHAPTER FOURTEEN

fraternity knew where they could get a beer on a Sunday!

My time serving on *H.M. Submarine Astute* would be an education in itself. I would make a few cock-ups, as everyone does at some time in their lives.

My job was to feed some sixty-five officers and men three meals a day and to make sure that nobody suffered from food poisoning. One of my difficulties was trying to get to grips with the many spices and ingredients that were available in Canada; they were somewhat different to what was issued to us cooks in the U.K.

We were off on a trip and I manned my diving station, ready to shut the main L.P. master blows when ordered to do so. This would be the trim dive. Every submarine carries out a trim dive after leaving harbour and reaching the open sea. The order to dive was given, each crew member reporting to the control room from their respective stations. My turn came and I yelled to the control room, "4.5.6.7. L.P. master blows shut!" The Captain, after getting the reports from the stations, ordered the main vents to be opened. The main vents were operated from what was known as the diving tree, operated by a leading hand of the engine room branch.

Air was expelled from the ballast tanks being forced out by the inflowing water. The Captain ordered the plainsmen to descend to 100ft. With a bow down angle of 10deg, this could be registered by reading the inclinometer that resembled a curved spirit level.

CHAPTER FOURTEEN

Levelling off at the desired depth, the order was given to check for leaks; the trim pump would be operated to pump water forward, aft, port or starboard, to get the boat on an even keel.

A trim dive was very important; this would ensure that the submarine was ready to perform its duties. It was also a bit nerve-racking, as one would be apprehensive in case someone had not secured a hatch correctly, or some other part of the sub's watertight integrity had been overlooked. On this dive everything went without incident.

Submariners were known to be a bit raucous when ashore, but when at sea the highest professionalism came into play; every man from the captain down had to work to the best of his ability. As for me, I was on a learning curve, having to deal with ovens that would or could not provide the temperatures to cook various dishes that were on the menu; this was often the case when the battery power was low, the power being used to maintain the boat's propulsion when dived; snorting helped replenish the battery power but sometimes was a little late to help me out.

However, our trip eventually took us to Prince Edward Island, positioned north of Nova Scotia; we were to be guests of honour at the annual Lobster Festival.

The islanders were in festive mood and provided us with a fantastic welcome. A parade had been arranged; the Captain and 1st lieutenant Slaughter headed the parade, being driven in a shining open-topped Cadillac!

CHAPTER FOURTEEN

They were enjoying themselves, giving what could be described as an imitation royal wave; the bands and floats followed, promoting the theme of the festival.

A local fisherman, grateful for our participation in the festival, came to the boat and gave us a gift of a large basket of fresh scallops. It was up to me to prepare and cook them for the crew, of course! This delicacy was a bit out of my normal expertise. I decided to make a batter and deep fry them. The boat was alongside the jetty and a shore-side power supply had been provided, so I got the deep fryer cranked up and proceeded to batter the scallops and put them into the hot cooking oil. The oil frothed up spittering and spattering in the middle of what would become a disaster! Unknown to me, the local press had been invited aboard for a tour of the boat. I got distracted from what I was doing. The 1st Lieutenant was the tour guide and three or four heads poked into the galley, one of them being a very attractive lady; she asked if it would be possible to try one of the scallops. I couldn't refuse, and I put in the frying basket and fished one out. To my horror the batter had slipped off! However, I kept my composure and offered the lady one rather uninviting looking scallop. She took it graciously and, being very kind, said it was delicious. The next day my name was published in the local newspaper. It read: "During my tour of the submarine I came across cook Paul Burgess in his galley that was no larger than a broom cupboard; cooking for a crew in such a confined space must be a daily challenge." She was not wrong!

CHAPTER FOURTEEN

Our stay in Prince Edward Island came to an end and we set off again to carry out exercises with the Canadian Navy. A couple of weeks later we returned to Halifax. The duty watch remained on board and the rest of us were transported to our barrack block in *Stadacona*. This gave the chance to get rid of the pungent smell that submariners exude when subjected to fresh air; even after having a long shower and putting on lashings of aftershave and phoo-phoo powder, the underlying odour of diesel fumes and other unmentionables were never completely masked.

Our clothing had to be washed. I forgot to mention that our sea-going clothing was a very relaxed regime; although we took some semblance of a uniform with us, mainly worn by the officers and the casing party, for entering and leaving harbour the clothing when dived was more of a civilian garb. Todd Slaughter, the 1st Lieutenant, would wear his favourite sweat shirt, emblazoned on the front with the logo, FORT LAUDERDALE WHERE THE BOYS ARE. As for me, I wore a black and white check shirt. As previously stated, the Submarine service was to a point a law unto itself, being somewhat a Navy within a Navy.

We were provided with sleeping bags. These also had to be laundered. We didn't have the luxury of getting into pyjamas, or any other night attire. We slept in what we wore during the day.

On the subject of sleeping arrangements, on some boats the crew outnumbered the amount of available

CHAPTER FOURTEEN

bunks. The off going watch would climb into the bunk vacated by his mate who had relieved him. This was called hot bunking, because the bunk hadn't had time to get cold. (A bit like sitting on a toilet seat after someone had just left; it was still warm!)

However, I digress. Our arrival in Halifax was on a Friday. After taking care of our laundry and ablutions, it was time to catch up on our mail from home. Bette had written several letters that I received all at once; putting them in order, I read them. The last one made my eyes come out like chapel hat pegs! I couldn't constrain myself and I let out a yell: "I'M GOING TO BE A DAD!" The lads that had heard me came in, slapping me on the back and giving out their congratulations! This was to be a time of celebration.

Submariners have many talents. One of our crew was a very good singer. He worked under a stage name called Gary Scott. When available he performed at the Jubilee Club close to the Halifax waterside. It was a very popular venue frequented by young and old alike.

I was invited along to the club with a bunch of the lads who always went to give Gary support. Needless to say, we never paid for a drink.

We wore civilian clothes. As far as the proprietor was concerned we were all part of his entourage.

A couple of the other lads had taken a private detectives course and had hitched up with a private detection agency; having access to the dockyard and able to mingle with Canadian sailors, they were useful

CHAPTER FOURTEEN

in surveillance and information gathering of sailors suspected of being unfaithful to their wives, the detective agency being contacted to prove or disprove the accusations.

After one long trip we arrived back in Halifax and the usual routine of returning to *Stadacona* took place, the only difference being that a couple of the spare crew lads had adopted a stray black kitten! I was not aware of this until walking down the corridor towards the bathroom wearing only my underpants, a towel slung over my shoulder and a wash bag containing my soap and shaving kit, I was attacked! The little bugger had been stalking me! The swaying of the towel draped over my shoulder had attracted him. Four paws with claws were climbing up my back. I let out a yell and the kitten let go and scampered off, leaving me with a scratched back. I was not the only one to be attacked in this way.

Another hazard negotiating the way to the bathroom was to be careful not to get shot in the bum by a pellet from a BB gun. This was a low velocity air pistol, and a few of the lads had them; it was accepted as a harmless prank, although when the pellet hit its intended target it was like getting a bee sting.

Sunday lunchtime in *Stadacona* was a fun time. The Bin would be open from 1200hrs until 1400hrs. *Astute* and *Alderney* were both in port together. One of our mates, Mickey Lydon, decided to have a lie in. This was not acceptable! A bunch of us invaded his room and

CHAPTER FOURTEEN

carried him in his bunk up to the Bin; parking the bunk outside, we dragged him inside.

The Bin was provided with chairs and tables laid out in a formal arrangement. This would change! Two submarine crews got together and put the tables in line ahead, surrounded with the available chairs. The beer started to flow. Mickey sitting in his vest and pants was starting to enjoy himself along with the rest of us.

What is known to submariners is a SODS OPERA, starting off to the theme music of Carousel. In chorus we would start off with, LAH, LAH, LAH, LAH, LAH, and so on; to the rendition of the tune one would stand up, take a swig of his beer and then sit down. This would take place around the table; as one sat down the other chap would stand up and so on. The upping and downing resembled the up and down movement of Carousel horses! The last man standing would be sung to in another way: "SIT DOWN YA C***, SIT DOWN!"

Another part of the opera was 'Barefoot daisy'; someone would be cajoled into taking off his shoes and socks, climb up on the table and run the length of it while the rest of the lads poured beer over his feet! The object of the game was to get to the end without slipping over; if he fell there were plenty of hands available to catch him.

The finale of the Bin session involved a mock American football game. A space was cleared in the middle of the room; there were no goal posts, and no football; instead, we used toilet rolls! I will let your imagination take you to the mayhem that this would cause—toilet rolls unravelling as they were thrown through the air, hanging off of light fittings, wrapped around chairs and tables and anything they came in contact with.

Our Canadian cousins were very tolerant, and in the main enjoyed our rather odd antics, although they weren't too pleased when we took the cannon balls away from the antique cannons that were positioned each side of the entrance to the main administration building and played bowls with them on the parade ground. A World War Two Doodle Bug (German Flying Bomb) was displayed in a prominent position within the barracks; we took it off its plinth and tried to launch it like a large glider! It was found with some underbelly damage; this was repaired and an enquiry took place as to how it was found close to the Submariners' accommodation. Our response was that high winds had been recorded and that the Doodle Bug was of a very light construction and had probably been blown off its plinth.

One prank, although never proved, was when the Commodore's flag was replaced by a pair of Canadian W.R.N.S. knickers. This was pushing things a bit far.

After one trip I got into trouble—not of my own making, I might add. *Astute* arrived back in Halifax after a month at sea; the usual routine was carried out and the duty watch remained on board, the rest of us being

CHAPTER FOURTEEN

transported to *Stadacona*. This was a Friday; being the early part of the month, our liquor issue was due.

Come Saturday morning I was up and about to go to the liquor store to collect my duty-free allowance. I was dressed in civilian clothes. The phone was ringing at the desk. No one was around so I answered it. On the other end was Shady Lane, the leading hand of the duty watch. On picking up the phone, Shady recognized my voice and asked what I was doing. I informed him that I was on my way to the liquor store to get my ration of booze. His reply was to ask a favour. "What sort of favour?" I asked. He asked me if I could get a box of beer and take it down the boat, continuing to say that I should get a cab. "We will reimburse you for the price of the beer and cab fare," he added.

These were shipmates so how could I refuse? Leaving the liquor store with my own supply and the box of beer containing 24 bottles of Olsen's best ale, I directed the cabby to the dockyard. After showing my I.D. to the dockyard security officer, the cab made its way to the jetty where the boat was secured. Carrying the box of beer, I crossed the gangplank and made my way along the casing to the fore hatch and I shouted down. Nobby Hart's head appeared and I passed the box of beer to him; he passed a fistful of dollars to me and I returned to *Stadacona*.

I had put my duty-free supply away in my locker and was about to relax when the intercom came to life requesting me to go to the desk to answer a telephone

CHAPTER FOURTEEN

call. Picking up the receiver, I asked who was calling. It was Shady. Before I could say anything, he said, "Chef, we made a BOO-BOO." My response was, "What do you mean?" Shady went on to explain that Toby the officer of the watch was calibrating the search periscope and had it beamed onto the cab that I was in. He saw me come aboard with the box of beer and hand it over to Nobby. When Nobby got to the bottom of the ladder Toby was there to intercept him, asking, "Who brought that on board? Don't tell any lies because I know!" Nobby had no alternative than to say it was the chef.

My response was, "What's the story (excuse)?" Shady was married and had a wife and child in Halifax. He was questioned by Toby as to why a box of beer was being smuggled aboard. Shady was thinking on his feet, and his explanation was that I owed him a box of beer and that his wife was going to visit the boat and take it home in the pram.

I had no alternative than to go along with the story. I put the phone down and waited for the next call that was sure to come.

It did. The cox'n was on the other end. (As previously stated, he was a compassionate man but was duty bound to carry out orders.) His words were, "Chef, you are placed under open arrest; get into the rig of the day—transport will arrive to bring you down to the boat."

I arrived on the boat and met with the cox'n. We went over the events that had landed me in the deep and

CHAPTER FOURTEEN

murky. I kept my mouth shut about the duty leading hand asking me to do a favour and bring a box of beer on board; I stuck with the original story that I owed Shady a box of beer and that his wife would come down the boat to take it home in the pram.

He instructed me to keep quiet about our conversation. He left to go and confer with Toby, and after some 15 minutes he returned. I was asked if I would accept the Officer of the day's punishment. I had no alternative than to agree.

I had to wait some time before I would be informed what my punishment would be.

In my estimation the cox'n was doing his very best to give me the benefit of the doubt in being the mediator between me and the officer of the watch.

Toby had already decided what my punishment would be, but it had to be approved by the 1st lieutenant; he left the boat and went to the wardroom at *Stadacona*.

My mate, the boat's steward ('Rubberwasp') happened to be serving a late breakfast to Todd Slaughter; according to Rubberwasp, Toby explained the scenario to the 1st lieutenant, who nearly fell off his chair laughing. After composing himself he gave his consent for Toby to mete out his punishment on me.

After waiting for what seemed to be ages, the cox'n escorted me to the control room. I was confronted by Lieutenant Toby Freer, and very formally charged with smuggling a box of beer aboard, and asked if I would accept his punishment. I replied that I would.

CHAPTER FOURTEEN

With bated breath, standing to attention, I waited for my sentence. Toby went on to say that I would be confined on board as part of the duty watch for the whole weekend; further to this I was ordered to clean the boat's decking from the after torpedo space to the forward torpedo space; this was the whole length of the boat, being some 200-plus feet.

I was supplied with a bundle of wire wool, a gallon can of white spirits, and a box of cleaning rags.

I started my journey through the boat, and on hands and knees, scraping and cleaning, I made my way through the various compartments. The engine room was the hardest on the knees; kneeling on steel deck plates with grooves in them is not very comfortable. However, I persevered and completed my task.

The duty watch were allowed to watch a movie. The Royal Navy supplied all ships with a projector and films of every description, although rather dated compared to what the civilian population were first given the privilege to see.

I asked if I could watch the film and this was denied. I was a man under punishment and was not allowed to do so.

I consoled myself with the thought that I had covered my shipmates' backs and that if I had told the real story they would have suffered a harsher punishment than me.

As an aside, the beer was held in store and passed out to the duty watch on Christmas day. Toby went on to become a very high ranking officer of Admiral rank.

CHAPTER FOURTEEN

Astute was about to become involved in one of the world's most perilous times; World War Three was threatening.

We were dived at the depth of 250ft. It was early October 1962 operating in an area of the Atlantic Ocean between Bermuda and the Eastern seaboard of the United States.

Eight small explosive devices were dropped on us. This was a signal for us to identify ourselves. The Captain made communication with the surface ship above us, using the underwater telephone. It was an American destroyer that requested that we surface. Our Skipper gave our code name and politely told the destroyer captain that before any further information or action would be taken he would refer the situation to higher authority.

Unknown to us, signals were going through the airwaves around the world; some two hours later a signal was received from CANFLAGLANT, the operational headquarters in Halifax, instructing *Astute* to surface and make passage back to Halifax.

We were still unaware of what was going on. Arriving in Halifax late Friday afternoon, it was bitter cold; thankfully we had been issued with our winter clothing that included string vests, long johns, double lined over trousers, a thick woollen lined hooded anorak, fur lined boots and fur lined mittens.

It was so cold that if you had a shower and washed your hair and then ventured outside before it was dry, icicles would form on it.

CHAPTER FOURTEEN

The lads were glad to be back in Halifax, and pleased that our trip had been cut short; the duty watch remained aboard while the rest of us were transported to *Stadacona*.

We went through the ritual of showering and trying to get rid of the usual submarine smells, etc. A few of the lads and I had a run ashore. Saturday gave a chance for the lads who had been duty watch after being relieved, to go to *Stadacona* and to go ashore if desired; Garry and some of his mates headed for the Jubilee Club to give a performance.

Sunday morning arrived. Those that had been ashore Saturday night were nursing their hangovers; some of us were looking forward to going to the BIN at lunchtime.

It was approximately 0930hrs when we heard the intercom from the tannoy come to life. It was the cox'n who made the announcement: "ATTENTION ALL HANDS! YOU HAVE 15 MINUTES TO GET YOUR STEAMING KIT TOGETHER. WE WILL THEN CLEAR LOWER DECK. TRANSPORT WILL BE HERE TO GET YOU TO THE DOCKYARD. JUMP TO IT!"

Our first reaction was, what the hell's going on? Our steaming kit consisted of the bare essentials, such as toothbrush, toothpaste, soap, towel, change of underwear, socks, and any other bits of clothing that could be stuffed into the steaming bag; these were like a small hold, all made of canvas that were held together with rope handles.

CHAPTER FOURTEEN

Transport arrived and the cox'n made sure we were all accounted for. We then set off to the dockyard; on arrival alongside the boat we disembarked from the transport lorries.

We were ordered to form two ranks. A small dais had been positioned on the jetty close to the gangway. The Captain and the officers appeared from the boat. We were called to attention as the Captain climbed onto the dais. He then ordered us to stand at ease.

He went on to say: "DUE TO THE DETERIATION IN EAST-WEST RELATIONSHIPS WE ARE GOING TO SEA ON A WAR FOOTING!" We looked at each other muttering under our breath, "What the f*** is he talking about!" After the initial shock the Captain allowed us to regain our composure. He then continued saying we will store ship. (As he was speaking a convoy of lorries were making their way along the jetty towards us.)

He continued, saying that after storing ship and taking on fuel we would go to Bedford Basin and take on our full complement of torpedoes. We achieved this in record time. As we were sailing out to sea our sister boat, the *Alderney*, was making her way in; at least we had a chance of a run ashore. The *Alderney*'s crew didn't have time to get that privilege and they had to do a quick turnaround.

When we were under way, the Captain made another announcement over the boat's intercom system; he went on to explain the situation we were faced with.

It had been confirmed by the Americans that the

Soviet Union was in the process of constructing missile bases in Cuba and supplying weaponry that could severely threaten the United States thus upsetting the balance of power throughout the free world.

President Kennedy had gone eyeball to eyeball with Nikita Khrushchev, the Soviet leader, telling him to dismantle the bases and remove the missiles; the Soviets had refused to do so and the Americans responded by setting up a blockade of Cuba; we were part of the blockade, only we were far from being anywhere near Cuba.

The submarine service operates in a clandestine environment so forgive me for not divulging where our area of operation was taking place.

Conditions on board were always cramped; with a full war complement of equipment including food to last up to three months, bread being a staple was stowed everywhere, even between the spaces of the torpedo tubes, wrapped up in cellophane to protect it from the atmospheric ambience that can only be experienced in a submarine.

Being a diesel electric boat we had to snort for at least 4hrs in 24 to maintain battery efficiency; this was done under the cover of darkness. During the snort time other operations took place: the gash was ejected—this was Rubberwasp's job; slop tanks were blown to get rid of the unmentionables from waste water from the galley and ablutions, not forgetting what had been deposited from the bodily functions of the crew.

CHAPTER FOURTEEN

Because of our mission it was necessary for the Captain to invoke the ultra-quiet routine; this meant that only those on duty could move about the boat in carrying out their duties; all off-duty crew were confined to their bunks; no messdeck games were allowed such as crib or uckers.

As for me, it could get rather difficult trying to cook three hot meals a day for a crew of some sixty-five men, especially when a temperature in the oven was needed to be 365deg, and all it would give was 250deg because the boat's batteries were getting low.

After about ten days into the trip the cox'n came to me and said, "I think you're going to have to start baking bread, chef. I had noticed that the bread we had taken on board had started to grow a greyish mould on the outer crust." I agreed.

I was already working a ten-hour day; this would add at least another six hours to it. There was no way that bread dough could be prepared during the day; it had to be done after the last meal of the day.

After cleaning the galley from the day's services, the tanky delivered the box containing the bread mix to the galley.

Bread baking is an exact science and requires the ambient and oven temperatures to be very precise; the bread mix contained the exact ingredients and measurements with the recipe enclosed.

Before starting to prepare the dough I went to the control room and asked the officer of the watch what

CHAPTER FOURTEEN

time we would be snorting; the reply was, "From midnight to four in the morning."

The damp warm atmosphere in a boat is ideal for what is known as proving bread dough, the interaction of yeast, salt, sugar and flour, creating a chemical reaction which allows the dough to rise and increase its size many times over; proving times may vary depending on the amount of dough. However, on this occasion I had done the preparation and had the dough proving in a large bowl with a damp cloth over it. I took a peep now and again to make sure all was well.

All was well until the order to snort was given. The snort mast was raised and a cold blast of air was sucked through the boat to feed the engines; it passed through the galley flat like a wind tunnel, and the dough that I had prepared and nursed for a couple of hours collapsed! I had to work fast. I got the oven up to temperature and worked like hell to knead and shape the dough into a resemblance of a loaf. (Submarines were not supplied with fancy bread pans; there was not any room for them!) I managed to put together seventeen loves and a batch of rolls, in spite of the adverse circumstances. Unfortunately, because the order to snort was premature to the time I had been informed, the bread and rolls came out not as I would have hoped: the crust was hard and the inside was a bit stodgy.

A few complaints were made and my response was, "Don't blame me, I never gave the order to snort!"—

CHAPTER FOURTEEN

because that's what knackered the bread.

Human nature never changes. We were involved in trying to avert World War Three and some of the crew took it upon themselves to moan about a loaf of bread! God bless them, I hope they are still alive today and have survived their wives' cooking.

Future snort times were strictly observed so that the staple of life could be prepared and baked without being exposed to outside sources.

The Cuban crisis came to an end, the Russians withdrew their missiles and dismantled the bases, and *Astute* was released from her operational duties and returned to Halifax, arriving a short time before Christmas.

We had not received any mail for a couple of months. Our mail from our loved ones gave us an account of what was happening in the civilian world during our time at sea. Newspapers like the *Daily Mirror* and other tabloids filtered through, giving accounts of the daily negotiations between Russia and America. I had a bundle of letters from Bette, all containing her feelings of anxiety. I was not alone; many of the other lads received similar letters from their wives and families.

Christmas day arrived. I had been invited to the home of a family that I had met at the Canadian Legion. I was dressed in civilian clothes and walked up to the regulating office at the main entrance to *Stadacona*, and reported to the duty officer for permission "to go ashore, sir." His response was, "No, not until you get a haircut!" I was gobsmacked! Where the hell could anyone get a haircut on Christmas day? I had just returned from a wartime patrol on a submarine that provided minimal facilities, least of all a barber's shop. (This was typical of the general service navy; they had no conception of how the submarine service operated, especially in Canada as they had no submarines of their own.)

I did an about turn and went to another gate used by the Chief and Petty officers. Since I was in civilian clothes, the guard would hopefully not notice that I was of a junior rank. As I walked through the gate I flashed my I.D. card and wished him a merry Christmas. I spent a very enjoyable day with the family that had invited me to spend Christmas day with them.

CHAPTER FIFTEEN

CHRISTMAS and New Year festivities were now over, and 1963 had dawned. *Astute* was again ready for sea, and we made our way out into the Atlantic. We went to diving stations. I manned the L P master blows, reporting them shut to the control room. The officer of the watch and the lookouts came into the boat from the fin sounding the diving klaxon and securing the hatch behind them. The usual 100ft depth was ordered by the Captain for trimming the boat. As the boat was diving, freezing sea water was cascading into the engine room through the engine room hatch. Jock McCann was on the hatch ladder trying to tighten the hatch securing cleats with a hammer, but with little effect, for water still continued to pour into the boat. The control room was informed of the problem and the order to surface was given. I opened up the L P master blows as fast as I could, reporting their condition; with the main vents shut the high pressure air was forcing its way into the ballast tanks; with the fore and after planes in the hard to rise position *Astute* returned to the surface. The engine room hatch was opened for inspection by the engineer Officer and the Chief artificer; the hatch and

CHAPTER FIFTEEN

hatch cover seals were inspected and it was discovered that a matchstick was the culprit for the leak! It had somehow been trapped between the two seals. After being removed, the trim dive was continued without incident.

On another occasion the boat had to make an unscheduled surface. It was a Friday and I had a deep fryer on the galley range; being Friday, fish and chips were on the menu. As the cooking oil was heating up a blue haze was being emitted; this haze permeated throughout the boat and my eyes started watering. I wasn't the only one—the lads in the control room were having difficulty seeing the depth gauges and compass bearings! The cox'n came to the galley to find out what was going on. I explained that I was using the cooking oil supplied from the stores in Halifax.

Needless to say, the boat had to surface to be vented to get rid of the toxic vapour! This took some thirty minutes; suffice to say that fish and chips were off the menu for the rest of the trip.

On our return to Halifax samples of the cooking oil were submitted for analysis to a forensic establishment; I was led to believe that the oil contained an ingredient used in tear gas, although I am unable to substantiate this.

Astute was nearing the end of her commission and would be returning home. As for me, I would remain in spare crew at *H.M.S. Ambrose*.

It was unusual to have two boats alongside at the same time. A cocktail party had been arranged on

CHAPTER FIFTEEN

Astute. Alderney was secured next to us, and the officers from *Alderney* were invited to attend along with dignitaries from Halifax, including the Mayor.

Rubberwasp (my mate Pat, the steward), asked if I could help him out with the event serving drinks and hors-d'oeuvres. I had no option than to agree—he was a good mate and I was happy to give him a hand.

The control room was the focus point of the event, the chart table being covered with a table cloth; the periscopes were raised to give a little more space and to allow the guests to have a peep through; the wardroom along with the Chief and Petty Officers' mess were made available for guests to have a sit down.

The duty watch were bunged up in the fore ends seamen's mess that was made into a makeshift cloakroom.

Rubbing shoulders with upper echelons of society was new to me so I asked Pat for a few tips; one was to make sure their glasses were always full.

Engines, as he was known, was seated in the corner of the wardroom and he called me over. I said, "Yes sir, what can I do for you?" His reply was, "I drink horses' necks." I said, "What's that?" and he replied, "It's brandy and ginger ale." I said, "Right you are, sir, I will take care of it."

For every one he had I had one too. The party was in full swing, with everyone enjoying themselves, when the 1st lieutenant approached me. He whispered in my ear that they were getting low on brandy, and I had to

CHAPTER FIFTEEN

go over to the *Alderney* with their catering officer and collect a half dozen bottles. I did as I was told, returning to *Astute* with a half dozen bottles of brandy about me. I couldn't resist slipping one to the duty watch bunged up in the seamen's mess.

The party was a great success, although the next day the 1st lieutenant enquired of me how many bottles of brandy we had borrowed from *Alderney*. I assured him that it was six; his response was that he could account for only five.

This was a little bit of retribution for me, having been punished for supposedly smuggling a box of beer on board!

It was early February when I was in the mess in *Stadacona* and called to answer the telephone. It was Taffy the duty signalman on the boat. On answering, Taffy said, "I have received a signal addressed to you." I asked what it said, and his reply was, "I'm not allowed to tell you; you have to come down to the boat. The officer of the watch will inform you of its contents."

Arriving on board I reported to the wardroom. Engines was the officer of the watch and he invited me to sit down. I complied and he passed me the signal, which read, WIFE IN HOSPITAL PREMETURE BIRTH SUSPECTED. I was in a state of confusion; this would be the eighth month of Bette's pregnancy, a very delicate time for any pregnant woman. I asked Engines if there was any way that I could get back to the U.K. to be with my wife to comfort her in this time of stress; he was very compassionate and advised me to talk to the 1st lieutenant who was my divisional officer.

I spoke with Todd, my divisional officer and showed him my signal. He made a decision to allow me to return to the U.K. on the boat as long as I could provide proof that I could return to Halifax after my leave that would be granted when *Astute* arrived back in *Dolphin*.

Astute was going to depart within the next 48 hours. I thanked him and went back to *Stadacona* to try and work out how I could get proof of my ability to return to Halifax after my leave.

Word had got around of my predicament. My mates on the *Astute* and the *Alderney* had a whip round and gave me enough money to put down a deposit on a return flight on Canadian Airways from London to Halifax.

I was delighted and very humbled by their generosity. I made it to the Airline booking office and secured my flight arrangements; my return ticket would be made available at Pickford's Travel agents in Oxford. The full cost of the flight would be 89 pounds, which I would be able to pay by instalments.

With my travel documents in hand I returned to the boat. I reported to the 1st lieutenant and produced the required documentation; he was satisfied with my information and gave me permission to return to the UK on the boat.

We had been at sea for three days when another signal was received addressed to me; it read, WIFE

CHAPTER FIFTEEN

OUT OF HOSPITAL IT WAS A FALSE ALARM. This false alarm had cost 89 quid, but to see Bette it was worth it!

Submarines returning from their commissions are not met with the *Fol de Rols* that accompany the capital ships like aircraft carriers or cruisers; instead, we slip in unobtrusively.

Any vessel returning from foreign parts are subject to a visit from H.M. Customs Officers. We were not exempt; we all had to fill in a customs declaration form listing anything bought abroad that would be brought into the country. Being a bit nefarious, all sailors were somewhat economical of what was declared on the customs form.

As for me I just wanted to get ashore to make my way to Scotland to be with Bette. I was cleared by Customs and with my railway warrant and small kitbag I made my way to Portsmouth station via the Gosport Ferry.

My journey to Scotland was uneventful. Arriving at Edinburgh Waverley station, I had to change trains. It was night-time, and freezing cold; snow was on the ground that had frozen. My train would take me to Inverkeithing where I would have to change to get the train to Cowdenbeath.

By this time I was knackered and didn't fancy waiting on a freezing station platform in Inverkeithing, so I decided to get a taxi to Cowdenbeath. Mr Kram had a taxi; he was Polish and had escaped the Nazi invasion in World War Two. His wife had a baby supply

CHAPTER FIFTEEN

shop in Inverkeithing. He was a very good man who would not overcharge me for a ride into Cowdenbeath.

I gave him directions to Park Avenue and I paid him for the ride and knocked on the door. Bette answered—she looked wonderful in the full bloom of pregnancy and awaiting motherhood. We hugged and kissed each other. Bette broke away and, looking out the window, she said, "Did you pay for the taxi?" I said, "Of course I did." She went on to say, "Well, he's still out there."

I went outside to investigate. Mr Kram's taxi was having difficulty trying to get up the brae with engine revving and tyres slipping on the frozen snow. I got behind the car and was able to give him a shove that enabled him to get enough traction to get moving.

Going back into the house, I asked Bette where her Mum and Alec were; she had forgotten to tell me that they had gone to meet me at the station! Not long afterwards they returned home and were surprised to see me there. I explained that I had got a taxi from Inverkeithing and apologized for their waiting for a train that I was not on. We all had a laugh about it.

Because of Bette's condition a bunch of pennies were on the dresser in the bedroom, in readiness to be used in the telephone box at the top of the street: if an emergency happened they could be quickly grabbed to make the call to the local midwife or ambulance.

One night I was awakened from a deep sleep. Bette's right leg gave a sharp jerk. Without hesitation I was out of bed, climbed into my clothes and was off up the street

CHAPTER FIFTEEN

with a fistful of pennies, convinced that Bette had gone into labour. I was about halfway to the phone box when I heard Bette's voice calling me to get back in the house! On returning she explained that the baby was moving around and had touched a nerve that triggered the leg jerk. It had happened before.

Unfortunately our baby decided not to enter this world while I was home on leave. My time was up and I had to make my way back to Canada.

I bade my farewells leaving Bette with tears in her eyes and a lump in my throat. I travelled to Oxford to visit Mum and the family for a brief visit and to collect my plane ticket from Pickford's Travel agents.

My flight back to Canada was scheduled on a Sunday. No one in the family was available to take me to London Airport, the reason being that Ernie, my stepfather, would be attending the Salvation Army morning service and Mum would be busy preparing the Sunday dinner; fortunately my mate Erick who lived across the street had a car and offered to take me to the airport.

Arriving back in Halifax, I reported to the administration office at *H.M.S. Ambrose*. I was informed that I would be put into spare crew; my duties would be working as an office boy with other duties as required.

In Navy terms, I would become a general dogsbody; this would include shuffling papers, making coffee and tea, and on occasion be part of the shore-side berthing party securing submarines that were returning to harbour.

CHAPTER FIFTEEN

I might add that when making coffee for the office staff the coffee percolator blew up in my face and I got scalded! Coffee along with its ground beans were cascading from the ceiling to the floor and everywhere in-between. After treatment for my burns at the sick bay I had to clean up the mess; needless to say I was not allowed anywhere near the coffee percolator thereafter—which didn't bother me at all!

Alderney was returning from a trip and I became part of the shore-side berthing party. It was still winter time and it was freezing cold. The boat made her way to the jetty. Ice had formed on her fin. The 2nd cox'n was in charge of the casing party and the bow man wetted his heaving line by dropping it into the sea. This was normal procedure: the heaving line was a personal bit of equipment that had what was known as a monkey's fist at the end of it. The seaman would weave a weight into the end of the rope and this would give it a good trajectory when it was thrown to the berthing party. The wetted line would add a bit more weight and assist in its trajectory; the heaving line would be attached to the main securing rope or wire cable that would secure the boat to the jetty.

Pulling the main rope or wire by the heaving line onto the jetty was our job; we had to secure it to a bollard (this being a post securely attached to the jetty); the boat's Capstan would be used to assist in bringing the boat alongside.

However, on this occasion the heaving line

CHAPTER FIFTEEN

immediately froze when being thrown towards the jetty! We were ready to retrieve it but it didn't arrive; the coil of rope returned to the boat like a boomerang. The 1st lieutenant from his position on the bridge was going nuts, as the boat was in danger of crashing into the jetty. Brummy, the 2nd cox'n with his nose bleeding from the cold and the icicle that he had brushed from his nose, yelled back, "If you can do any better sir, come down here and try!"

After calming down *Alderney* was berthed safely. Another boat had arrived to relieve the *Astute*. She was the *Auriga*. I was supposed to have been drafted to her, but things can change.

As all submariners we shared stories of the various situations that we had faced and endured, and we knew that the *Auriga* had a problem with her slop tank during her passage to Canada. The consequence was that the crew had to carry out their bodily functions by sticking their bums over the fin until the boat got to St Johns in Newfoundland, where repairs could be carried out.

As for me, when serving on *Astute* we were supposed to be at 250ft with the fore and after planes clutched in George. (This was the automatic depth keeping mechanism, not unlike the automatic pilot fitted to air liners.) However, on this occasion George fell asleep; we had silently crept up to a very dangerous level where we could be vulnerable to the keels of surface ships that could be passing over us. Fortunately the Skipper was on his toes; he had noticed from the depth gauge in his cabin

CHAPTER FIFTEEN

that the boat was nearing the surface, so he entered the control room ordering emergency stations, giving the order to emergency dive and flood Q. This was the rapid dive tank that could take a boat very quickly below the surface. The inboard vent operated, expelling the air that had been in the tank into the boat. This was not the best smelling air one would want to breathe.

As previously stated, things can change. My biggest change happened on March the 18th, 1963, when I received a signal that I was the proud father of a baby boy. He was weighed at nine and a half pounds and twenty-two inches in length. Bette and I had an agreement that if the baby was a girl, she would choose the name, whereas if it was a boy, I would choose the name. I named him Alan David Burgess. It would be some months before I would get to see him! However, it was a time for celebration. I was not the only new father, for the wife of one of the other lads had given birth in the same time give or take a couple of days; however, his had tipped the scales at twelve pounds. The Bin had a lot of revelry with our mates being very generous with liquid refreshment.

On April the 3rd I was drafted to the *Alderney*. Her chef Robbie was due for discharge; he had served his time. Being married to a Canadian girl, he requested that his discharge from the Navy take place in Canada. This was granted and Robbie left the boat to take up his civilian life as a recruit in the Halifax police force.

CHAPTER FIFTEEN

As for me, I was his relief. I knew a number of *Alderney*'s crew—Major Marjoram, Chippy Freeman, Soapy Watson, just to name a few; they were a great bunch of lads.

Alderney had recently returned from a trip where she had very narrowly escaped a disaster. One of her hovering tanks had failed to vent and this took her into a deep dive far beyond the maximum diving depth that the A-class submarine was designed for; with the skill of her skipper (known as Harry), and the expertise of the crew, she managed to surface and limp to Halifax.

On inspection, it was found that the excessive pressure on the hull had cracked the engine frames, so temporary repairs were carried out in the Halifax dockyard. These repairs involved welding spacers onto the ribs of the boat in the engine room; sixteen hydraulic jacks were welded to the engine casing, eight per engine; in theory, the engines would be held in place as the boat made its way back across the Atlantic to England.

Alderney was prepared for her return journey to England when another disaster struck; it was April the 10th, 1963, when a SUBMISS signal was received and we were ordered to report to the boat. We prepared for sea and waited to be informed if SUBSMASH was to be signalled; some four hours later it was.

I need to explain that a SUBMISS was indicated when a submarine failed to report after two hours of its scheduled time, and an alert would be given; if no signal was received within another four hours a SUBSMASH would be signalled. Any allied vessel within the vicinity of the last known position of the distressed submarine would make its way to carry out search and rescue operations.

We were informed that the submarine in difficulties was the *U.S.S. Thresher*, and was positioned somewhere off Cape Cod, her last known position. We were about to let slip when another signal was received; it was devastating, informing us to stand down. *U.S.S. Thresher* had sunk with all hands, this being some 129 souls; we were gutted and grieved for the crew along with their families, friends and the American people.

CHAPTER SIXTEEN

ANOTHER LAD joined *Alderney* about the same time as me. He was a Scouser. (A Scouser is a native of Liverpool.) Anyway, Scouse and I became good mates.

His birthday came along a few days before we were due to return to England. We had a run ashore to celebrate; we had carried out one birthday celebration on board where the tot time ritual had been carried out.

Being dressed in uniform, we were able to get away with a few pranks. Unfortunately Scouse got away from me; we were about to leave a bar, to find another one that Scouse wanted to go to; I needed a pee, and after leaving the toilet, Scouse was nowhere in sight. I went outside into the street and in the darkness with the help of a street lamp I was able to catch up with Scouse who, in his partially inebriated state, had got into an altercation with a police officer. When I arrived to sort out the mess, the police officer had drawn his gun! Scouse and the policeman were standing toe to toe with Scouse having his index finger stuck in the barrel of the police officer's revolver! Scouse was saying something like, "Shoot, you b*****d, let's see what happens!" I intervened and apologized to the officer for Scouse's behaviour; after I helped to remove the offending finger from the gun barrel we were allowed to carry on our way, with a warning from the police officer that if he encountered any more trouble caused by us he would have us arrested.

We finished the night off at Joe Como's Fish & Chip shop; this establishment was not far from *Stadacona*. Joe was very tolerant of the Submarine fraternity, who would congregate there after a night out on the beer. When we arrived, Sharky, another of our mates, was standing on a table, giving his rendition of 'Lloyd George Knows My Father'—a song reminiscent of World War One.

It was time for *Alderney* to leave Canada and make headway for home. Leaving Halifax, we had mixed feelings; the people had been very good to us, and some of the crew had married Canadian girls; some others had Canadian girlfriends; we also had some Canadian crew members who would be separated from their families. This was a sailor's lot! Each would deal with it in his own way. As for me, I was looking forward to be reunited with Bette and to see my baby son.

Leaving the jetty for the last time, we headed out into the Atlantic. Although we were going to be on a surface passage, a trim dive was mandatory; before this could be carried out the jacks holding the engines in place had to be wound down and the boat changed over to the electric motors. A gentle and fragile trim dive was executed and the boat levelled off at 100ft. The trim was

CHAPTER SIXTEEN

corrected; this done, the order to surface was given, and *Alderney* was gently nudged to the surface. The jacks were extended, the main engines engaged, and the course was set for our return to England. An Admiralty tug was sent to escort us in case the temporary repairs carried out in Halifax failed.

Alderney made her way across the Atlantic at a steady 15 knots. Sometimes I would take the wheel to help guide her home; most of the crew were in a joyful mood looking forward to being reunited with their wives, families, and friends.

Alderney arrived back in England safely and was secured to a jetty in *Dolphin*, her home shore base.

I was granted leave and made my way to Scotland. Bette was waiting for me, and presented me with Alan our baby son. I was so proud of her and our baby! Bette had bought a Silver Cross pram for the baby out of the allotment allowance that I had made out for her.

I was eager to show him off and made a number of trips down Cowdenbeath High Street, pushing him along in his very elegant pram.

My leave came to an end and I travelled back to the boat. Arriving at Portsmouth Dockyard station, I would have to catch the ferry across the harbour to Gosport. I had a bit of time to spare so I went into the Fleet Club to have a quiet drink. I bought a pint and, looking around for a seat, I noticed Peanuts sitting on his own. I went and sat with him and asked how he was doing since he had returned on the *Astute* from Canada.

CHAPTER SIXTEEN

His reply was somewhat distressing; he went on to say that when he got home, his wife had taken in a lodger that was nothing but a hippie—and she had gone the same way. With a soulful look, he continued, saying, "What can I do, chef, with thirty-six budgies (he had an aviary), an electric train set, and a wayward wife?" I was stuck for words. I tried to console him as best I could. Unfortunately servicemen from whatever force, be it Army, Air force, or Navy, sometimes have to face this type of situation after a long separation.

It was time for me to leave to catch the Gosport ferry; I bade my farewell to Peanuts and wished him well, hoping that his domestic life would work out satisfactorily.

Arriving back on *Alderney*, I found the majority of the crew had been dispersed to other submarine bases; as for me and the remainder of the crew, we were to remain with the *Alderney* (sort of caretakers, until the Ministry of Defence decided what to do with her); I was relieved from cooking duties as we would be victualed ashore in *Dolphin*; my duties would be watch keeping as a trot sentry.

I was teamed up with my old mate Scouse Wilkinson. (He of the police officer incident in Halifax!) We would be working with the other lads twenty-four hours on with forty-eight hours off, followed by forty-eight hours on and seventy-two hours off. Two of us would be on the boat for the duration of the duty except for meal times when one would be allowed ashore to go for a meal; the boat would never be unattended.

CHAPTER SIXTEEN

Scouse and I were able to work out our own routine as for kip time during our duty watch; during the daylight hours we took turns checking telemotor pressures and the various inspections within the boat; because of the varying tide levels the ropes and lines securing us to the floating pontoon had to be adjusted.

We had a fishing rod that we used to give us a bit of a relief from our relatively mundane duties; this was positioned on the pontoon, and the rod had a bell attached to it that would jingle if a fish took the bait.

It was just after midnight when Scouse relieved me from my watch. I was about to snuggle into my sleeping bag in my bunk when I heard him shouting, "CHEF! CHEF!" I jumped out of my bunk and made my way to the fore ends. Scouse was standing at the foot of the fore ends hatch, and the watch coat he was wearing was oozing water with squashed jellyfish and squid, along with a bunch of seaweed attached to it; he was still wearing his cap with water spurting out of it through the vent holes! I said, "What the hell have you been at, you stupid sod!" He replied, "I just relieved you and got on the casing when the bell was ringing on the fishing rod. I jumped from the boat to get to the pontoon. I missed and fell in the dock!"

He was lucky; the watch coat had trapped a bubble of air that propelled him to the surface. He was beside himself laughing, saying, "I came back up under me hat!" He was standing in a puddle of water that had dripped off him. I told him to go and get dried off and

CHAPTER SIXTEEN

I would take over his watch. Needless to say, the fish he thought he had caught got away.

I would serve on *Alderney* until September 1963. I applied for married quarters so that Bette could be nearer and we could have a more normal married life; unfortunately this was denied: the reason given was that I was not guaranteed to be in the Portsmouth area for longer than a six-month period.

However, I was able with the help of my Mum to get Bette and Alan accommodation in Oxford. This was in Hayfield Road. Bette would have duties to perform; the house was occupied by a lady of some 80 years old; the house was older than its occupant and had no electricity. Gas lamps were provided in the downstairs' living rooms, along with a gas stove in the kitchen.

Bette had been brought up in a similar environment in Scotland, so fortunately she was able to adapt to her environment; life was hard for all of us.

Oxford was some 90 miles from *Dolphin*. I would hitchhike home on weekends when I was off watch, to spend time with Bette and Alan. To hitchhike home would usually take about 3 hours.

On this occasion I left *Dolphin* at 12 noon. It was pouring with rain. My mate Bungey Williams who was serving on one of the boats operating from *Dolphin* had a Vincent Black Shadow motorbike and sidecar. He would normally give me a lift as far as the A30 outside of Winchester, where we would part company; he would head off to London and I would start thumbing it on the A34 towards Oxford; unfortunately Bungey didn't have a weekend off this time, so I had to hitchhike all the way.

By the time I got to the house I was like a drowned rat. I went inside and Bette was nowhere to be seen. Aggie the old lady appeared and I asked her where Bette was. "She had to go out," was her reply. I took off my soaking wet clothes and waited for Bette's return. She eventually returned with Alan in his pram. She was soaking wet and in tears.

After taking off her wet clothes and making sure that Alan was settled down, I made a pot of tea. Bette went on to explain that she was waiting for me to get home to take care of Alan so she could go to the chemist on Walton Street to get the baby milk powder that Alan needed as she was getting low on it. Being a serviceman's wife, she could not be sure if leave might be withheld for any number of reasons; this was our lot and we had to live with the uncertainty that all married service families had to deal with.

My weekend leave came to an end; I left Bette in the early hours of Monday morning to get to Carfax in time to catch one of the Southdown coaches returning with other lads from all parts of the country to their ships and establishments in the Portsmouth area.

Portsmouth Navy Days were approaching. This was the time when the public were invited aboard to meet the men and view the ships. *Alderney* (although still

CHAPTER SIXTEEN

crippled) was designated to be the submarine open to the public.

Those of us left aboard had to give her a good clean up. We did a good job. The 1st lieutenant was in charge of the boat, and after his inspection the boat made its way with a skeleton crew from *Dolphin* to one of the main jetties in Portsmouth Harbour, using the main motors for propulsion. (The engine frames had not yet been repaired.)

Alderney found her berth and was secured alongside; the British public converged on Portsmouth dockyard in droves, all eager to do what visitors do—to have an insight into how the British Navy operated and how we sailors lived.

The majority of our guests were very polite and interested. Unfortunately there is always one that can be obnoxious! This one was very loud. I was positioned at the bottom of the fore hatch ladder where the guests were entering the boat; I would direct them from the forward torpedo space through the boat to the other lads who would explain the boat's function and equipment.

Mr Loudmouth, as I will call him, started off saying at the top of his voice, "I've come to see what my tax money is spent on!" I was a little annoyed by his demeanour and attitude.

My response was very cool, calm and collected. I said, "Welcome to my home." I showed him to my bunk space; this was in the passage opposite from the

CHAPTER SIXTEEN

steward's pantry. I opened the curtains that afforded a bit of privacy and I went on to explain that the strap above his head could be pulled down and attached to the bunk frame to stop me from falling out when on a surface passage in rough weather. I went on to inform him that I shared my bunk space with a few other of the boat's integral parts, which included the telemotor, oil relief valve, the fresh water relief valve, and an electrical panel fuse board. I went on to explain that when taking on fresh water, the relief valve would operate if the supply was not turned off quick enough when the tanks were full; the same thing would happen when topping up the telemotor system; consequently, I explained, I could be like a sardine pickled in oil or have a flooded bunk and swim around like a fish. I finished off the introduction to my home by saying it's amazing what the taxpayers' money can provide. Subdued, Mr Loudmouth continued quietly on his tour of the boat.

Navy days came to an end. *Alderney* returned to *Dolphin* and birthed in Haslar Creek.

I applied for married quarters so that Bette and I could have some semblance of married life; this was denied, the reason being that I didn't qualify because I was not guaranteed to be in the port area longer than six months.

I would miss the qualifying period by one month, the reason being that I was to be drafted to the *Osiris*, a new boat being built by Vickers Armstrong in Barrow in Furness.

CHAPTER SIXTEEN

My time with Bette and Alan would be confined to the odd weekend leave; however, this was the Navy and Navy families learned how to cope with long separations.

It was a Sunday and I was the only one on board. My mate Scouse had gone up to *Dolphin* for his tea. I had done my internal rounds of the boat and made my way to the casing. I checked the breasts and springs securing the boat to the jetty. Looking up, I saw a bunch of fellows in civilian clothes leaning over the jetty guard rail. I enquired who they were and they told me they were a cricket team from the London Fire Brigade and had been playing a match against the *Dolphin* eleven; they were passing the time awaiting their transport to return them to London. In some ways I supposed that being the only one on board I was the Captain, so I offered them a tour of the boat. They jumped at it! I gave them a good tour of the boat, explaining how the chart table worked. I raised the search periscope and they took turns looking through it. I must have done a good job, for when it was their time to leave and I escorted them to the gangplank, the senior officer turned and thanked me for an excellent tour; shaking me by the hand he gave me a fistful of money! I was overwhelmed by their generosity. Unbeknown to me they had a whip round! I was humbled and grateful at the same time.

The amount of money came close to five pounds,

CHAPTER SIXTEEN

which was a very nice windfall and would be put to good use on the next weekend leave that I would be with Bette.

One Monday morning I was having breakfast in *Dolphin* when a message was broadcast through the tannoy system. The announcer requested that anyone with O, RH negative blood in his veins report to the sick bay. This was my blood group so I complied and reported to the sick bay. I knew that I had a comparatively rare blood group. Out of the whole ship's company of *Dolphin* and the submarine crews that were tied up alongside, there were only two of us that had the required blood group; strangely, we were both cooks.

On reporting to the sick bay Tiffy we were informed that a horrific accident had occurred and blood was urgently needed; we were transported very quickly to the Royal Navy Hospital Haslar. A check on our blood group was carried out and the next thing I was lying on a bed in a room; needles were poked into me and the blood was extracted.

As a reward for our blood donation the Surgeon Commander in charge of the case ordered that we were to be given twenty-four hours leave for recuperation.

Because of the repayment that I had to make on the flight ticket when Bette was taken into hospital with the suspected premature birth of Alan, and the fact that by returning to the UK prematurely I lost my overseas living allowance, our finances were rather stretched.

CHAPTER SIXTEEN

One of the lads suggested that I should contact the R.N.B.T. (This was a charity set up to assist sailors' families in need; the full name of the charity was the ROYAL NAVY BENEVOLENT TRUST.)

I went to their office in Portsmouth and was interviewed by a rather stern gentleman. I explained to him my predicament, and enquired if a grant could be made available to pay off the air flight ticket, as this would be of great help. His reply was, "Have you been in crown debt?" I hadn't a clue as to what he was talking about, and my reply was no. His response was sharp and short, saying that there was no way the trust could provide me with a grant.

I left the office dejected, and a little perplexed as to why my request for help had been rejected; however, life goes on, and in due course Bette and I paid off the Canada Airways loan.

However, that was in the past. My draft to the *Osiris* was approaching, which meant that I had to re-qualify in S.E.T.T. training.

CHAPTER SEVENTEEN

I REPORTED to the tank training officer as ordered. I was already conversant with the procedure, and to my surprise I met up with Soapy Whatson. He had been drafted to the tank and was one of the swim boys. Soapy had served in Canada where we had previously met, along with a couple of the other lads who had also been drafted to the tank.

I went through the basics as a refresher. When it comes to your safety you don't forget! However, the escape from the 100ft depth was going to be a bit different.

As I ascended from the escape hatch Soapy and a couple of the other swim boys grabbed me and held me for a couple of seconds. I knew a prank was about to be played on me, and I wasn't wrong! They let me go and as I slipped away from their grip Soapy gave me a gentle twist on my torso. I spun through the water like a cork popping out of a champagne bottle! When I hit the surface, needless to say I re-qualified in my S.E.T.T. training.

CHAPTER SEVENTEEN

It happened that my mate Chappie was spending a bit of time in *Dolphin* before being drafted to the *Dreadnought,* our first nuclear powered submarine; we both had a weekend leave granted so we left *Dolphin* on a Friday afternoon and hitchhiked together to Oxford.

We got as far as Newbury and decided to go into a pub for a drink. We got a couple of pints and decided to have a game of darts. An elderly gentleman and his friend challenged us to a game. The old gentleman was wearing what could be loosely described as riding gear. Chappie and I took up the challenge and said that the losers would buy a pint for the winners, to which our opponents agreed.

We won! The old gentleman, true to his word, offered to buy us a pint, but also gave us another option: instead of having a drink, he offered us a tip on a horse that was running at Plumpton on Saturday. Newbury was racehorse country, and if anyone in the know knew about horse racing, this would be the place.

Time was getting on and we had to get on the road. (We had another 30 miles to go to get home.) We took up the offer of the tip and the gentleman took out a small paper pad from the inside pocket of his jacket and with the pencil that he had tucked behind his ear jotted down the name of the horse, and the time of the race.

Bette was now living on Marston Road in a house owned by Mr Williams. Bette was a live-in housekeeper and had moved a couple of times after leaving Hayfield Road; she had lived in Abingdon for a few months, and

CHAPTER SEVENTEEN

now was taking care of Mr Williams who was an elderly gentleman.

However, on the Saturday morning Mr Williams and I made our way to the local bookies. I shared my tip with him, and Mr Williams put his money on the nose. I was a bit more cautious and put a half crown on an each-way bet; we went to the Friar Pub for a lunchtime pint and to watch the race. Our horse came in at a good price. I picked up something like thirty bob while Mr Williams picked up twice as much as I did.

My draft and orders arrived to report to Barrow in Furness to join *H.M. Submarine Osiris*.

Osiris was in the process of being fitted out and the crew was gradually being put together. We were accommodated in civilian lodgings paid for by the Admiralty. The people of Barrow were very friendly towards us and provided us with as much comfort in their homes as was possible. I was fortunate to be billeted with the cox'n in the home of a very pleasant and happy family.

Again, no Married Quarters were available in Barrow for any of the married members of the crew. Bette had to carry on the best way she could without me being close by.

Our day was taken up in the dockyard offices looking over the plans of the boat to gain knowledge of her construction. After the dockyard workers had left for the day we toured the boat to view what progress had been made, each of us being interested in the part of

CHAPTER SEVENTEEN

ship where we would be employed; as for me, it was the galley.

I would also work on putting together menus; these would be checked over by the cox'n and the 1st Lieutenant, who by the way was my boss on the *Astute*. As the crew gradually came together, I would meet up with a number of lads that I had served with in Canada.

Osiris was ready to start her sea trials. She was still in the manufacturers' hands. The Captain and senior officers would be on board for these trials. All catering arrangements were carried out by civilians. The first sea trial would last for a couple of days.

During this time the rest of the crew would report to the dockyard and carry out our daily duty of scanning the boat's plans and familiarizing ourselves with the boat's layout.

The 1st Lieutenant, Todd Slaughter, had left his car in the charge of one of the electrical departments' leading hands while he was away at sea on the trials.

During this time a message was received—a new crew member would be arriving at Barrow railway station; he had to be met and shown to the lodgings where he would be accommodated. I volunteered for the job, and instead of using public transport to collect our new shipmate, I persuaded the leading hand to let me have the 1st lieutenant's car to pick him up.

With some reluctance he handed over the keys of the car and I drove to the station. The train arrived and to my surprise our new shipmate was an acquaintance of

CHAPTER SEVENTEEN

mine—Geordie Howe. We had served in Canada together, in spare crew and on the *Alderney*.

This was a time for celebration! After putting his kit in the trunk of the car we set off for the Dreadnought bar; this was the local hangout for the majority of submariners billeted in Barrow; it had been named after *H.M. Submarine Dreadnought* which, as previously stated, was our first nuclear submarine.

In our haste to get into the pub I hadn't realized that I had parked the car in a no-parking zone! We had a couple of pints and I was able to fill Geordie in on what was going on with the boat and the crew; compared with most of them we were old hands. Then it was time to leave the pub and get Geordie to his digs.

Getting into the car I noticed something stuck in the windscreen wiper blade. I got out and retrieved it. OH, SHIT—it was a parking ticket!

After dropping off Geordie at his digs I went back to the Dockyard and returned the car into the safe hands of its custodian. The parking ticket was crumpled up and discretely disposed of.

Osiris returned to Barrow after her first sea trial. Adjustments had to be made in a number of areas; with a new boat this was to be expected—everything had to be in good working order before the Admiralty would take her over.

It was November the 22nd, 1963 and news was being broadcast throughout the world that PRESIDENT

CHAPTER SEVENTEEN

KENNEDY had been shot during a visit to Dallas in Texas. I watched the news on the television in the home of my host family. I had arranged to meet up with Geordie and a few of the other lads in the Dreadnought bar.

I remember that on the bus I said a silent prayer for him, asking God not to let him die; unfortunately my prayer went unanswered.

Meeting up with the lads in the pub we all thought that the balloon had gone up, and that the Russians were behind the assassination in retaliation for the Cuban crisis.

We readied ourselves to being involved again in a situation that could be the onset of World War Three; fortunately, it didn't happen.

On a lighter note, one of the lads, Jimmy McQuigan, had heard of a pop group called the BEATLES! He was an enthusiastic follower of them, and they were doing a gig at Barrow Town Hall. He coerced us into going along with him to see the show.

I had been fortunate to be able to buy a car; it was a 1946 Morris Eight series E. I drove it from Barrow to Oxford to be with Bette when I had a long weekend leave, occasionally giving a lift to the chief petty officer in charge of the signals department; he lived in Shrewsbury, which was a bit out of my way, but nevertheless it helped him.

Osiris was about to go on an extended acceptance trial. This would be for a duration of two weeks, the catering being provided by the manufacturers at

CHAPTER SEVENTEEN

Vickers. The 1st lieutenant decided that I shouldn't be idle in Barrow, and sent me on a temporary draft to *H.M.S. Pembroke* to do a refresher course at the cookery school.

I was given a weekend leave before I had to report to *Pembroke*. I loaded up my car with my kit with the addition of a small Mobo Rocking Horse that my landlady in Barrow had kindly given me for Alan; her children had grown out of it.

I loaded up my little Morris Eight, including the rocking horse, and I set off on the first part of my journey to Chatham.

My first stop would be Oxford (or so I thought) because I had been given a long weekend leave on my way.

I made my way through Ulverston, where Stan Laurel of the famous Laurel & Hardy duo came from; I was making my way to the newly opened M6 motorway. Travelling on the M6 close to Warrington, a nasty knocking sound could be heard coming from the engine. I checked the car's gauges and the oil pressure gauge was reading zero! I was lucky that a layby was just ahead of me. My old car gave me enough power to drive into it but it was failing fast.

Fortunately the layby was provided with an AA emergency telephone box. I made a call and explained my predicament, and within a half hour a tow truck arrived. I explained to the driver what had happened; after checking the car out he confirmed my worst suspicions—the oil pump had packed up and the main bearings were shot.

CHAPTER SEVENTEEN

After securing the car to the tow truck the driver asked where I would like to be dropped off. I replied that I should go to a local police station, and he obliged. On arrival the driver accompanied me to the reception desk; the duty sergeant looked at me: I was standing there in uniform, with a pusser's suitcase in one hand and a rocking horse in the other! The driver explained my predicament to the sergeant.

A phone call was made to the duty Superintendent, who came to the desk. I explained to him what had happened to my car; this was confirmed by the tow truck driver.

I could not be in better hands. The first words from the Superintendent were, "Have you eaten?" My reply was, "Not for a while." He turned to the sergeant and instructed him to take me to the station canteen, assuring me that he would take care of my travel arrangements.

He was as good as his word. After being provided with a substantial meal he gave me a tour of the police station, which was very impressive; one of the three-minute warning systems was installed that was connected to Fylingdales in Yorkshire, the U.K. early warning system designed to alert us of an incoming ballistic missile from the Eastern Bloc.

I was issued with a railway warrant that would take care of my travel arrangements. The train I would catch was due in Warrington at 2300hrs; this was the overnight train from Edinburgh to London. I would have to change trains in Birmingham.

CHAPTER SEVENTEEN

It was time to leave. The Superintendent called for his car, and his driver took my suitcase and rocking horse and put them in the trunk. The Superintendent explained that he had to check with his beat officers on the way to the station, assuring me that I would be in time to catch my train.

As the car approached a beat officer would appear as out of nowhere; information was passed between the police officers and the Superintendent; the good people of Warrington could sleep in peace and be assured that their safety was in good hands! I thank the Warrington police force, especially the Superintendent and his men for the help and hospitality afforded me in a time of need, not forgetting the tow truck driver.

CHAPTER EIGHTEEN

ARRIVING IN OXFORD with my suitcase and rocking horse, I got a taxi to take me to my address in Marston Road. The taxi driver was Jackie Nichols; later in my *MISHMASH OF LIFE* I would be living next to his daughter, Hilda! Bette and I would become good friends and neighbours with her and her family.

As for now, Bette and I had an enjoyable weekend and got a lot of pleasure watching Alan playing on his rocking horse; he was of an age where he was in the stage of romping and not walking.

My weekend leave came to an end and goodbyes had to be made which were always difficult.

However, duty called. Arriving in Chatham, I made my way to Pembroke Barracks. So much had happened in my life in the six years when I was first drafted to *H.M.S. Pembroke* as a raw recruit.

I carried out the usual joining routine and was allocated a mess, and informed to report to the cookery school at 0830hrs on the following morning. After stowing my kit in my locker, I took in my surroundings;

they hadn't changed much from the last time I was there.

It was early evening and I decided to go to the N.A.A.F.I. for a pint. On arrival I was met with a sight for sore eyes: a bunch of submariners were sitting around a couple of tables they had put together. Soapy Whatson was one of them along with a couple of other lads that I had served with in Canada; they called me over to join them and greeted me like a long lost brother.

They were part of the crew being put together for the *Ocelot*, a new submarine being built in Chatham dockyard, not far from Nelson's *H.M.S. Victory* that had been built in the same dockyard in 1705.

Because of the *Ocelot* being built in Chatham, the lads were billeted in Pembroke Barracks, not like us with the *Osiris* being built by Vickers Armstrong in Barrow where we were billeted with the civilian population.

After a few beers and talking over old times we got into a bit of revelry; barefoot daisy came into play and one of the lads climbed onto the bar counter top with rolled-up trousers and no shoes or socks and did his dance routine along the bar with us pouring the ritual beer over his feet! When he slipped and fell we were there to catch him.

It got time for the bar to close and Soapy said to me, "What mess are you in?" I said, "I'm bunked up in a general service mess." He replied, "Not anymore you're not! We're going to give you a mess change!" Under Soapy's direction the lads descended on my bunk space,

CHAPTER EIGHTEEN

emptied my locker, stripped my bedding and transported everything to their mess! I was back in the company of fellow compatriots.

I was tired and turned into my bunk while the rest of the lads continued with their revelry; some alcoholic beverage had found its way into the mess.

It was way past lights out. Barrack routine orders were always strictly enforced; being submariners, this was something that faded from memory! The revelry continued until the Master at Arms and his Regulating patrol arrived and put a stop to the fun.

In the next mess to ours were some of the *Royal Yacht's* crew who were on a course of some kind; they were upset that our lads had continued to be a bit boisterous after lights out when little boys should be tucked abed. (What a shame!) Submariners are not little boys; indeed, our life was very different from anything close to normal.

Unfortunately Soapy and a bunch of the lads were put on Captain's report; charges were read out and the Captain's comments were not very well received by the submarine fraternity, he being a general service captain. He started his deliberations by saying that the submarine service used to be the cream of the service, but intimated that the cream appeared to have gone sour! The punishment meted out was extreme and harsh. Soapy lost his leading hand rank while other lads were stripped of their good conduct badges; this was caused by some pompous arse that wore the *Royal Yacht Britannia* cap tally.

CHAPTER EIGHTEEN

Needless to say, the *Royal Yacht* crew were warned not to walk alone at night for fear of reprisals.

Submariners were not in the habit of carrying out reprisals on inferior members of her Majesty's Navy. The *Royal Yacht* crew had nothing to fear.

As for me, I reported as ordered to the cookery school. The officer in charge was a bit perplexed as to why I was there. I explained the reason and his response was, "How long will you be here for?" (This gave me an opportunity to pull a flanker.) I said, "A week." He said, "Very well, I will put you in the bakery training department." I had no objections.

The instructor was an ex-submariner and we got on well together. I became an assistant instructor, helping the young recruits in their endeavours to become cooks in Her Majesty's Royal Navy.

I had fiddled an extra week's leave and went back to Oxford to spend some more time with Bette and our baby son.

Back in Barrow, *Osiris* was being prepared for commissioning. This would be on Friday the 13th, which was somewhat unique, as she was launched on the 13th and her number was S 13. A special tie was commissioned to celebrate this event.

On commissioning day, the ceremony would be attended by Barrow's civic dignitaries, the host families that had accommodated us, and any family and friends of the crew that could attend. (Bette was unable to.) The

CHAPTER EIGHTEEN

Bishop of the Barrow Diocese would perform the blessing of the boat. I was detailed to meet him at the dockyard gates and escort him to where *Osiris* was berthed.

Prayers were said and the Naval Hymn ('For those in peril on the sea') was sung; some of our guests became a little emotional, especially our host families that we had become attached to and them to us.

It came to the moment for the Captain to address his crew. Lieutenant Commander Fry was our skipper.

After giving thanks to the boat's builders and to our host families, he got down to business. He started off by saying that the average age of the crew was 21years old. He continued, saying that being the captain "the buck stops with me. If I have a bad crew, I have bad officers; if I have bad officers, it will be my fault. I will not tolerate bad officers or crew." I warmed to him; this was a man that I would respect.

With him and Todd Slaughter as the 1st Lieutenant, I felt comfortable; if ever there were a couple of pirates these would be it. My faith would be proved right.

Submariners, being who we were, nicknamed our Captain 'Sammy Fry and his little fishes'.

After the commissioning ceremony, a dance and buffet had been arranged for the crew and our host families; this was a farewell to the many people who had shared their homes with us.

Barrow was a friendly town and we left it with many happy memories; now came the time for our shake down trials.

CHAPTER EIGHTEEN

This was the period where the Captain had to mould his crew into an efficient cohesive force, from his officers down to lowly me; we would be put through a rigorous training procedure. Many of the lads were not long out of the submarine training school at *Dolphin*; it was up to the more experienced members of the crew to help them accomplish a high degree of efficiency.

Not only the crew were being tested—the boat also had to perform to our Captain's standards. Sammy was ruthless in his demands on the boat and his crew. At 02.00hrs emergency stations were called and we were out of our bunks like a shot! I was down in the battery tank compartment shutting the sluice valves designed to protect the batteries from the ingress of salt water that could turn into phosgene gas if it got into the battery acid; as a cook on a submarine, you may have a ladle in one hand and a wheel spanner in the other!

Deep dives had to be carried out. The Kyles and Lochs of Scotland were perfect for this exercise. *Osiris* had been going through a number of trials in the North Western Atlantic. We were due to carry out a deep dive when it was noticed that a chunk of our casing around the base of the fin was flapping around. (This was made of fibreglass.) Before the dive the Engineer Officer, Lieutenant Baines, and the Chief Stoker, Ernie, were on the casing with a large saw cutting away the flapping damaged piece of the boat's structure; when cut off it was discarded to Davy Jones' Locker. (Dumped overboard!)

CHAPTER EIGHTEEN

The deep dive went ahead without the full casing. The skipper wanted a steep bow down angle at full speed, the crew were at their respective diving stations. This was not a normal dive; we would descend in a spiral; this was like a coiled bedspring, going down not to a bedframe but to the bottom of one of Scotland's Kyles.

The dive was becoming dangerous. The angle of the dive went to 28-plus degrees when the fore and after planesmen reported losing the bubble on their inclinometers. I was sitting in the galley sink bracing myself with my feet against a bulkhead; one of the lads lost his footing and had no option than to run downwards and finished up with his feet stopping his momentum by running up the fore ends bulkhead.

Sammy with his usual aplomb got the boat steadied and gently got *Osiris* sitting on the bottom of the Kyle.

What had happened was that the after planes were overtaking the fore planes. This meant that the boat was in danger of doing a loop the loop; that's okay for an aircraft, but for a submarine in high density water, it was not a good thing to be happening.

After sitting on the bottom for a short period while we checked for leaks, *Osiris* gently lifted off the bottom. Sammy had not finished with us; he ordered main motors full ahead and ordered the cox'n to steer on a reverse spiral back to the surface.

Because of the damaged casing, *Osiris* was ordered back to Faslane. *H.M.S. Maidstone* was the resident submarine depot ship; we had a replacement part for

CHAPTER EIGHTEEN

our casing being transported to us from Chatham Dockyard; it was taken from the *Ojibwa* that was under construction for the Canadian Navy; being an Oberon class boat it was a perfect fit.

Our work up trials included exercising in the North Western approaches. For a while we operated out of Londonderry. *H.M.S. Stalker* was a decommissioned World War Two L.S.T. (landing ship tank) that acted as an accommodation ship for submarines; it was manned by civilians who provided the catering arrangements, etc.

Because of the rip tides that forced their way down the Foyle we were not allowed to cross the gangway onto the boat after dark in case we fell in after imbibing a few pints of Porter when ashore.

Stalker would supply overnight accommodation. This was very sparse; a bunk and a mattress was all that was supplied.

I had been ashore and returned to *Osiris*. My mate Alex was trot sentry. As I approached the gangplank, he said, "Hang on, Chef, you can't come on board, it's too late; you'll have to kip on the *Stalker*." I didn't want to give him a hard time so I went to the *Stalker* where I found an empty broadside mess with a bunk, and I climbed onto it. (I wish I hadn't!)

I woke up with a mouth feeling like a lavatory brush. After swilling my mouth with a couple of glasses of water and having breakfast, I made my way back to the *Osiris*. A couple of hours later I started to itch in the scrotum area of my body. I stripped down to my socks and carried out a self-examination of my pubic area. I noticed these minute little black things! Oh shit, I had been invaded by what was commonly known in the Navy as crabs (pubic lice). I stripped off and shaved myself in the affected region; fortunately I knew a Petty Officer sick bay attendant on one of the Frigates that was tied up alongside; he was able to give me some A.L. 63 (commonly known as DDT powder). I dusted myself with it and it worked! I vowed that I would never spend another night on the *Stalker*.

On one occasion the I.R.A. decided to pay us a visit. It was a dark murky night and they drove by in a fast car taking pot shots at the boat. Although the trot sentry was armed with a Sten gun, he didn't have an ammunition clip; this could only be issued by the officer of the watch. Fortunately nobody was hurt during the raid and no damage was done to the boat.

It was time to leave Londonderry. We made our way into the Atlantic and headed to the West coast of Scotland, carrying out various exercises on the way; because of the adverse angle of the boat when we carried out our first deep dive, strap hangers (similar to the ones on London tube trains and busses) had been fitted to the bulkhead. *Osiris* eventually returned to Faslane.

Captain Fry was doing a good job getting his crew into a cohesive and efficient body of men. He had gained respect from the lower deck, especially on one occasion when, in the middle of the night, he called for emergency stations; with stopwatch in hand, he timed us as we got to our positions. A couple of Officers were not quick enough in his expectations of them and he let them know it!

Our running up and shake down trials were in their final stages; we had been at sea for two weeks and pulled into Campbeltown to collect mail; we were anchored offshore and a boat appeared bringing our mail to us.

The 1st Lieutenant asked the skipper of the boat that had delivered our mail if he could provide his boat and crew to give us a run ashore; the skipper was hesitant in his reply and from out of nowhere a bottle of brandy appeared.

The bribe worked! Shore leave was granted to those of us off watch, and my only problem was that I didn't have a uniform with me—the reason being that it was thought that no shore leave would be given on this trip.

Fortunately one of the lads on duty watch offered to lend me his. He was a sparks and about the same size as me. I went ashore that evening as a signalman; the 1st Lieutenant also joined us—probably to make sure that we all returned to catch the boat back!

The first stop was the nearest pub. By the time we arrived it was about 6.30 p.m. In those days the rural pubs used to shut at 9 o'clock. However, word travels fast and the village hall was opened up to accommodate us and to put on an impromptu dance.

Parked outside the pub was a milk float. The driver was inside. Annie, the driver and local milk maid, was a

CHAPTER EIGHTEEN

good sport and joined in our revelries! When it was time for the pub to shut, we bought a load of bottled beer to take with us to the village hall. We climbed onto the milk float that became a beer float, and off we went to the village hall. Some of the local girls had come along to join in the fun.

A rather large lady was in charge of putting on the music which came from an ancient Danset record player. Scottish reels like The Gay Gordon was popular with the local lassies; we were very grateful to the people of Campbeltown for their hospitality and tolerance.

At some time during the evening I found I was missing my watch. I was on my hands and knees looking under chairs for it. Todd (the 1st Lieutenant) saw me and said, "What the hell are you at, chef?" I replied that I was looking for my watch. He then got the music stopped and ordered everyone to look for my watch! After two minutes the music started up and everyone continued with the dance.

Annie was unable to stay to the end of the dance as she had to tend to her dairy duties that would commence very early in the morning.

I was still minus my watch. Anyway, all good things come to an end and it was time to get to the jetty to catch the boat back to *Osiris*.

My mate Rubberwasp has rubber legs; he fell down in a heap and I managed to pick him up. I got him over my shoulder and carried him to the jetty. Unfortunately he decided to empty the contents of his digestive system

CHAPTER EIGHTEEN

down my back! I was worried as to what the sparks would have to say about the mess his uniform was in.

The following morning our commandeered liberty boat paid us a visit, delivering a churn of fresh milk. Taped to the lid was my watch with a note from Annie, explaining that she had found it on the floor of her milk float! I was very grateful for her generosity in providing us with fresh milk and her honesty and integrity for returning my watch.

As for the soiled uniform, I presented it to Rubberwasp. (Being a Steward he knew how to get things cleaned!) It was returned to its rightful owner in pristine condition.

Osiris was now very close to completing her trials. The next and final stage would be F.O.S.M.S. inspection (Flag Officer Submarines), so the boat returned to Faslane.

CHAPTER NINETEEN

MARRIED QUARTERS were available in Faslane. I put in an application for one and I was informed by the accommodation Officer that none were available; however, he said that my name would be added to the list. In any case I was able to find accommodation for Bette and Alan. This was a holiday caravan in a family's back garden in a village close to the base. The name of the village was Rhu Ellen. Helensburgh was the closest town.

This accommodation, although a bit cramped, was better than what Bette had to contend with when living in Oxford. She had to endure some harsh situations. Because the accommodation was below the standard required by the Navy it didn't qualify for any subsistence living ashore allowance. Unfortunately it was the only rental property available at the time. Nevertheless, we coped.

It was made clear to us that the caravan was being let out to holidaymakers that had been booked in for the end of July. I had hoped that by then I would have been allocated a married quarter, but I was wrong.

CHAPTER NINETEEN

The time was approaching for us to leave the caravan and the owners were very good to us and found alternative accommodation further down the street. This was one room in a large house; the lady who owned the house had a son serving on *H.M.S. Maidstone*, our depot ship; again, one room in a house didn't qualify for any funds from the Navy.

During this time *Osiris* was preparing to become a fully operational submarine. This is a time of great concentration: all sailors have to deal with the task ahead. Domestic situations take a back seat out of necessity for the safety of the boat and crew.

F.O.S.M.S. inspection was very thorough. The boat was stretched to its limits. Although the deep dive wasn't angled to the twenty-eight degree bow down angle that we had experienced during our running up trials, we cut that in half; even this brought a mild rebuke from F.O.S.M. to the Skipper, who said, "Captain Fry, you are not the only one on this submarine—you have to consider your crew." Every department got the eagle eye from the Admiral's staff. We were put into every conceivable situation imaginable, passive and active; however, at the end of the inspection we were given a good report and became a fully operational submarine.

Bette and I had been married for close to eighteen months by this time. During this period we had spent something like three months together, split between weekend leave and the odd week's leave. Living close to the base, we were together more than we had been in our married life.

Being an operational boat, *Osiris* had to earn her keep. Exercises had to be performed to maintain readiness in the event of an international crisis. Crew performance was always intense during these times; however, we did have some lighter moments.

One of the lads wanted to get married. His name was Alex and came from Bishop's Stortford. Unfortunately his local vicar refused to carry out the wedding ceremony, the reason being that he hadn't been christened. We were having a chat about it when I came upon an idea! I suggested that he could get christened in the base Chapel. The sin bo's'n (Padre) was a good chap and had gone to sea with us a couple of times, and I volunteered for Bette and me to be the Godparents.

We approached the Padre and Alex explained his predicament. The Padre was very sympathetic and agreed to perform the Christening.

Come the Sunday morning service, Alex, Bette, me and baby Alan were in attendance along with a few lads from the boat to give support. The regulars were a bit surprised to see such a large congregation. (The Padre was used to a fluctuation in the number of his flock that could attend his mattings; sometimes most of them would be at sea.)

However, after his sermon he pronounced that a christening was to take place and the congregation were invited to remain to witness it; pointing to Alan, he went on to say, "You may think that this little child is the one to be christened, but this is not so!"

Alex, Bette and I were called up to the font. (This was a ship's bell turned upside down, held in a wooden cradle.) A lady in the congregation had taken care of Alan for the duration of the ceremony. Alex was duly christened, and Bette and I had become his Godparents.

Living in one room of a house, our resources were limited when it came to having a celebratory meal. We managed to put together a couple of Vesta Curries. Alex was grateful for our efforts; we were happy that he now had the documentation required by his local vicar for him to marry his beloved fiancée.

Alex was also the captain of the boat's football team. A match had been arranged against a local team. It was a Sunday morning. The night before there had been a hard frost. The pitch started to thaw out and was becoming a bit squishy; under the turf was a thin layer of shale that was as sharp as a razor! I was playing in midfield. The game had been an even match, and was a three-three draw at half time.

Early in the second half the opposition made an all-out attack on our goal. Foxy our goalkeeper came off his line to narrow the angle of the anticipated shot and he slipped on the slick surface of the pitch; fortunately he was able to slow the ball's momentum, but it was now out of his control and heading towards the goal. I

CHAPTER NINETEEN

took off running and caught up with the ball and was able to give it a back heel. I saved the ball from going into the net, but lost my balance and skidded along on my knees. The sharp shale lacerated the skin! The game came to an end; we had won the game by a narrow margin, four to three.

I needed attention to my lacerated knees. Our depot ship *Maidstone* had gone to sea, but there was a First Aid caravan positioned on the base, manned by a sick berth attendant. I went to it to get a bit of First Aid. The sick bay tiffy was unsympathetic, though he cleaned away the mud and then poured iodine into the wounds on both knees. It stung like hell! He applied a couple of dressings and sent me on my way.

I went home for a while to get my kit together. *Osiris* was about to leave in the late afternoon for a two-week patrol, so I bade Bette and Alan farewell and caught the bus back to the base. The bus stop was at the bottom of the road.

During the trip the cox'n dressed the wounds to my knees, giving me hydrogen peroxide to dab onto them and a bandage to stop the blood and other body fluids from seeping into my trousers. (In those days the 1st Lieutenant and cox'n were responsible for the boat's crew's medical care; they had in fact undergone a very extensive First Aid training course.)

A submarine is not very conducive to assist in a wound's healing process, the lack of fresh air being one of the problems; however, the cox'n did his very best in

CHAPTER NINETEEN

helping to keep my injured knees from becoming further infected.

On returning to Faslane we found the *Maidstone* was tied up in her usual berth, her sea time completed. The cox'n instructed me to go to the *Maidstone*'s sick bay to get treatment for my knees.

I carried out his instructions, reporting to the sick bay. I was met by an acquaintance of mine, who was now a Petty Officer. (We had first met at *H.M.S. Dryad* when he was a leading sick berth attendant.)

After having a brief chat about where our career paths had taken us, he asked what my medical problem was. I explained about my knees and how they had come to be in such a state. He instructed me to sit down and roll up my trousers to expose my knees, and the bandages were delicately removed.

He proceeded to press in my groin and under my armpits. His next remarks got me a bit worried; he said, "Sit there and don't move, I'm going to get the MO." Within a few minutes the Doc arrived and checked out my knees. The skin around the knee caps was a whitish grey colour. He proceeded to check my groin and other parts of my anatomy. After the examination, he said, "I want you to sit still; your body is in the last line of resistance." A cot was prepared in the ship's sick bay ward. I was turned in, and the treatment started: I was given a number of injections of various concoctions, the Doc reassuring me that he would do his best to save my legs!

It was suspected that my knees were being infected

CHAPTER NINETEEN

with Gangrene. Fortunately for me the treatment worked. I spent several days in the sick bay, and then had to follow up with a series of penicillin injections.

When I re-joined the boat, she had been moved to a floating dock in Gareloch Head for degaussing. When this was completed, she was returned to the Loch and tied up alongside the A.F.D. (Admiralty Floating Dock). She needed a lick of paint. I became part of the 2nd coxn's painting crew.

I was painting the fin from the top down, using what was called a long tom. This was a paint roller attached to a broom handle. When you had painted as far as you could from the top of the fin you would then go onto the casing to paint the lower half. An old dinghy was supplied to the crew to scull around in to paint the hull down to the waterline. The dinghy looked like a kaleidoscope caused by the many colours of paint that had splashed over it during its many years of service! The encrusted paint was thicker than the wood it was built of.

My encounter with it came when I was reaching over from the top of the fin when my long tom slipped out of my hands; it bounced off the fin, onto the casing and finished up in the Loch. I climbed down the ladder as fast as I could, got onto the casing and jumped into the dinghy; untying the securing rope, I pushed off to retrieve my long tom that was floating down the Loch. I had a problem: there were no oars! I was adrift in Gareloch in a dinghy with no oars trying to retrieve a long tom paint roller.

CHAPTER NINETEEN

I used my hands as paddles and managed to catch up with the long tom. Grabbing hold of it, I was able to use it as an oar to propel me back to the boat. On arrival I was met by the Jimmy. He had a grin on his face. His remark was, "Burgess, I don't know whether to charge you with abandoning ship without permission or to recommend you for retrieving Admiralty property!" This was typical of Todd Slaughter, my 1st Lieutenant who, as I have previously stated, was among one of the best officers I had ever served under.

After degaussing and the painting was completed, *Osiris* returned to our Faslane base. Shore leave was granted and I was able to have some time with Bette and Alan. We made the best of the time we had together.

Sunday morning came around and it was time to say goodbye to Bette and our baby son. The Captain had received his orders for *Osiris* to carry out an operational duty that would be a period of up to three months.

I walked away from our one-room home in School Road and waited at the bus stop for the bus to take me to the base.

I was dressed in uniform. This I would change out of on the depot ship. (We had lockers allocated for this.) Standing at the bus stop I felt despondent at leaving my wife and child with tears in their eyes; parting was always difficult. I am sure I was not alone on this emotional seesaw; all service families had to cope with the departures in their own way.

I was aware that a so-called peace camp promoted by

CHAPTER NINETEEN

the C.N.D. was established near Shaldon. On this particular Sunday the so-called peace marchers decided to march on the Faslane submarine base. I was an obvious target, waiting for the bus to come, standing waiting in my uniform! The mob with banners flying and chanting in their well-practiced vehement epithets, they proceeded to spit on me and give me the odd elbow in the ribs as they marched along on their supposed peace march to take care of all mankind. (I wondered what would have happened to them if they did the same thing in Russia!) Of cause Monsignor Kent, the leader of the C.N.D. in Britain who condoned the behaviour of these thugs, would offer up some lame excuse to the general public that he didn't condone this type of action.

As for me, I stood my ground and accepted what had happened to me as part of the job. We had been instructed not to react in these situations. I found consolation in that the job I was doing was giving the freedom for these misguided morons to carry out their vitriolic actions.

After going onto the *Maidstone* and cleaning up from the spittle that had been ejected onto me, I changed out of my uniform into the gear that I would be wearing for most of the trip; like the other lads, the essentials were put into our steaming bags: a bar of soap, toothpaste and brush, a change of underwear, and a few other things to try and make life bearable during the trip.

We went to harbour stations and the boat was let slip from the jetty, sailing out of Gareloch on a surface

CHAPTER NINETEEN

passage into the Clyde and gently passing Great Cumbrae Island, then Little Cumbrae, Arran, and the Isle of Mull; reaching the North Western approaches and well out of sight of land, we carried out our trim dive; after surfacing we maintained a surface passage until nightfall.

The order for diving stations was given. The crew responded and I reported the master blows shut. The handle to the Kingston tanks had been removed as these were used as extra fuel tanks. We would not surface or breathe fresh air for the duration of the trip.

This was a secret mission. Our S13 identity number that was usually emblazoned on the fin had been painted out. We were on our own and travelling incognito. After the boat had settled down and the course set, the Skipper made an announcement over the tannoy; he gave a brief outline of what task we had been commissioned to carry out, and emphasized that we all had a part to play in the success of the operation.

One of the duties of my mate Rubberwasp was to ditch the gash. This was done at night when the boat was snorting. The slop tanks would also be blown during this time—done by one of the engine room lads. We always knew when the slop tanks were blown, for a very obnoxious smell would find its way into the boat when the tanks were vented inboard. Deodorizers were installed but they were not very efficient.

When the order to 'ditch gash' was given each mess would bring the bags of gash to the gash ejector, each

CHAPTER NINETEEN

bag being weighted from the crushed cans that I had used the contents of in the days meals. The telemotor operated can crusher was installed in the galley; it was very important to weight the bags, for any floating to the surface could give the boat's position away to an enemy ship that might be looking for us.

Rubberwasp was very diligent in his duties. Unfortunately, he encountered a problem with the gash ejector; a bag had got hung up on the hull valve; consequently it couldn't be shut. The intermediate valve and lid could be secured, but with the hull valve not operable meant that the gash that accumulated would have to remain in the boat.

We would have to live with the problem, although my mate Geordie who had the job as tanky was a qualified shallow water diver. (By shallow water I mean that he was certificated to dive to a depth of 30ft.) We approached the 1st Lieutenant, and put forward a proposition. I was the spokesman, and I said, "Sir, in view of the problem with the gash bag, Geordie and I volunteer to go over the side to release the bag." With his usual grin he said, "How do you propose to do it?" My reply was, "If we could surface and put a rope over the side we could put on a load of clothing and a couple of breathing sets; after a tot of rum, we would go over the side using the rope to release the bag."

His response was, "You're a couple of brave bastards! Look at the water temperature—you wouldn't last two minutes. Besides, we're under orders not to surface

CHAPTER NINETEEN

under any circumstances until our operation is completed."

Living conditions on a submarine are not the best in normal conditions, and now we had to accommodate the gradual accumulation of everyday gash. It was decided to stow it in the forward torpedo space, tucking each bag daily between the torpedo tubes, keeping them as far away as possible from the living accommodation; nevertheless, the smell would gradually permeate throughout the boat, and we got used to it.

Because of the duration of our trip, fresh water was strictly limited. *Osiris* could distil 30 gallons of sea water per hour, only when on the surface or when snorting; the crew were limited to 1 inch of water per day for personal ablutions such as brushing your teeth and basic washing of your face to freshen up; we slept in the clothes we stood up in, the only luxury being to take your shoes or boots off before climbing into your bunk. Nobody was able to know when diving or emergency stations could be called; we always had to be ready to respond to any event, to save the boat and ourselves.

A leading cook had been drafted to us; he was a Scots lad who got nicknamed Galley Boots. Because of the duration of our operation, the cox'n split us into two shifts. I would be responsible for bread baking and breakfast, and would be required to work through the night and early morning. Galley Boots would be responsible for providing dinner and supper. I had no problem with this arrangement as I was a bit nocturnal.

CHAPTER NINETEEN

It was very rare for a cook to receive an accolade. I only had two that made me feel very humble. One was from the lads on the *Alderney* when I made my version of turkey stuffing during our journey from Canada back to England; the other was on this trip. When the Captain summoned me into the control room, my first thoughts were that I was in trouble. The Captain said, "Chef, my wife has had me on a diet of which bread was severely restricted. I have now broken my diet; the bread you have baked is excellent! Keep up the good work."

Being a cook on a submarine had many challenges. We had tinned food products that had been canned in 1933; these cans had the date stamped on them along with distinctive arrows, not unlike the ones printed on prisoners' suits from bygone years.

Sometimes when the boat had been dived for a long period running on battery power, it became difficult to get the temperature of the galley range and ovens to a level required to cook the meat and vegetables; this delayed the service to the crew, who could get frustrated as each watch was on a strict routine to relieve each other; nevertheless we did the best we could with what we had.

On these extended trips, keeping the crew occupied during the off-duty hours was a challenge for the Skipper. Fortunately for us, Captain Fry was very creative; besides the film shows that we watched over and over again, at least when the projector worked, he set up a brains trust activity that was designed to involve

CHAPTER NINETEEN

all departments throughout the boat; the wardroom was the venue. (Being invited into officer country was a privilege.) The format was a general knowledge quiz. I survived a few rounds but got knocked out by the Jimmy who went on to win the contest. I forgot to mention that the Skipper was the quizmaster.

When we were forced into the ultra-quiet routine, when all off-duty men had to take up residence in their bunks, reading books became the overriding preoccupation. As for me, I got into the James Bond books by Ian Flemming: *Casino Royall*, *Gold Finger* and so on; when finished, we would swap books with each other, and somehow I ended up with *Lady Chatterley's Lover*.

On a couple of occasions the Captain decided we were in need of some spiritual guidance, and a Sunday church service was arranged in the fore end torpedo space. I got nominated to read the lesson.

I read the words from the good book. Looking around me, taking in my surroundings among racks loaded with torpedoes that could wreak havoc on humanity, and being aware of the putrid smell emitting from the gash bags that were stowed between the torpedo tubes, I prayed that the good Lord would have mercy on us.

Another activity came into play. One afternoon the 1st Lieutenant gathered the off-duty watch into the fore ends, and we stood around (there was nothing to sit on), wondering what this was going to be about; we were soon enlightened: it was to be given the opportunity to

CHAPTER NINETEEN

give a talk on a given subject. It could be one of your own choosing or one delegated by the Jimmy.

My Godson Alex started off by choosing his own subject. Coming from a family of pig farmers, he gave a talk on pig rearing, expanding on the different breeds, such as Whites, Saddlebacks, Berkshires, and so on. As for me, the Jimmy chose the subject that I was to talk about, which was to enlighten people about what to look for when buying a second-hand car!

I started off by explaining the basics, checking the obvious, body, paint and interior condition, moving on to inspecting the tailpipe of the exhaust system; any excessive build-up of oily soot could indicate an engine problem; when the engine was started, listen for any knocks or clattering noises; go for a test drive and change gears frequently to make sure that the gears were smooth and that there was no clutch slip; make sure that the gauges were working showing no indication of low or high oil pressure, or any signs of overheating indicated by the temperature gauge; take a ride sitting in the back seat and listen for any grinding noise coming from the rear axle and differential; on a straight road, let go of the steering wheel to check that the steering geometry was correct. (If the car remained in a straight line it was correct; if the steering was sloppy the car would wander off course.) Brakes were important and had to be tested, not only the footbrake but also the handbrake; tyres would also be needed to be inspected to make sure that adequate tread was on them to give good traction and that no splits or cuts were visible. After the test drive when the engine was warm, lift the bonnet and check for any oil or water leaks, from gaskets or hoses; lights and indicators had to be in good working order. I finished my talk and was complimented by the Jimmy, although he had the last comment by saying "if any of you buy a car, be careful where you park—you may get a parking ticket, especially if it's outside the Dreadnought bar in Barrow!" With this comment my face came over with a red blush! I had a feeling that he knew it was me that had got him a parking ticket in Barrow.

We had a couple of other bits of equipment to use if we wanted to; one was a rowing machine, which was set up in the torpedo space; the other was a sun ray lamp.

Galley Boots, the silly sod, fell asleep when he was using it and got a blistered forehead and cheeks; he looked like Beetroot Head from the Worzel Gummidge stories, and this was not the only mishap that he would be subject to.

The boat was snorting and the slop tanks had been blown; unfortunately they had not vented properly, consequently leaving them with a slight pressure. Galley Boots went to the heads to do the necessary, and on completion he got hold of the salt water hose to flush his unmentionables into the tank; with water flowing, he operated the flap valve on the toilet, and there was a gush of vented air that had been trapped in the tank—and what he had deposited in the toilet came back along

CHAPTER NINETEEN

with some other excrement! Poor bugger, he was covered in shit! We were already stinking from the gash that we were unable to get rid of, and this only added to it.

As stated, we were operating in an area that was inhospitable to us. A destroyer from an unfriendly nation had picked us up on their detection devices, and we went deep and found a layer to hide under. (A layer is a variation in the density of sea water.) This can give a false reading to surface ships trying to locate submarines; we would be held in this position for a number of days.

Being unable to snort, the batteries were losing power and trying to feed the crew was becoming difficult as the galley range could not be brought up to a sufficient temperature to cook the food that was required.

We did manage, but all meals were cooked low and slow; ultra-quiet routine was put into operation, and the air was getting very thin, so breathing was becoming difficult. The CO2 concentration in the boat was getting to a dangerous level, and the Skipper ordered the CO2 absorption unit and oxygen generator to be operated; this eased our breathing problems. Because of our predicament, radio silence was enforced, and *Osiris* was unable to transmit her routine messages; because of this, a sub miss alert had been issued.

Fortunately for us, the offending ship gave up

CHAPTER NINETEEN

looking for us and sailed away, and we continued on our mission.

On completion, *Osiris* made her way back to friendlier waters, surfacing somewhere off Norway. A blast of fresh air came into the boat when the upper lid of the fin was opened. The first thing was to ditch the bags of gash and their putrid contents overboard; thereafter we made a surface passage back to Faslane.

Before leave was granted, the Captain thanked us for our dedication to duty under difficult circumstances; he then went on to emphasize that we had been on a secret mission and that if he heard any whisper of what we had been about he would have Naval Intelligence and the special investigations branch on us like a ton of bricks. We got the message.

The majority of the crew were given permission to go onto the depot ship, *H.M.S. Maidstone* to get cleaned up. Having a shower was a luxury that we had been denied for the past two to three months! Trying to get rid of the accumulated noxious smell that had impregnated our bodies, we used a lot of soap and water, aftershave lotion and phoo-phoo powder, to mask the underlying body odour; this helped, but it would take a few days of being in the fresh air before we would return to normality.

Submariners could always be recognized by the pale and sallow colour of their skin, except for Galley Boots who was still nursing his sunburnt face from his over-exposure to the sun ray lamp.

CHAPTER NINETEEN

I have explained many situations that occurred during this trip. There were a couple that also come to mind; one is that when dived deep, and life was becoming difficult, a whale decided to try and make love to us! This would be hilarious if a submarine and its crew became a father to a whale! Another incident happened when there was a pressure in the boat; one of the lads was in the process of opening a bottle of Heinz Tomato Ketchup, and when the cap was released the bottle exploded and the bottom of the bottle blew out. His lap was covered in ketchup and shards of glass; with the tomato ketchup all over his lap, it was difficult to ascertain if his blood was mixed in with it! Fortunately it wasn't; we got him cleaned up, and no skin penetration was found in his nether regions.

I digress. After getting cleaned up I went to School Road in Rhu. I entered the house and Bette and our baby weren't there. The lady of the house informed me that Bette had gone to visit her mother and family in Cowdenbeath. I was able to get a few days leave and made my way to Cowdenbeath.

Bette was having a difficult time; living in other people's homes was not a very good way to live.

We returned to Rhu and made the best of what we had. I made enquiries as to when a married quarter would become available; unfortunately I was informed that it would be some time.

When I had left the boat to go to Cowdenbeath, a

CHAPTER NINETEEN

situation had occurred involving a few of the crew.

It was a ritual in the Chief and Petty Officers' mess that they would bottle part of the rum issue. I was privileged to be included in this as my tot was included in their daily ration. This was neat rum, and not diluted to the one-to-one ratio being one part rum and one part water for the mess decks. On arrival back at base the bottled rum would be opened and shared between the mess members that had remained on board.

After the trip the boat had to be de-stored; this included all perishable goods such as frozen meat and other victuals that would be returned to the Naval stores depot.

Unfortunately some of these stores found their way into the boot of the Chief E.R.A.'s car; he was Canadian and had a very distinctive vehicle—a red-painted American built Ford Fairlane; there were not many if any of these cars being driven on the roads of Scotland.

After having a good few tots of rum from the mess bottle, the silly sods, instead of going home to their families and married quarters, decided to go into Helensburgh to continue their revelry.

On the return journey home an accident occurred. A little Austin Seven got in the way of the big Ford Fairlane, and caused a collision.

The local police attended to sort out the mess, but because Navy personnel were involved in the incident, Naval authorities were called. On arrival they noticed a strong smell of rum emitting from the breath of the

CHAPTER NINETEEN

Navy contingent. The Provost Marshal's staff who attended ordered the boot of the Ford to be opened for inspection. (Apparently there had been suspicions of a rum racket taking place from the base.) No rum was found, but the misappropriated meat and other edible stores from *Osiris* were.

Navy discipline can be harsh; the Captain is all powerful in administering it in accordance with the Admiralty's code of conduct.

Punishment was meted out. The chief lost his rank and a couple of the others lost theirs. Brigham, who was a three-badge man, lost his good conduct badges accumulated over a twelve-year period of service; he had served close to twenty years and was now being sentenced to 60 days in detention quarters at Portsmouth. (D Qs as it was known throughout the Navy was not a nice place to be incarcerated in; the discipline and strict regime were designed to teach its occupants the error of their ways.) Brigham didn't deserve this harsh punishment; he had been caught in a web not of his making. The Captain had to administer the punishment as laid down in the disciplinary code and gave the most lenient sentence that he could.

I was approached by the cox'n and informed that I would be part of the prisoners' escort, along with my old shipmate Mickey Lydon who would be the leading hand in charge of the escort; another stoker would make up the complement.

Brigham had been held in the cells on the *Maidstone*.

CHAPTER NINETEEN

Travel arrangements had been made and Navy transport would take us to Glasgow where a compartment had been reserved for us on the daytime train to Euston station in London. On arrival we would transfer to Waterloo station and report to the regulating office, from where we would board the train to Portsmouth.

We were dressed in our No.1 rig with the addition of white webbing gators to tuck our bellbottoms in; we wore a white belt around our waists, and displayed the badge of office, this being a wrist band with the insignia of a crown in the centre and emblazoned with the letters N.P. on either side of it.

We collected Brigham from the cells. He had his kit packed; it was his responsibility to carry it, and we boarded the transport to Glasgow's Queens Street Station.

After showing our railway warrants to the ticket collector, we found the reserved compartment on the train; we were in the process of settling down when we were interrupted by two civilian prison officers, who were escorting one of their own prisoners.

We had already been to the restaurant car and purchased a 24-can box of beer, which we tucked under the seat; our new travelling companions were also allocated seats in our reserved compartment.

The train gently pulled away from the station and started its journey to London. We took off our white gators, belts and Naval Police wrist bands. Brigham was a shipmate, and we were determined to treat him as one and do our best to save him from as much embarrassment as possible.

Out came the beer, and we offered the two civilian prison officers a can and asked if it was okay to offer their prisoner one; they didn't object.

The civilian prisoner looked like a nice young lad but remained very quiet. After a while he said that he needed to go to the toilet; he was handcuffed to one of the officers who escorted him to the toilet. During his absence, Mickey struck up a conversation with the remaining officer.

He explained that he and his partner were officers at Barlinnie Prison—a notorious prison in Glasgow and home to a lot of hardened criminals of every calibre. Mickey had knowledge of one particular inmate that had been found guilty of murder and had been hanged within the prison's confines; it turned out during the conversation that the officer we were talking to had been the one designated to take care of the prisoner before his hanging.

Being inquisitive, we asked the question about the lad that was in their charge. The officer explained that he had been given a seven-year sentence for armed robbery; he had been given compassionate leave under escort to visit his young daughter who was in a Manchester hospital dying of Leukaemia.

Arriving at Manchester Piccadilly station, we bade them farewell with some sadness and compassion for their prisoner.

CHAPTER NINETEEN

Our journey continued and we finished off the beer and lapsed into a restful state. We were nearing Euston station and it was time to freshen up and get dressed into our formal rig to carry out our escort duties.

We reported to the regulating office at Waterloo Station, and were informed of the time of the train to Portsmouth, and were checked that Brigham was still in our charge.

Arriving in Portsmouth, we were transported to the detention quarters. The entrance was not very welcoming; the bell was rung and the door was opened by the duty Master at Arms. We entered the foyer and handed over Brigham into DQs with the relevant paperwork. Mickey got in return a sign off document stating that the prisoner had been escorted and delivered as ordered.

This was not one of the happiest moments in my service to her Majesty, but it was a necessary one; rules and regulations have to be applied and obeyed. I for one had fallen foul of them a couple of times and had borne the consequences. Having said that, I also had successfully avoided some of them.

After delivering Brigham, we went to the Trafalgar Club and stayed the night. It had been a long day.

The next morning we travelled to London. We had been given a couple of days leave before we had to return to *Osiris*. Mickey took us to a pub called The Black Cap, situated in one of London's districts that had many Irish inhabitants. We had a meal of—would you

CHAPTER NINETEEN

believe it?—of Irish stew! After the meal we split up and I made my way to Oxford to visit Mum and the family.

Returning to Scotland, nothing had changed in regard to Bette and me being allocated a married quarter. Living in one room with a baby and a husband that was away for long periods was not a good recipe for a sustainable marriage, and the stress was starting to show on Bette.

I had a decision to make. I had two loves; one was Bette and my son, the other was the Navy and all that it brought with it for good and not so good.

I had signed on for a nine-year engagement. After making some enquiries I found that I could revert to doing a seven and five commitment, although to do this a fee of £125 would have to be lodged. The seven years served would be compensated by being put on reserve for five years; for this I would be paid one shilling a day, and be willing to be recalled in the event of any national emergency. I opted to transfer to the seven and five contract.

Leaving the Navy was like a reluctant divorce! If only a married quarter had been made available and Bette had been given the opportunity to make a home for us, I would probably have continued with my Navy career for the full twenty-two years. This was not to be so.

This MISHMASH of my life was at an end, and I was about to start a new one as a civilian.